Preparing to Teach Writing

Preparing to Teach Writing

James D. Williams
University of North Carolina,
Chapel Hill

Wadsworth Publishing Company
Belmont, California
A Division of Wadsworth, Inc.

Education Editor: Suzanna Brabant
Production Editor: Leland Moss
Designer: Andrew H. Ogus
Print Buyer: Barbara Britton
Editorial Assistant: Marla Nowick
Technical Illustrator: Willa Bauer
Compositor: Alan Noyes
Cover Designer: Andrew H. Ogus

Printed in the United States of America   **49**

1 2 3 4 5 6 7 8 9 10—94 93 92 91 90 89

Library of Congress Cataloging-in-Publication Data
Williams, James D. (James Dale), 1949 –
    Preparing to teach writing/James D. Williams.
        p.   cm.
    Bibliography: p.
    Includes index.
    ISBN 0-534-10026-0
    1. English language — Rhetoric — Study and teaching. 2. English language — Composition and exercises — Study and teaching. 3. English teachers — Training of.   I. Title.
PE1404.W54   1989   88-25027
808'.042'07 —dc19   CIP

*This book is dedicated to the memory
of my mother and father,
Jessie and Elmer Williams.*

Contents

PART TWO
Toward a Contemporary Methodology

Preface

For the Teacher

When I first started teaching composition in 1972 at a California high school, I knew almost nothing at all about what I was supposed to do. Like most English majors, I had been trained in literature, not literacy. Composition hadn't even been covered in my methods course, which had focused instead on teaching poetry and fiction. Trying to stifle my growing panic over the prospect of teaching several writing classes a day, I asked friends and colleagues for suggestions, and they were usually happy to share with me their personal anecdotes about favorite lessons. What I really wanted, however, was a "cookbook" of lesson plans that I could draw on day by day, something that I could follow step by step, without having to think too much. I now believe I was fortunate that none existed.

Under the circumstances, my teaching was a haphazard process of trial and error largely influenced by the assorted success stories I had heard. My classes seemed to be going nowhere. If something worked, I had no idea why it worked, which meant that I usually couldn't replicate it for another class. If something failed, I had even less idea why it failed, so I had no clear notion of what I should be avoiding with students.

Only toward the end of my first year, after I had started studying rhetoric, did I begin to make any progress. I discovered that numerous teachers and researchers were seriously investigating written discourse, using research designs from the social sciences to examine what characterizes good writing, what distinguishes good writers from poor ones (other than finished product), and what methods of instruction work best to improve writing performance. It was becoming clearer to me that effective teachers must do more than follow a "cookbook" of lesson plans. They must be able to draw on research and theory as they develop and explore their own teaching strategies, because pedagogical recipes have to be seasoned to suit the individual needs of individual classes and students. I started to realize that theory and research inform the teaching process, helping us know which seasonings to use.

When I began training credential candidates to teach writing, I was determined to help them avoid the frustrations I had experienced during my first years of teaching. By that time, work in composition studies had undergone a significant shift away from anecdotes to empirical, quantifiable research. Numerous studies provided insights into the factors that underlie the complex behavior we call writing, clarifying both the act of composition and the process of composition instruction.

I quickly discovered, however, that very little of the research was available to students in textbook form. A few texts summarized some of the research, but they didn't do a very good job of addressing applications in the classroom. Many more texts discussed methodologies, but they generally said little about research. They essentially offered a summary of methods that was removed from any principled analysis of the research and theories that provide a framework for effective teaching. In other words, the available texts failed to integrate three critical components of classroom success: theory, research, and practice.

Preparing to Teach Writing developed out of my work with teachers and teacher candidates over the years. With each passing term I found it increasingly difficult to ask my students to synthesize a thick pile of diverse articles related to composition, and I saw serious shortcomings in the texts I had to choose from. So I wrote this book to come as close as possible to being all one needs in a course about teaching writing. It does what other books on composition instruction have not adequately accomplished: It balances an in-depth discussion of theory and research with a detailed presentation of effective teaching methods.

Coverage

Preparing to Teach Writing is the most comprehensive text of its kind on the market. It offers readers a detailed treatment of the theories, research, and methods that shape composition studies today.

The text is divided into two parts. Part One examines research and theories that inform writing pedagogy. It draws on findings from a number of different disciplines relevant to teaching writing, such as sociolinguistics, cognitive psychology, rhetoric and composition, psycholinguistics, even philosophy. The goal is to give readers the foundation they need in research and theory to develop their own lessons and activities as they grow as teachers. With this thought in mind, Part One cites the most current, up-to-date studies available, some as recent as 1988. These references should prove useful to anyone interested in doing further reading, and they also act as empirical anchors in an area often plagued by unsupported opinions. The bibliography reflects the interdisciplinary nature of the ongoing investigation of language studies and is one of the more extensive to be found in a textbook.

Part Two translates the information in the earlier chapters into classroom methods. It elaborates the pragmatic approach to composition instruction, which emphasizes the recursive, social nature of composing. Because Part One serves as the foundation for Part Two, providing the rationale for classroom activities, the methods are tightly focused. The aim is not to offer a wide range of possible approaches to teaching composition, but rather to offer an analysis of several approaches that appear to work, given what we currently know.

Key Features

Preparing to Teach Writing is designed to be the most effective text available for training writing teachers. It has several features that readers will particularly appreciate:

Chapter overviews: Each chapter begins with an overview of the material, a device known to improve comprehension and retention.

Balanced, integrated discussion of theory and practice.

Historical overview of current trends and philosophies in composition.

Comprehensive treatment of theories, research, and strategies.

Emphasis on the social nature of composing that goes beyond process.

A tone that treats readers as professionals.

Full chapter on writing assessment.

Numerous examples of student writing, including an appendix with ten full-length student essays.

Thorough treatment of nonmainstream students.

Chapter summaries: Each chapter ends with a conclusion that integrates the topics just discussed into the fabric of the text as a whole, helping readers better connect theory and practice.

How to Use This Book

Preparing to Teach Writing is a valuable tool for everyone teaching or planning to teach composition, whether in public schools or colleges. It is designed particularly, however, for students pursuing a public school teaching credential.

Most states currently require all candidates for elementary, middle, and high school credentials to complete a course in composition theory and instruction. The course typically introduces students to a wide range of topics, from the role of grammar in writing instruction to constructing assignments, style, sociolinguistics, and process methodologies. Students have to master a great deal of information in this course, because its goals are large: to introduce students to the research and theories that have shaped contemporary writing instruction, and to introduce them to the current techniques for teaching writing.

Preparing to Teach Writing meets both these goals. Its two-part division allows students first to explore the issues that inform composition pedagogy and then to explore how these issues are actually worked out in the classroom.

In manuscript form the text has been used by credential candidates at both UCLA and the University of North Carolina at Chapel Hill. Their experience suggests that *Preparing to Teach Writing* is more helpful when the material is covered in sequence, beginning with Part One and continuing with Part Two. Although the book balances theory and practice effectively, there is no question that students will benefit significantly if actually given the opportunity to use the methods outlined in the text, rather than just read about them. I therefore encourage teachers to adopt a workshop approach for the course; it will reinforce the strategies and methods that students are studying, giving them hands-on experience with how theory can be translated into practice. Microteaching activities, which allow students to take on the role of an instructor, are useful in this regard as well.

I would like to thank my editor, Suzanna Brabant, and the many reviewers whose comments helped me finish this book: Professors Kathleen L. Bell, Old Dominion University; Allen Berger, Miami University; Leila Christenbury, Virginia Commonwealth University; Edward R. Fagan, Pennsylvania State University; Sylvia Gilman, Biola College; Roy C. O'Donnell, University of Georgia; Richard Straub, Florida State University; Robert Whitman, Vanderbilt University; and Kristin R. Woolever, Northeastern University.

Acknowledgments

Several people have figured significantly in the development of this book. I would like to thank Lou Waters, Hans Guth, and the late Phil Cook, who as my teachers at San Jose State believed in me before I had learned to believe in myself; Ross Winterowd, who challenged me to think when I arrived at the University of Southern California as a graduate student and then gave me the freedom I needed to chart my own course; Sue Foster and Jack Hawkins, who trained me in the art of intellectual rigor; and Erika Lindemann, for being a friend and for writing her own book about teaching composition that helped show me the way.

James D. Williams
Chapel Hill
June 4, 1988

PART ONE

Setting the Scene: Developing a Theoretical Framework

CHAPTER 1

Perspectives on Teaching Writing

Seeing Writing in a Social Context

Teaching writing is not particularly easy, but it can be both fun and rewarding for those who accept the challenges involved. One of the more difficult challenges is the fact that language in general and writing in particular are the most complex of all human behaviors. Yet many people, especially students, are convinced that using language is actually quite simple because, after all, even first graders can speak to each other very well.

There are also, of course, more mundane, yet nevertheless significant, challenges: classrooms that invariably are too crowded, a curriculum that more often than not fails to consider the functional nature of language, growing numbers of students who speak little or no English, and a society that takes an inconsistent position regarding the idea of excellence in written communication. On the other hand, we can experience the personal reward that comes from helping students master the single most important element of their lives as thinking, educated human beings—language.

Anyone who would teach should know that a characteristic of language, especially children's, is that it is used significantly as a means of social definition. Through language, children discover how the world is organized, who they are, and how they fit into the existing social structure (see Clark & Clark, 1977). The seemingly simple act of writing

3

one's name, for example, can have profound significance for a child, because the visible presence of that name provides an existential reality of tremendous importance for a developing sense of self.

Although all of us constantly use language to establish, evaluate, and maintain social relationships, this self-definitional function is concentrated during two major periods of life. The first is in early childhood, from about age three to seven. The second is adolescence. With this point in mind, we shouldn't be surprised by the fact that many teenagers pay special attention to song lyrics and discover that keeping a diary or a journal is an important part of their lives.

Helping young people better understand themselves is one of the richest rewards for teachers, more gratifying than teaching the date Columbus reached the Western hemisphere or the parts of speech. The power of language instruction is its inextricable link to who students are and who they are in the process of becoming. It is a part of their everyday lives in a way that so many other subjects are not.

One of the goals of this book is to enable you to realize that reward by giving you as much information as possible about language, writing, and teaching writing. Its basic position is that language is a social activity, something that people do with other people for an identifiable reason. In this framework, writing is only one mode of language use; the others are speaking, listening, and reading. But rather than present the four language modes as separate elements, *Preparing to Teach Writing* aims at integrating the modes through a "whole language" approach to discourse.

To cover as much of the subject as possible, the information about language and writing offered in *Preparing to Teach Writing* ranges from the general to the specific. With this information, you can go on to personalize what you've learned for the individual classes and students you'll be working with in the years to come. This chapter is designed to offer a brief introduction to a few of the concepts we'll take up in more detail later.

As suggested above, everything we do involves language to one degree or another. This has always been true: Whether sounding the alarm about an emergency or passing along advice, we need language skills. The need for writing competence (and indeed for formal education), by contrast, varies according to the social and economic demands of a given culture. In the rural parts of many third-world countries, for example, writing ability is not a high priority; information, whether it be about a change in taxes or a birth in a neighboring family, tends to be passed on orally.

An oral culture, of course, is not necessarily an impoverished one. The opulent Greece and Troy that we know from Homer's *Iliad* were oral cultures. Yet as a society grows, accumulating more and more information, writing becomes increasingly important. Human memory, capable though it is of prodigious feats, simply cannot accommodate everything. Books, articles, letters, memos, and the like can therefore be thought of as an artificial extension of memory. Writing and reading are necessary to preserve and retrieve that information. As a society becomes more dependent on technology, financial markets, and modern manufacturing, literacy, particularly writing ability, becomes a requirement for national and individual prosperity.

The history of our own country provides a model of the connection between literacy and growth. Throughout the pioneer days of westward expansion, well into the 20th century, when the economy was agrarian, relatively few people could read, and far fewer could write. In fact, during the 19th century people were considered literate if they could simply write their names.

But as the nation shifted from agriculture to industry, technology, and world finance, a corresponding demand was placed on our schools for highly literate people who could read, write, and speak well. Today the demand for communicative excellence is so great that business and industry have established communication standards that will take our schools some time to meet; in the interim, companies like Lockheed, TRW, IBM, and Price Waterhouse are hiring private educational consultants to set up training programs designed to teach their employees how to write better.

Given this reality, it's a bit ironic that the advent of video and computer technology has prompted some pundits over the last few years to argue that we are returning to an oral–visual culture where reading and writing have no place. And every once in a while we hear of a few school districts, fearing to fall behind the times in the face of such predictions, that have initiated classes in computer programming to prepare students for what lies ahead, reducing instruction in other areas (like writing) in the process. To date, however, there is no evidence to suggest that the demise of the written word is at hand. On the contrary, the need for people who can write clearly and intelligently is greater than ever and appears to be growing daily.

It's important to recognize, of course, that there is more to teaching writing than satisfying the economic needs of a modern society, even if its survival depends on written communication. In the final analysis, we are working with individual minds and spirits that require our utmost attention and care, which explains in part why most teachers balk at the suggestion that they perform the work of "social engineers."

The Product View of Teaching Writing

Helping students use written language to grow socially and intellectually is one of our goals. Helping them write better is another. Realizing these goals requires that we work closely with students as they attempt to master written discourse. Until the last 15 years or so, the way writing was taught made this harder to do.

Generally speaking, writing instruction was viewed primarily as teaching students punctuation, spelling, and correct usage (distinguishing between *lie* and *lay, who* and *whom, effect* and *affect,* and so on). Class time was devoted to spelling drills, vocabulary exercises, and discussing assigned reading of published works that served as models of good writing. Then the class was given topics, went home, and wrote an essay, one that imitated the reading assignments, after a fashion, or analyzed them.

The teacher read through the finished papers, marking punctuation, spelling, and usage errors in red, often making abbreviated marginal notes like AWK for "awkward," AMB for "ambiguous," and MM for "misplaced modifier." After handing the papers back, the teacher would spend a few minutes commenting on the errors, concluding that it was obvious everyone needed more work, and then it was back to the drills, the exercises, and the discussions. The focus throughout was on the finished product, with class time spent telling students what the finished product should look like.

This approach to teaching writing, which has come to be known as the "product view," operates on a number of assumptions that writing teachers and scholars have come to reject over the last few years. (It's worth noting here, however, that perhaps most educators in fields outside composition studies continue to embrace the product view.) It assumes, for example, that good writing is the result of knowing how to spell and punctuate, and of knowing the parts of speech. It also assumes that there is a positive correlation between being able to discuss a published piece of writing, identifying the thesis, tone, organizational features, and so forth, and being able to write a well organized essay with a clear thesis. We might think of this as the equivalent of assuming that someone who reads music will be able to play Mozart.

There is no question that all teachers must be fundamentally concerned with the final product of writing instruction. Nor is there any question that we want students to spell and punctuate accurately. But good writing consists of more than accurate spelling and punctuation. Experienced teachers are very familiar with the error-free student essay that says absolutely nothing—form without substance.

As the research discussed in the next few chapters will suggest, the biggest problem with the product view is that by focusing attention on the results rather than the means, it asks us to believe that we can teach writing simply by telling students what writing is about. In contrast, work over the last 15 years suggests that teaching writing effectively has two crucial requirements: that we provide students with situations where language can be used meaningfully, and that we focus attention on and emphasize the act of writing itself, not finished essays.

The Process View of Teaching Writing

Beginning in the 1960s, composition scholars began reassessing the effectiveness of the product approach (see Braddock, Lloyd-Jones, & Schoer, 1963; Rohman & Wlecke, 1964). Within a few years, writers like Peter Elbow (1973), Janet Emig (1971), and James Moffett (1968) were advocating a move away from an emphasis on product. Although each took a slightly different position on composition instruction, they held numerous points in common.

These writers argued, among other things, that a finished essay was the result of a complex *process* of activities. This process included several stages of composition development. During the planning or prewriting stage, writers generated ideas and organization. During the writing stage, they put these ideas into some rough order. Then, during the revision stage, they honed organization and expression. Finally, during the editing stage, they corrected surface errors like spelling, punctuation, and usage.

Effective writing instruction, it was argued, would focus not on the completed essay but on helping students through these various stages. To achieve this aim, classrooms were to become "writing workshops" where students shared their work with one another and where the teacher intervened regularly as compositions were developed through several drafts. The emphasis was on *process* rather than *product*. This approach to composition instruction, known as the "process view," has supplanted the product approach in most of the nation's universities and in a large percentage of its school districts.

Underlying the process view is the understanding that writing, like most complex skills, is a nonlinear process. Writers do many different things simultaneously as they are constructing a text. For example, on the basis of *protocols*, what people tell us they're thinking about as they compose, we know that good writers consider the purpose of the text, think about who will read it, and try to make certain that their intentions, what they want the text to do, are clear.

All this mental activity goes on at more or less the same time, with the mind flicking back and forth from one point to another. And if this weren't enough, good writers are also paying attention to word choices, paragraph development, punctuation, and how individual sentences sound. That seems like quite a lot of mental activity, doesn't it! But actually, this description is only a rough outline of what the process of writing involves.

Again, as with most other complex skills, people bring any number of bad habits or poorly learned techniques to the writing process. Weak writers, for example, have a tendency to assume that the only reader of their essays will be the teacher, who already knows what the topic is, so they fail to identify the topic explicitly in their text. As a result, their writing seems confused or incoherent.

You can tell writers that they have not identified the topic, or whatever, and then expect the problem to be rectified in the next essay, but this usually doesn't work very well. Pointing out the mistakes in a paper after it has been graded is about as useful as mentioning to beginning cooks that their soufflés didn't rise because they left out the eggs. In fact, it is probably less useful, because writing an essay is more complex than baking a soufflé, which means there's a greater likelihood that the next time around the writers will be so busy juggling all the other elements of the process that they simply forget the comments on the earlier paper.

In the soufflé analogy, the key to ensuring that the cook is successful lies in carefully monitoring the entire baking process and intervening when the ingredients are being mixed and the eggs are left out. Not only is it still possible at this point to save the soufflé, but people also tend to learn better when the instruction comes during an action. Most of a coach's teaching, for example, takes place during practice, not after.

The process view suggests that those who want to teach writing effectively need to think of themselves as coaches. They need to intervene regularly in the writing process, immediately correcting those things students do wrong and praising those things they do right, giving reinforcement when it is most useful and most beneficial. In practical terms, such intervention requires that teachers ask students to produce multiple drafts of an assignment. Class time is devoted to revising drafts on the basis of feedback that the teacher as well as fellow students provide. Typically, the instructional emphasis in a process-oriented classroom is on writing, talking about the writing, and rewriting.

Some readers may ask whether making writing meaningful and focusing on the process of developing a paper will turn all our students into brilliant writers. No, it won't. But it will allow us to do a more effective job of instruction in the time we have with a class.

The Pragmatic View of Writing Instruction

One of the biggest challenges we face as writing teachers is enabling our students to understand that writing competence is valuable outside the classroom and that it has an important place in their lives now and in the future. Students become bored, frustrated, and angry when they perceive lessons as irrelevant and meaningless. The process view helps in this regard because it allows teachers to communicate more easily the idea that good writing is related to mastering skills students can take with them into other writing situations; they aren't merely completing assignments as a form of busywork.

A difficulty with the process view, however, is that by its very nature it tends to focus attention on the internal processes of individual writers. Thus some scholars see it as being overly psychological and argue that it does not adequately address how society or context influences the writer. Peer work groups may in theory answer this criticism, because they allow students, clustered in groups of four or five, to interact with one another as writers and audience, with members offering constructive advice on how to improve drafts. In practice, however, we find that even in the most successful classes, group members may sometimes fail to provide meaningful input, and writers may often fail to respond to group members in a realistic manner.

There is no question that the psychological factor is important and that the process view has made a major contribution to composition pedagogy. Yet there is also no question that we have to recognize that *texts* have various effects *on writers,* because language is primarily a social action, not a psychological exercise. We get things done with writing, such as canceling a magazine subscription, confirming a hotel reservation, and so on. Writing allows us to share our feelings with others, establishing (or in some cases dissolving) bonds.

In addition, the very *form* our writing takes can link us to a social and cultural heritage that goes back centuries. Anyone who would write a poem, a letter, an essay, or a report draws, consciously or not, on the existing conventions for that form, which in most cases have a long history. The very act of using these conventions can establish a person's social identity. For example, those who write briefs are in the legal profession; those who write financial reports are in business.

In this regard, a growing number of writers are suggesting that the process view has little to say about how the writer creates as a member of society (see Bizzell, 1984; Cooper, 1986; Holzman, 1986). James Reither (1985), for example, tells us that "writing is not merely a process that occurs within contexts. That is, writing and what writers do during writing cannot be . . . separated from the . . . [social] situations in which writing gets done, from the conditions that enable writers to do what they do, and from the motives writers have for doing what they do" (p. 621).

Teachers who see writing as a "way of knowing," as a way of learning more about a subject, are, in a sense, embracing the position Reither describes. Unfortunately, they too often fail to emphasize the necessary role-taking it involves. If students can stop seeing themselves as "students"—empty vessels waiting to be filled—and start seeing themselves as historians, musicians, accountants, or whatever, they will approach a related writing task as a professional would, with care and dedication. That is, if they stop separating themselves from the "situations in which writing gets done," they stand to learn a great deal about a given subject, because a writer who is part of a meaningful context is usually quite thorough.

For those tens of thousands of students who have no personal inclinations that would allow for this sort of role-taking, an emphasis on the social context of writing still seems to have the potential to accomplish something marvelous. If these students cannot see themselves as engineers or managers, perhaps they can at least stop seeing themselves as students and start seeing themselves as writers.

Recent work in linguistic pragmatics, the area of study devoted to how people use language meaningfully in everyday situations, has provided a number of significant insights into the ways individuals and society interact through language, and some of these insights are beginning to influence what goes on in writing classes. The focus is on integrating the psychological with the sociological, giving us a "psychosocial" approach to language, and on understanding how the mind affects and is affected by society. The psychosocial approach treats writing as inextricably related to speaking, reading, and listening. Equally important, it aims to link literacy with the daily activities of students so that reading and writing become more meaningful to them.

The titles of Thaiss and Suhor's *Speaking and Writing, K–12* (1984) and Bailey and Fosheim's *Literacy for Life* (1983) illustrate this focus. And published as they were by our major professional organizations, the National Council of Teachers of English and the Modern Language Association, they also illustrate the profession's interest in connecting writing to other language skills.

The pragmatic view of writing instruction, then, uses the process view as its foundation and builds on it by increasing the emphasis on the social aspects of writing. It advocates the position that written discourse, like oral discourse, is highly functional. The implication for instruction is that every task be related to the "real world." In practical terms, a real-world emphasis means that students' compositions will do something in the tangible sense of performing a social action.

The pragmatic view also advances a whole-language approach to teaching: Reading, speaking, listening, and writing are interrelated activities in the classroom. In this respect, the pragmatic view is inherently psychosocial. At the present time, the pragmatic view appears to be the next step forward in theory and pedagogy. It has as a major goal helping children see that writing has a purpose beyond fulfilling the demands of a school assignment. *Preparing to Teach Writing* incorporates the pragmatic view and actively argues for a functional, psychosocial methodology in writing classes.

The following anecdote suggests one way the pragmatic view may be translated into practice. One of my former credential candidates, a history major, began his student teaching by asking his eighth-grade class for a writing sample. He felt very strongly that all teachers, not just those in language arts, should be dedicated to helping develop children's language abilities, a sentiment formally expressed in what is known as the *writing-across-the-curriculum movement* or the *language-across-the-curriculum movement*. The class had been studying U.S. government, and one of the students, whom we'll call Joey, submitted the following:

> The U.S. consitution is an importent dokument. It give us many rites. Like speech and freedom. Witout the Consitution we might as well be rushans. What our president Raygin call the "evil empire." But some-time it seem that the consitution give us to much freedoms. Many time crimnals don't go to jail for doing bad things when they should go to jail. Thats not right and the consitution should change it.

In a conference two days later, my student asked Joey to recall the things he had been thinking about when he wrote this paper. The purpose was to gain additional insight into Joey's composing process. Joey's response was typical for a student who has come to believe that product is all-important and who has come to see writing as a nonfunctional enterprise: "I was thinkin' I don't spell so good and was wonderin' if I had written enough."

My student knew his work was cut out for him. According to the course guide, the next major study unit dealt with U.S. involvement in Southeast Asia. He asked his class whether they would like to have some pen pals from the Philippines who could give them some firsthand knowledge of life in one part of Southeast Asia. The students were enthusiastic, and a letter to a school principal in Manila began an exchange of letters that continued long after the unit on Southeast Asia was concluded.

Students on both sides of the Pacific were interested in learning more about the culture and lifestyle of their counterparts, and for the American children the letters from Manila seemed to reinforce significantly what they were learning about history and government. Just as important, they suddenly had a purpose for writing. Written language had become meaningful. Composing the letters was always a collaborative project, with children working together in small groups, sharing letters they had received from abroad and also sharing the letters they were writing. The children were encouraged to include in their letters pertinent class experiences. My student circulated among them as they composed, offering suggestions when necessary, answering questions when asked.

The effect on writing performance was tremendous, as the sample below shows. Like the previous sample, it was written by Joey, just over a month after the paper about the Constitution, at a time when Ferdinand Marcos was still in office:

> Dear Emilio,
> Thank you for your last letter. Since I got it we have been studying more about your country. And I have been thinking about what you said about how nice it must be to live in America. We seem to have more freedom than you and its easier for us to make money and buy the things that make life comfortable. I think things would be better for you if you did not have martial law. Then maybe the government would not have all the money. It must be tough with the army and the police telling you what time you have to go to bed and stuff. . . . I don't know why our president helps keep your president in power. I think he don't want to lose the navy base that keeps alot of our ships on one of your islands. . . .

What we see here is that when written language becomes meaningful, writing performance improves on all levels. For example, Joey's concern over the impression his spelling might have on Emilio motivated him, for perhaps the first time, to write with a dictionary close at hand.

Research and Teaching Writing

Having taught high school myself, and having trained teachers for several years now, I recognize the powerful urge to plunge immediately into the study of teaching methods and strategies, leaving the study of research and theory to another day when one has more time. I also recognize that this day mysteriously never seems to come. Teaching is hard work, and after seven hours in the classroom with dozens of children, catching up on research and theory in composition takes a special effort .

It is entirely possible, of course, to teach writing without knowing the slightest thing about research and theory. One could, for example, simply follow a list of instructions: "Step 1: Students will take out pen and paper. Step 2: Students will arrange themselves into groups of four," and so on. In fact, many educational programs and many district instructional guidelines attempt to do just that, establish a set of procedures that are termed (quite oddly, it seems to me) "teacher-proof." In Los Angeles, for example, the district uses a teacher-proof "workshop pack" put together by a group of educational consultants. The pack includes a list of six steps or procedures, summarized below, that teachers are to follow whenever working on writing:

1. Get students to identify purpose and audience
2. Have students brainstorm
3. Have students organize and outline the essay
4. Have students write a rough draft
5. Get students to revise the rough draft
6. Have students edit the final draft

There are many problems associated with the lockstep approach to education, more than can be adequately dealt with here. It should be fairly obvious, however, that this approach doesn't allow for much individual variation among students or teachers, even if, as above, the steps more or less describe the general aspects of a given behavior.

But the point is that without some understanding of what researchers and theorists have learned about how and why people use language in general and writing in particular, a teacher has no way of evaluating the effectiveness of any set of guidelines or procedures. Do students really benefit, for example, from writing an outline? Do they really produce better essays if before composing they state something to the effect that "The audience for this paper is a group of teenagers from broken homes who are trying to give up smoking"?

Simply assuming that the answer to such questions is yes on the basis of the fact that the procedures are provided by one's school district is a mistake. Yet without some awareness of what scholars can tell us about writing instruction, we are usually forced to make that assumption. The inherent danger to effective instruction seems greater when we consider that local policies, such as those concerning teacher-proof programmed instructional packets, are commonly the result of political decisions at times far removed from the issue of pedagogical soundness.

Over the last 15 years or so, a tremendous amount of research has been done on what language is, how it's used, and how people write. The results of this research can inform the decisions we make in the classroom about writing, decisions that affect the lives of our students. Many of the studies are discussed in the next few chapters. The findings and conclusions presented here are important for all teachers because we all deal with language, regardless what subject we teach. Language is the basis for knowledge. As for writing instruction, the research presented here can inform our teaching, not only explaining why some strategies work and others don't, but also giving us the means to develop new strategies as we grow as teachers.

CHAPTER 2

Rhetoric and Writing

Overview

Rhetoric has been part of formal education in the Western world since the ancient Greeks, but the nature of rhetorical study has changed from period to period, reflecting different societal needs and requirements. That is, rhetoric has changed as societies have changed. As a result, an understanding of rhetoric must take into account historical factors that have influenced how it has been defined in a given historical context.

In ancient times, rhetoric was initially defined as the "art of persuasion," but even in classical Greece there were several conceptions of what the term actually meant. One defined rhetoric according to one's interest, whether it was law, politics, or philosophy. Philosophical rhetoric, often referred to as *dialectic*, emphasized debate in an effort to reveal "truth" and was advocated by Socrates and Plato.

Throughout the ancient period, dialectic was largely ignored in favor of pragmatic rhetoric, which was used in arguing court cases and persuading audiences. By the end of the Roman period and the beginning of the Middle Ages, however, linguistic needs had altered significantly. The elaborate judicial system of Greece and Rome disappeared, so there was little need for a rhetoric concerned with legal matters and persuasion. The focus of language study came to be written texts, particularly the Bible. Led by Saint Augustine, scholars concentrated on interpreting the Bible and on debating their interpretations with one another in an effort to establish biblical truth. The Middle Ages therefore saw a shift in rhetoric to dialectic, as well as a shift in emphasis from speech to writing.

In many respects, modern rhetoric retains significant features of medieval dialectic. Not only do schools continue to emphasize writing to the near total exclusion of speech, but a major portion of that writing is based on the interpretation of texts. Over the last 50 years or so, there has been renewed scholarly interest in rhetoric that is frequently referred to as the "new rhetoric." Writers like Kenneth Burke, Chaim Perelman, and James Kinneavy have given us several fresh perspectives. Yet their work is closely associated with the philosophical rhetoric of Plato and Aristotle, and its chief concern is establishing a system by which one can discover available arguments to answer proposed questions or defend proposed theses. It continues, in other words, to be highly dialectical.

Our linguistic needs today are slightly different from what they were when Perelman and Olbrechts-Tyteca (1969) defined rhetoric as argumentation aimed at gaining the "adherence of minds," and they are certainly different from what they were when Burke (1931) defined it as using language to bring about cooperation.

Within the specific domain of writing pedagogy, our needs are also shifting. In an effort to move writing instruction beyond empty exercises and drills, and ultimately beyond an emphasis on individual process, we require a rhetoric that draws on classical oral traditions, one that will allow teachers to utilize students' oral competence.

The definition offered in this chapter is linked to the idea that language is an action. Viewing writing as an action suggests that effective writing is going to involve goals and plans as writers develop strategies to produce desired effects. Moreover, it suggests that writers need to have a sophisticated understanding of audience in order to be successful. The last part of the chapter therefore discusses some of the implications associated with language as action and examines the relationships among a writer's intentions, the context in which he or she attempts to fulfill those intentions, and discourse plans.

What Is Rhetoric?

Before I became a teacher, I understood *rhetoric* to be speech that sounded good but conveyed nothing. It seemed to be the specialty of politicians who when queried about their stand on civil rights, nuclear power, or high taxes would speak with conviction without ever answering the question. Their responses were examples of "empty rhetoric," a flourish of words without substance.

Once I started teaching, I experienced a different kind of rhetoric. This other rhetoric was books that were collections of essays arranged by mode: "Definition," "Comparison and Contrast," "Persuasion," "Argumentation," "Narration," and so forth. I didn't know that these two uses of the word were related and didn't think any more about it until years later when I began my doctoral work. Then, for the first time, I started wondering just what rhetoric is all about.

To understand what rhetoric *is* one must know something about what it *was*. For example, the connection between these two uses of *rhetoric* is largely historical, linked to traditions that have their origins, like so many other aspects of Western civilization, in ancient Greece. The history of rhetoric suggests that change and the promise of change are our central concerns in arriving at a viable definition of rhetoric for our own time.

Change in language, of course, operates on numerous levels. One of the more visible is vocabulary. *Floppy disk, modem,* and *software* are now such common terms that even people who don't know how to operate a computer generally know what they mean. Yet only a few years ago these terms didn't exist. They arose out of social and linguistic changes linked to the spread of computers from a handful of scientists and engineers to the public.

On another level, the need for literacy has changed since the 19th century, when the amount of information transmitted in writing was much smaller than the amount transmitted today. Literacy was not a particularly pressing issue because most people lived and worked on farms where its place in day-to-day living was small. Businesses operated on a significantly smaller scale and generated significantly less paperwork. Reading was limited owing to the scarcity of books, and writing, with the exception of letters to friends and relatives, was limited owing to the lack of need. If one didn't know how to write, as was true of many, it was possible to dictate the letter to someone who could, and the sender would then sign his or her name.

Today, however, businesses produce mountains of written discourse daily in the form of reports, proposals, letters, memos, and transaction records. By some estimates, 75 percent of all jobs in the United States involve writing to one degree or another, so literacy has become a major social and economic concern. In *Illiterate America*, for example, Jonathan Kozol (1985) describes how the American military has been forced to "dumb down" operation manuals for sophisticated weapons systems like the B-1 bomber, giving them a comic-book format and cartoon characters that young recruits can understand. The estimated annual cost in terms of wasted man-hours runs into the billions. The so-called Big Eight accounting firms likewise spend millions of dollars each year to hire communication consultants to teach new accountants, college graduates all, how to write.

As a result of shifting societal and linguistic needs, rhetoric itself changes, thereby making any definition subject to contextual qualification. Thus, the question "What is rhetoric?" is meaningful only in relation to the cultural characteristics of a given society in a specified period. Our linguistic needs are different from those of the past, and a contemporary definition of rhetoric must account for those needs if it is to be viable. We can't rely on previous insights and conceptualizations, because chances are they won't be entirely relevant to how we use language today. This isn't a particularly startling insight, of course. In classical Greece, for example, rhetoric was by and large viewed as the use of language for purposes of persuasion. But almost from the very beginning there existed different emphases and purposes, and thus slightly different notions not only of what rhetoric did but of what it was.

Classical Rhetoric

The first formal conceptualizations of rhetoric seem to have developed out of the ancient Greeks' fondness for litigation. Disputes over property and business transactions were common, and the court dockets were always full. There were no lawyers, so litigants usually argued their cases themselves, although in some circumstances they were allowed to make use of a *synegoros*, or private advocate. Rhetoric was initially viewed, therefore, as a means of improving one's oral presentation before the court in order to win a legal case. It was fundamentally a means of persuasion.

It's important to note that at the heart of this rhetoric was argument from *probability,* not from fact. Indeed, by some accounts it was the introduction of probability into legal arguments that most significantly characterizes early formulations of rhetoric (see Guthrie, 1971). We get some sense of how probability arguments work if we imagine a situation in which, say, a 70-year-old grandmother is accused of robbing a couple of thugs. In response to the charges, she could ask: "Is it really likely that a frail old thing like me could rob two ruffians like them?" It just doesn't seem probable.

In most instances there exists a range of probabilities from which arguments can be constructed, so rhetoric in this account becomes not only a means of persuasion but a means of discovering probable arguments based on what normal people do under normal circumstances. Aristotle had in mind something along these lines in Book II of his work *The "Art" of Rhetoric,* for here he describes human psychology with the aim of showing how to appeal to an audience's emotions. The fact that Aristotle tells us the function of rhetoric is "to find out [*theoresai*] in each case the existing means of persuasion" (1975, I.i.12–14, p. 13) prompts George Kennedy (1980) to conclude that for Aristotle, rhetoric was "a theoretical activity and discovers knowledge" (p. 63).

We can understand how in our own judicial system the existence of factual evidence related to a case would theoretically provide very little need for rhetoric; the case could be decided strictly on the basis of the evidence. If half a dozen people saw the grandmother rob the thugs at gunpoint, her argument from probability would have little value.

But the court system of ancient Greece was not above corruption and bribery; in fact, bribery was rampant in important cases. Such a situation made direct evidence, like eyewitness testimony, highly suspect (see Kennedy, 1980). As a result, litigants would often shun the use of direct evidence if it were possible to build a strong case exclusively on probabilities. Moreover, the ancient Greeks were particularly fond of arguing probabilities, because demonstrating that one probability was more probable than another generally involved very subtle and clever lines of reasoning that seem to have appealed to something characteristically Greek.

In the fifth and fourth centuries B.C., democratic changes in the Athenian constitution turned the courts into arenas of frequent political conflict. Cases were no longer argued before a single judge but before a group of 500 jurors drawn from a panel of citizens (see Sealey, 1976). Athens had no political parties as we know them, but citizens banded together in quasi-political social clubs, often based loosely on kinship, that vied for political power.

When one group was becoming more influential than another, it was a common tactic for rival groups to file a series of suits, commonly charging treason or public malfeasance, and so consume the defendants' time in litigation that they had little time left for political ambitions. Demosthenes, the great Athenian leader of the fourth century B.C., is said to have been on trial more than a hundred times. Arguments before the court in such cases therefore had political undertones, and in many instances overtly dealt with political issues. Such confrontations were frequently continuations of arguments begun in the governing assembly. Thus rhetoric as a "means of persuasion" related to pragmatic decision making had both a legal *and* a political function.

The many handbooks on rhetoric produced during the ancient period were designed to communicate the principles of persuasive discourse. These texts consistently emphasized the social aspects of rhetoric, taking into account the fact that a speaker is part of the group to whom he speaks and suggesting how he can use his position (*ethos*) as a member of that group to construct persuasive arguments. (NOTE: We are using the pronoun *he* in this section simply because in ancient times women were not allowed to participate in these activities.)

Another common feature is that these handbooks could be quite technical. For example, they divided and classified speeches into several parts, such as *narrative, exposition,* and *argument.* In the exposition section the orator explained the problem to be addressed; in the argument section he made his case.

As rhetoric became increasingly defined as composition, particularly during the 19th century, and as students had fewer and fewer opportunities to practice elaborate discourse, teachers turned increasingly to abbreviated forms as rhetorical exercises. Typically, these exercises consisted of practicing the individual divisions that in another time had been only part of a whole discourse. These divisions eventually developed into composition modes, and today we may assign an *argumentative essay*, a *narrative essay*, or an *expository essay*. "Rhetorics" consisting of collections of essays classified by mode are of course based on these classical divisions. The most common rhetorical modes are narration, description, comparison and contrast, definition, process, analysis, and argumentation.

At about the same time that legal–political rhetoric was being formulated, two different kinds of rhetoric were developing among Greek philosophers, who had needs quite different from those of politicians and litigants. These philosophers were concerned with the concept of reality, and their effort to explore the nature of truth, virtue, and knowledge emphasized rhetoric as a theory of knowing.

The nature of reality itself, however, was viewed differently by different philosophers, and we can conveniently divide the views into two categories of belief. Socrates and Plato are in the first category, which is based on the notion that everything is absolute and that change occurs only at a superficial and ultimately trivial level. Most important, Socrates and Plato believed that there is an absolute truth, an absolute virtue, and so on. In their view, language should be used as a tool to separate truth from falsehood—that is, to determine the true and absolute nature of reality.

Although we may think of them as practicing what has been called "philosophical rhetoric" (Kennedy, 1980), Socrates and Plato actually ridiculed rhetoric as it was currently taught, claiming it was used to trick audiences into believing that the worse argument is the better, which they maintained was inherently evil. The goal of Socrates and Plato's approach was the discovery and defense of *truth*. Their philosophical rhetoric achieves this goal by pointing out the wisdom of one's own position and the foolishness of all others. Although the limited scope of this summary imposes a degree of oversimplification, we can say that philosophical rhetoric is, in essence, the rhetoric of debate, of presenting a thesis and defending it. Debate of this sort is also commonly known as *dialectic*.

In the second category of belief is a group of philosophers known collectively as Sophists, who practiced what we may think of as sophistic rhetoric. Unlike Socrates and Plato, they believed that all things are relative and that the truth concerning any issue depends on one's point of view. If a question arises regarding the truth of a matter, each person involved is "right," because each sees one facet of the truth.

We commonly express this idea when we note that there are "two sides to every story."

Rhetoric for the Sophists, then, was a tool for examining the various sides of an issue. Because each side holds an element of truth, in the sophistic view people who would practice rhetoric are obligated to explore that truth fully in order to understand it. By understanding multiple aspects of truth, or rather by understanding all sides of an issue, one acquires wisdom. Indeed, the name Sophist is related to *sophia*, the Greek word for wisdom. Thus to the Sophists, the person who mastered rhetoric also mastered knowledge and could view reality more clearly than someone limited by a single perspective.

The Sophists linked wisdom with the proper way to live one's life, so sophistic rhetoric also placed great emphasis on the speaker's moral character, unlike the rhetoric of the law courts and political assemblies, and quite unlike the philosophical rhetoric of Plato. In fact, Isocrates, the most influential of the Sophists, taught that only a good man could become a good rhetorician.

The effect of this conception of rhetoric was not quite so grand as it sounds, however. In practice it frequently resulted simply in highlighting the cleverness of the speaker. If reality is relative, then the substance of a speech is not particularly important, because reality shifts according to the point of view one is advocating. For example, is it better to be loyal or disloyal? Most of us would probably say it is better to be loyal, but what of the soldier ordered to commit an unconscionable act, like shooting civilians? In this case wouldn't it be better if the soldier were disloyal and disobeyed the order?

The Sophists apparently took special delight in arguments of this sort, which challenged accepted ways of thinking and provided an opportunity to demonstrate their wits. The potential for greater and greater elaboration and increasingly contrived arguments is fairly evident, and it seems that this potential was often realized. The focus became not so much a "good man" speaking as a clever man practicing his eloquence. As a result, we have in English terms like *sophistry*, meaning a plausible but misleading argument, and *sophist*, which has come to mean one who is skillful in devious argument. The emphasis sophistic rhetoric placed on the speaker led some rhetoricians several centuries later to view rhetoric solely in terms of appealing presentation, until a speech or a piece of writing was almost entirely form without substance, or what I referred to earlier as "empty rhetoric."

Medieval Rhetoric

In spite of pragmatic difficulties, sophistic rhetoric and the rhetoric of the law courts dominated language study until the Middle Ages. The ability to deliver a well prepared speech was deemed more important than the ability to debate opponents in the pursuit of some philosophical truth. In the Middle Ages, however, the focus shifted to dialectic, or the sort of philosophical debate advocated by Plato, for several reasons.

When the Roman Empire collapsed, the sophisticated court system that had been part of the ancient world for centuries collapsed with it. As a result, there was simply little or no need for legal rhetoric. Furthermore, although there had been few opportunities for open political discussions in the Empire, even fewer opportunities existed in the feudal states that sprang up after its fall, so this aspect of rhetoric also disappeared. Both Greek and Roman rhetoric had manifested an inclination to dwell on literature and literary devices, and the fall of the Roman Empire, coinciding with the spread of Christianity, turned what previously had been an inclination into the dominant focus. The largely public rhetoric of persuasion and decision making became the largely private rhetoric of literary interpretation.

This shift was very much the product of Saint Augustine, who argued that rhetoric could be put to use in preaching and, more important, interpreting the Bible. His initial goal was to attack and refute heresies, but his writing and teaching had implications that reached beyond contemporary struggles to establish a Christian doctrine, which in A.D. 400 still did not exist. He viewed rhetoric as a critical tool for discovering scriptural truths and defending them against the misinformed and the unenlightened. Thus we see that dialectic was at the core of his concept of rhetoric. Saint Augustine epitomized the Christian scholar, whose task was to determine the true reading of the Bible and to defend that truth against detractors.

Over time, of course, texts other than the Bible became the subject of rhetorical analysis. And the Middle Ages even saw the development of two new strands of rhetoric: the art of letter writing (*ars dictaminis*) and the art of preaching (*ars praedicandi*). But the fundamental characteristics of the rhetoric advocated by Saint Augustine in the fifth century A.D. did not change significantly. Rhetoric became principally concerned with writing, and it became almost entirely concerned with dialectic. Higher education during this period, for example, greatly emphasized debate guided by a higher moral purpose and a search for truth. Students were expected to engage in disputations on a regular basis, debating such questions as the justice of war, the use of poison in war, free will, redemption, and so on (Kinneavy, 1971).

In many ways, the influence of Augustinian rhetoric extends even into our own lives, because certain important aspects of education remain essentially unchanged from the Middle Ages. For one, education is still concerned primarily with writing, not speech. In fact, the dominant view has held that *rhetoric is composition.*

Teachers still ask students to establish and defend theses, although the medieval emphasis on moral purpose and the search for truth has largely disappeared. Still, the process itself may be characterized as mastering dialectic principles. Our writing classes are not exceptions. The typical term paper that calls for research and documentation is an example of the dialectic process, as is the essay in which students express a point of view and support it.

Defining a Modern Rhetoric

If we were to formulate a definition of rhetoric appropriate for the Middle Ages, it might be something along the lines of "the art of disputation." This is quite different from "the art of persuasion" characteristic of ancient Greece. But what of our own time? What definition best conceptualizes the way we use language as we interact with others? Several definitions exist, each with its own historical context, but two of the more interesting come from the 1930s and 1960s.

During the height of the Great Depression, Kenneth Burke (1931) viewed rhetoric as using language to bring about cooperation among people, whose nature he deemed it is to be in conflict with each other. Several years after the Depression, Burke (1950) expressed this view most elegantly when he wrote: "Rhetoric is concerned with the state of Babel after the Fall" (p. 23).

We better understand the idea that rhetoric brings about cooperation when we consider the dire social conditions of that time. With the economy a shambles and millions of people out of work, social unrest was widespread. Many doubted the government's ability to alleviate their despair. Yet the country needed everyone to cooperate if the social fabric was to hold together. Burke's "rhetoric of cooperation" found a living representative in President Roosevelt. His radio addresses urged people to make a unified effort to mobilize the nation, assuring them that by helping one another life would eventually get better.

The 1960s were quite far removed from a spirit of cooperation. Political activism dominated social interaction worldwide, and one movement after another competed for public attention. Civil rights, the women's movement, antiwar demonstrations—each had its own agenda. Moreover, each movement characteristically faced a largely apathetic or even hostile public, so there was little opportunity for persuasion and almost no mood for cooperation. Rhetorical success was measured in terms of whether or not an audience would simply listen to what one had to say or read what one had to write. In this context, we find Perelman and Olbrechts-Tyteca (1969) defining rhetoric as argumentation aimed at gaining the "adherence of minds."

There is a sense, however, in which cooperation on some level and adherence of minds are fundamental to language events. The philosopher Paul Grice (1975), for example, has argued convincingly that language exchanges involve what he calls the "cooperative principle." According to this principle, people cooperate with one another to provide information relevant to a given situation.

Accordingly, if someone asks you how to drive from campus to your house, you're not going to give him or her the chemical formula for salt, because that is an irrelevant and uncooperative response. As for adherence of minds, you may have developed an idea that will benefit the world for the next thousand years, but if no one will read your exposition of that idea, if you cannot gain the adherence of minds, you have accomplished nothing. In both cases, we must take into account the fact that language users exist in a society of other language users. Moreover, language itself is a social event defined, shaped, and constrained by the culture in which it occurs (see Giroux, 1983).

For the time being, at least, we seem to have reached a point of social and political stability very different from the 1930s and 1960s, such that those who would make a speech or write an essay are likely to receive a reasonable hearing or reading. Indeed, a significant feature of discourse today is that practically everyone has the opportunity to step into the public forum, and increasing numbers have the actual experience. The media's insatiable demand for "features" has democratized rhetoric to such an extent that even the man or woman in the street has the chance to convey some message or opinion or recollection, and, perhaps more important, there appears to be an audience of one kind or another willing to listen. It therefore seems that cooperation and adherence of minds have become established presuppositions and cannot be the focus of an adequate definition of rhetoric today.

To be viable, our definition must be broad enough to embrace both speech and writing. It must also allow for a social view of discourse. Finally, it must provide the potential of a balanced emphasis among the three parts of any discourse: speaker or writer, the discourse itself, and the audience. Rhetoric is severely limited if, like classical legal rhetoric, it emphasizes the discourse, or, like sophistic rhetoric, it emphasizes the speaker or writer. With these points in mind, I would define contemporary rhetoric as *the conscious control of language to bring about an intended effect in an audience.* The remainder of the chapter will discuss the pedagogical consequences of this definition.

Language as Action

When we think about language at all, we probably don't think about it as being an action. It seems to have little in common with hitting a baseball, or sewing a dress, or driving a car, which are easily identified as actions. Yet understanding language as an action is crucial to understanding the role rhetoric plays in writing, as well as to exploring a few of the problems students have with writing.

Consider the characteristics of actions. They involve an agent. They produce some sort of change in the world. In addition, to be truly considered an action, they must be intentional; that is, the agent must intend to engage in an action and to produce some sort of change.

This last point seems especially important, for without intention we may have an event, but not an action. We can understand the distinction if we consider, say, a girl playing baseball. As she comes to bat, we could identify her intention to hit a home run.

Now let's suppose she hits the ball and sends it out of the park, thereby realizing her intention. But what if the ball sails right through a neighbor's window and hits him on the head while he's reading the newspaper, knocking him out cold? Can we say that the batter performed the action of knocking the neighbor out? Not really. The batter's action was simply hitting the home run. Breaking the window and knocking out the neighbor were *results of the action,* because the batter had no intention of doing either. On this basis, an action is performed only when one intends to do something and actually does it (see Searle, 1983).

We see how this analysis relates to language when we consider that anyone who uses language is an agent, since words do not spring forth out of thin air but are produced by a speaker or writer. Moreover, most language is intentional, and by nature is primarily functional. That is, we typically use language to affect our environment, whether it be through making requests, issuing directives, supplying information, or making assertions.

Assertions are especially interesting because, unlike requests and directives, for example, their functional nature is not readily apparent. Much school-sponsored writing asks students to formulate a series of assertions that they are then supposed to support. If you were to say "There is a robin on my balcony," you would be making an assertion, but how is it functional? How are you performing any action other than merely mouthing some words? Well, first you are asserting a particular representation of reality consisting of a state of affairs in which there is indeed a robin on your balcony. But in hearing your statement (or reading it, as the case may be), the audience must formulate a mental picture of your asserted representation of reality, such that *your* representation in effect becomes *its* representation. If this process doesn't occur, your assertion will simply not be comprehended; the words won't have any meaning.

It seems reasonable to propose that in asserting "There is a robin on my balcony" you are expressing your belief that in fact there is a robin on your balcony. You are asserting, in other words, the validity of your representation of reality. The mental model that the listener or reader formulates must also include your assertion of validity. *Your* belief becomes *his or her* belief. In this adoption of belief lies the element of change characteristic of an action, and in this sense your assertion is most certainly functional because you have transferred to the audience your representation of reality and your belief in that representation.

Interestingly enough, you need not actually hold that belief, you need only instill it in your audience. This is the point about rhetoric that the Sophists noted, for which they were so criticized by Socrates and Plato. One begins to understand on the basis of this analysis why the ancient Greeks viewed language as both powerful and potentially dangerous. To appreciate their view more fully, you need only move from the simple example of the robin and consider assertions related to ethics, values, and belief systems. To get others to view the world as you do is perhaps the most powerful aspect of language, and it underlies all forms and definitions of rhetoric, including dialectic.

Speech and Writing

The functional aspect of language applies to both speech and writing. If one examines conversations carefully, it becomes apparent that speech is used primarily to create a social bond vital to cultural continuity (see Brown & Yule, 1983; Labov, 1972a; R. Lakoff, 1973). Typical conversations convey very little new information, and they often reinforce facts that the participants already know, as in talk about the weather, taxes, sports, families, high prices, and so forth. The goal is to create a sense of shared experience that translates into an act of communion, which we may term "social action." In addition, speech enables people to define themselves in relation to the rest of society, establishing a social niche. We can say, therefore, that speech is essentially interactional (see Brown & Yule, 1983; Hudson, 1980; Levinson, 1983).

Although successful writing also establishes a bond between reader and writer, this is not, at least for nonfiction prose, its primary function. Essays and reports are generally designed to present a new insight, a new point of view, or new information to readers. They consist of a series of assertions, each with a cluster of supporting statements designed to give readers reasons for accepting those assertions. Or, stated another way, written discourse aims at getting readers to adopt the writer's representation of reality as their own. So whereas conversations tend to be reciprocal exchanges, writing is unilateral or transactional (see Brown & Yule, 1983).

Even so, there is a sense in which writing must also be seen as a social action. For one thing, it is not private but inherently public, designed to be shared with others. Outside most classroom settings, the act of writing itself is a shared activity; most writers, with the unfortunate exception of many students, produce prose that has benefited from the feedback of friends, colleagues, or editors. The popular idea that writing is a solitary activity is simply a myth, a vestige of the Romantic period when poets like Byron, Coleridge, and Wordsworth wanted the world to believe their work was the product of lonely inspiration (see Faigley, 1986).

We may question whether it is even possible for a writer to work in complete isolation, cut off from an audience and from a sense of audience. Whatever discourse one can produce is inextricably tied to one's linguistic and cultural heritage. A writer may choose to ignore that heritage, but anyone who makes that choice must pay a price: One must present one's views or information blindly, with only a vague notion of whether the reasons used to support assertions will be accepted or rejected. Unless amazingly lucky, the writer will fail, because there is a method involved in writing, a method of social relations that include, among other things, intentions, purpose, audience, and writer.

Purpose and Intentions

It has become a commonplace in composition that most student writers find it very difficult to recognize any purpose for their writing other than finishing an assignment. In our elementary schools and our high schools, we can watch students' eyes grow dull and their jaws become grimly set whenever they are asked to write.

It's often the case that a teacher will give an assignment, whether a simple narrative or some sort of argument, and the finished papers will not be narratives or arguments at all, even after the class has spent time talking about how to write the essay. The required number of words or pages will be turned in, and the three- or five-paragraph essay may have a semblance of structure, but no narrative, no argument. What seems truly remarkable is that the writers are surprised when the teacher points out that they didn't do the assignment. How can we account for such occurrences?

Part of the problem appears to lie in a faulty understanding of the rhetoric of speech and writing. It's important to emphasize, however, that there is no suggestion here that speech significantly interferes with writing, a surprisingly popular but mistaken view (see Dillon, 1981; Shaughnessy, 1977; Hirsch, 1977; and Ong, 1978, for this view, and compare it to more recent work by Edelsky, 1986; and Farr & Janda, 1985). The matter is more complex than that, as the next several sections will show.

Our students have an implicit understanding of oral rhetoric. They know that spoken language is performative, that it is used to get things done. They know that if they ask someone sitting next to them in the school cafeteria, "Can you pass the salt?" they will get the salt shaker, not a box of Cracker Jack. By the same token, they know that if they ask their parents whether they can stay up late to watch TV, or stay out late on a date, they will have to do some persuading, providing the parents with good reasons why permission should be granted. Parents know just how creative children can be in discovering good reasons, and generally the more desirable the goal, the more inventive children become.

The fact that children use oral discourse to get things done on a daily basis, that they use it to manipulate their environment in order to attain some goal, should be ample evidence of their rhetorical competence. They know how to produce an effect on their audience. How is it, therefore, that their written discourse seems so lacking in rhetorical awareness?

In the classroom, students practice writing in various rhetorical modes, ostensibly to learn how to narrate or compare or describe, as though they have never performed these tasks before, as though they have no fundamental rhetorical competence. Moreover, they practice the same mode-oriented writing tasks year after year, even into college, as though there is nothing else to learn, and after years of trying, they still haven't got it.

This situation seems to be in part the result of insisting that speech and writing are inherently different, as so many teachers and textbook authors do. But believing that students are blank slates with no understanding of rhetorical devices makes about as much sense as believing they have no understanding of grammar. It is equivalent to forcing a native speaker of English to go through drills on subject/verb/object word order to learn how to produce an English sentence. The fact that many students are indeed subjected to such drills says much more about the state of language arts instruction than it does about student competence.

One result of the supposed rhetorical ignorance of students is that many teachers tend to make the rhetorical context of assignments as detailed as possible. This tendency is apparently part of the widespread belief that good writing lies dormant in students, waiting for a good assignment to bring it forth (see Hillocks, 1986).

Assignments may specify, for example, the composition of the audience ("the school newspaper"; "members of the PTA with more than one child in school") and/or the aim of the composition ("an argument designed to persuade, but not necessarily convince"; "a description that focuses on the sounds of a favorite spot"). Students aren't fooled by these assignments, however. They understand that the teacher is the real reader, regardless of what the assignment says.

Interestingly enough, research indicates that assignments with a great deal of rhetorical specification yield worse essays than more general assignments do (see Brossell, 1983; Metviner, 1981; Woodworth & Keech, 1980). This finding is linked, it seems, to what we may think of as "cognitive overload."

Writing is such a complex task that it makes great demands on cognitive processing—that is, on the mental mechanisms used to process information. A highly specific assignment increases those demands because the writer must keep in mind an additional set of details. Apprentice writers generally don't have much experience in handling a large number of abstract mental operations simultaneously. The result is an overload of cognitive function.

Whereas it seems that rhetorical context is often too greatly emphasized, the functional, performative aspects of written discourse are seldom noted in our schools, much less stressed. Within the context of the composition class, what does an analysis *do*, for example? Or comparison/contrast? Or definition? What is the goal of such tasks from the student's perspective? What effects are to be produced in the audience?

Students cannot answer these questions, even though answering them is fundamental to producing a well written essay, because they have not been shown that writing, like speech, is functional. Ironically, in light of many teachers' tendency toward overspecified rhetorical context, these questions are fundamentally rhetorical, but after so many years of practicing modes unrelated to any real writing task, students have come to see writing as an arhetorical enterprise, a mind-numbing drill where the important concerns are the number of words to be completed and whether or not one can write on both sides of the paper (see Britton et al., 1975).

This is not to say that writing teachers have no set goals in mind when giving assignments, nor that they view writing as being arhetorical. But the goals are frequently not articulated to students, and when they are, the students fail to perceive them *as goals* in the performative sense that they relate to their own language activities. The purpose and the intention of the task are the teacher's purpose and intention, not theirs. Essentially, students are being asked to formulate what we may call "nonperformative intentions," intentions unrelated to the functional nature of language, intentions divorced from a specific action *in their world*. Such intentions are inherently arhetorical.

Argumentation provides a compelling example. In their oral discourse, children use argument and the various associated rhetorical strategies in order to manipulate their environment. The world imposes constraints on their behavior, and they try to overcome them. They try to "win." In the classroom, however, the emphasis is on establishing a thesis, or a "truth," and defending it. There is no concern with winning because in the realm of the intellect there is nothing to win, per se. But if winning is not the purpose of the language event, what, in the student's mind, *is* the purpose? What intention should he or she have in producing the essay?

As long as classroom writing remains arhetorical and nonfunctional, there can be no satisfactory answers to these questions. The intention of a given writing task will be implicit in the assignment, but it will be the teacher's intention, which generally has more to do with practicing a particular mode than it does with the ways students use language to perform acts.

The difficulty this imbalance presents is obvious when we seriously consider how hard it is to take on the role of another and truly understand her intention. To make that intention one's own to the extent that it becomes the motivation for linguistic action may be well-nigh impossible (see Flavell, 1968, 1985; Williams, 1985). But meaning requires intention. Without an intention, composing is meaningful only inasmuch as the act of putting words down on paper becomes the purpose of the writing task, which isn't meaningful at all. It results in merely simple representation, realized through the act of putting words on a piece of paper. This is not a rhetorical act. It is nothing more than an assertion: "The words I have put on this piece of paper represent an argument."

There are certain types of acts that we can perform merely on the basis of saying we perform them. If we say "I apologize," we have performed the act of apologizing in the utterance itself. Notice, however, that if we say "I fry an egg," no egg is thereby fried. The second case does not count as performance, simply an assertion. Whether an egg gets fried or not has nothing to do with claiming to fry one. Other, quite specific conditions must be satisfied before we can say we have performed the action of frying the egg.

Too many of our writers fail to make this distinction. The reason may lie in the fact that the rhetoric of oral discourse is rather liberal in allowing us to make assertions without being overly concerned with validity or support. Thus when asked to write an argumentative essay, the assertion "I write an argumentative essay" assumes for our students all the conditions of satisfaction, just as "I apologize" meets the conditions of satisfaction of apologizing. The representation of reality fulfills the intention.

We can even see this reliance on representation in the structure of student argumentative essays. They characteristically consist solely of claims and assertions without reasons or evidence for support. The essays fail in part because we cannot say "I fry an egg" and thereby fry an egg or "I write an argumentative essay" and thereby write an argumentative essay; the capacities of representation are exceeded. We do not have the ability to bring about states of affairs merely by representing them as having been brought about.

In large part, our intentions and actions, linguistic and otherwise, are governed by a set of "by-means-of relations" that our students often ignore. Going back for a moment to the example of the batter, the action of hitting the home run involves a complex set of these by-means-of relations. The child hits the home run by means of stepping into the batter's box, by means of watching the pitch, by means of swinging the bat, and so forth.

In regard to writing, by-means-of relations are rhetorically performative. We can say "I will persuade by means of x," and "I will describe by means of y," but in each case what fills the slot for x or y will be rhetorically related to meaning and purpose. Therefore, we cannot say "I will write an argumentative essay by means of *writing*." The conditions of satisfaction would include at least in part "I will write an argumentative essay by means of writing an argumentative essay by means of gaining adherence of minds, making claims, establishing reasons, providing evidence and proofs, etc."

The causal nature of actions complicates matters for students and teachers alike. Actions cause things to happen; they bring about change in the environment and the individual. We become aware of causation in the performance of actions. Therefore, the experience of causation is inherent in just about everything we do. The problem is that it becomes relatively easy to attribute a causal relationship to events that are not clearly intentional, thereby confusing intentional actions and simple performances.

By way of example, we may think of those football games we've seen where a player picks up a fumble and runs 60 yards or so, in the wrong direction, for a touchdown in the opposing team's end zone. We can imagine that as he is running down the field the player must feel rather proud of himself, convinced that he is the cause of at least six points and perhaps winning the game.

That feeling lasts until he discovers his mistake, when it is replaced by surprise and dismay. The intention in this case was to score points, but certainly not for the other team, and it seems just as certain that the player thought he was fulfilling that intention as he ran down the field.

For him, the act of running was the means of fulfilling the intention, and in the performance of that act he experienced the causal relation between running and points on the scoreboard. Only afterward does he perceive that the causal experience is false.

Something similar happens with student writers. When they begin working on a writing assignment, the act of putting words down on paper provides the causal experience of having fulfilled the intentions inherent in the assignment, calling for narration, analysis, description, or what have you. This act, in other words, has the effect of producing a causal experience such that generating words is equated with satisfying the conditions of the assignment.

Based on their causal experience, apprentice writers may confuse the "intentional act" ("I *am writing* a narrative essay") with the "intentional content" ("I *have written* a narrative essay"). They will believe they have succeeded in satisfying the conditions of the assignment, producing a narrative essay, even if they have not, because they have the experience of performing an act they label "writing a narrative essay."

In too many instances, the act doesn't even change from one assignment to another; students merely change their labels. As teachers we will recognize that their belief is false, but recognition may not come quite so easily to students. Indeed, as experience shows us, they are surprised when told that they have failed to satisfy the requirements of the assignment, because they have the causal experience of having performed the act.

Admittedly, these are complex concerns. I've known more than one teacher to look somewhat befuddled after considering language as intentional action and to mutter, "I never realized teaching writing could be so complicated." It is complicated, of course, in spite of the common conviction that teaching writing should be easy. But one doesn't teach students the technical details of purpose and intention and cause presented here. One uses this information to develop teaching strategies that enable students to take advantage of the language skills they already possess.

The aim is to help them understand the rhetorical nature of writing. For very young children, this can be as straightforward as practice in observing the details of language that appears in their world: labels on clothes and packages, signs at school and in stores, and so forth. For older children it may involve practice in drawing inferences and conclusions on the basis of a small body of data. But in both cases, the focus must be on the rhetorical aspect of language, on action and purpose.

Discourse Plans

The importance of planning is a natural consequence of the definition of rhetoric as the conscious control of language to bring about an intended effect in an audience. The plan that underlies a completed discourse represents a figurative bridge between intentions and effects, and it is a fundamental part of rhetoric. In the pragmatic view, plans must exist in some form or another before students start writing; that is, we do not simply ask them to write and then try to help them discover or impose a plan after the fact.

We can begin tracing the relationship between planning and rhetoric by noting that there is some evidence that rudimentary discourse plans exist as models internalized on the basis of developmental experience with language. Ann Matsuhashi (1981), for example, reports that students in her study were more successful at writing narrative reports than at writing argument because they have a well established "familiarity with a script for narratives of personal experience." She suggests that the difficulties students had with argument and exposition were the result of the lack of "an internalized script" (p. 129). Linda Flower and John Hayes (1981) make a similar suggestion, arguing that competent writing develops out of generalized writing plans, perhaps in the form of a story grammar.

Along similar lines, Steve Krashen (1985) bases his claims for a positive correlation between reading and writing on the notion of internalized discourse models. In his view, which will be discussed in more detail in Chapter 3, good writers were avid readers as children, perhaps specifically as adolescents. Reading, he believes, develops a set of models or plans for various types of discourse. It gives children genre familiarity. When avid readers sit down to write, these models provide the structure for organization and development, and all that remains for the writer to do is supply the information. With the plan for a narrative clearly in mind, a child doesn't need to concentrate on beginning, middle, and end but can get on with the details of the narrative.

Although the idea that writers use internalized plans or models to structure their discourse may seem like simple common sense to most people, not all scholars agree that it truly reflects the reality of composing. Theorists like Ann Berthoff (1981), Peter Elbow (1973), and Ken Macrorie (1970), for example, suggest that plans inhibit the production of good prose. In their view, it is impossible to know anything about what one will do with writing until the act of writing is completed. Then one discovers both plan and purpose in the finished product.

In spite of the considerable influence this notion has had on composition instruction, the research studies referred to above offer strong evidence that some set of internalized models govern language use (also see Williams, 1987; Witte, 1985, 1987). This evidence becomes more compelling when one considers that it is well supported by extensive research in cognitive psychology. Philip Johnson-Laird (1983), for example, has conducted numerous studies that suggest all mental processes, especially those that involve reasoning, are based on generalized models of how the world is structured.

Internalized plans no doubt develop significantly from reading, but they necessarily develop as well from speech. As noted, children may develop the strategies and techniques of argument long before they have any experience with argument in written form. In this respect, we are probably dealing with a general developmental phenomenon linked to maturation.

Planning in Speech and Writing

Both speech and writing require plans, but writing is relatively more planned than speech, which means that one of our tasks is helping students learn how to elaborate discourse plans. There are many instances where utterances occur quite without planning, as in the case of an expletive related to stubbing one's toe in the dark. Yet there are no instances, as far as I can determine, where writing occurs spontaneously, unless we were to consider doodling or the repetitive signing of one's name, characteristic of many people during adolescence, as writing. Both these cases, however, seem more akin to automated behavior, and as such could not be deemed writing.

The rhetorical aspect of most language endeavors leads us to understand that when we talk about discourse planning we are actually talking about *degree* of planning, which varies not only between speech and writing, but between different types of speech and different types of writing, depending on situation, goal, and audience. Some oral discourse will, like a single expletive, have essentially no planning. Spontaneous disagreements that arise in the middle of talk about where to go for dinner provide one example. At the other end of the continuum we have lectures, speeches, classroom presentations, interviews, and the like that are so very well planned that it is difficult to distinguish the degree of planning from what we find in the best written discourse.

The degree of planning related to speech and writing can also be distinguished on the basis of intention. Oral discourse can be successful as both representation and communication even if one does not formulate an intention prior to making an utterance. That is, if you stub your toe in the dark and utter "Damn!" you succeed in communicating a message, if anyone is listening, even though just prior to, and in the process of, uttering that exclamation you had neither intention nor plan to communicate anything at all. It is impossible to perform the same feat in written discourse for several reasons, the most significant being the absence of instances of spontaneous writing.

As soon as one *decides* to write, one has formulated an intention based on the logical properties of the act. We can understand this concept better if we consider that writing, unlike speech, always has an intentional object. Thus when one decides to write, the conditions of satisfaction specify not only the requirement (that one write) but the thing required (that one write *something*). Therefore, one decides to write a letter or a journal or a report or a shopping list or an essay.

We cannot make the same claim for utterances. Individual utterances obviously have objects in the sense that they are *about* something, and they share this characteristic with individual written expressions, but "speaking about something" is not the same as "speaking something." One case is not intentional, whereas the other is. Note in this regard that we cannot say "I have decided to speak a letter," or "I have decided to speak a shopping list." The fact that we can substitute only the verb *dictate* in such sentences is revealing and supports our semantic awareness, based on mental models of how such things operate, that dictating is quite a different task from speaking. But the real difference is rooted in the fundamental concepts of planning, goals, and intentions—or, in other words, rhetoric.

Prewriting

One result of scholarly interest in writing plans has been an emphasis on "prewriting." The aim of prewriting activities, of course, is to help students develop a plan for producing an essay, to help them with the process of elaboration. These activities take different forms, depending on the inclination of the instructor. The predominant forms consist of: (1) class discussion of a topic before students begin to write; (2) free-writing activities designed to stimulate thought and ideas; and (3) brainstorming, often in association with outlining or clustering.

Clustering is much like outlining in that it emphasizes jotting down ideas that may be relevant to the topic, and it connects these ideas in a more or less systematized fashion, with the relationship between circled or clustered ideas depicted through connecting lines. Class discussion appears to be most popular at the elementary level, whereas a combination of class discussion and clustering appears to be favored at the high school and college levels.

Prewriting is such an intuitively reasonable prerequisite to competent composing, and it has become such an enshrined part of writing pedagogy, that many teachers can't avoid feeling uneasy when they discover that there are no reliable data to suggest that prewriting activities of the sort mentioned above have any measurable effect on writing performance. J. F. Gauntlett (1978), for example, studied 315 high school students who engaged in prewriting activities that involved "sensing, imagining, feeling, talking, and writing" (p. 29). As a control, he also studied 257 high school students who did not engage in prewriting activities. Gauntlett found no significant differences between the writing of the two groups after four months of work. Other researchers have obtained similar results (see Alloway et al., 1979; Olson & DiStephano, 1980).

It's entirely possible that these studies were confounded by factors unrelated to prewriting per se, but we have no way of determining this.

It seems more likely, however, that the lack of measurable effect may be related to the nature of the prewriting activities. Free writing offers a case in point. In spite of its popularity among writing teachers, the available research suggests that free writing is not a particularly effective technique for improving writing performance (Hillocks, 1986). Moreover, although in theory prewriting is a technique for generating things to say and ways to organize them, in practice the emphasis often seems to be on the form and structure of the prewriting activity. Students developing an outline of their brainstorming, for example, will worry greatly about the placement of headings and subheadings, confusing the form of the prewriting activity with the form of the essay.

It seems extremely easy for brainstorming, free writing, and clustering to become systematized to the point where they simply fail to help students plan. Although the very notion of "systematized free writing" or "systematized brainstorming" sounds contradictory, it isn't if students come to believe that no writing can take place unless the designated prewriting activity is completed. Under such circumstances, prewriting represents yet one more specified part of an assignment, thereby doing nothing but adding to the difficulty of the task.

By way of illustration, not long ago my colleague Ross Winterowd and I collected research data from elementary and high schools in the Los Angeles area that included about 500 narrative and argumentative student essays written in class on topics we provided for participating teachers. In each of the schools, brainstorming has for several years been the prewriting technique of choice among teachers, and when we conducted our pilot study we noted two things. First, every student in the pilot produced either an outline or a cluster that reflected the results of his or her brainstorming. Second, every student spent so much time making the outline or cluster neat that very little time was left for actual writing.

The goal of brainstorming is idea generation, and writing the ideas down is an option that has significantly less importance under timed writing conditions than under nontimed conditions. Producing an outline or a cluster is a memory aid for ideas and organization. Presumably, most students won't forget their ideas five minutes after generating them, as one might after a day or two, and timed writing assignments tend by their very nature to impose organization. One might assume on this basis that prewriting would be limited to assignments that take several days to complete, either inside or outside class. But it appears that prewriting, as well as the other "stages" discussed in Chapter 1, has become part of *all* writing tasks, even impromptu ones, in numerous schools across the country.

In our research, we wanted students to write as much as possible, so when we gave topics to the teachers participating in the actual study, we included instructions for students stating that they should not produce formal outlines or clusters as part of their brainstorming, but at most should jot down a few notes and then begin writing.

Even though they understood the details of the study, our teachers balked at this suggestion on the grounds that the formal outline or cluster was a vital part of the writing process; without it there was, they maintained, no prewriting. After some discussion, the teachers agreed to forward our instructions. Yet over 90 percent of the students ignored the instructions and developed a formal outline or cluster. Although several analyses and explanations are possible, I would argue that for these students (and teachers) prewriting, in the form of an outline or cluster, has become a systematized part of the writing process, as inviolable as the introductory paragraph. If prewriting becomes systematized, of course, it no longer functions very well to generate ideas for content and form.

There is another reason the studies mentioned above may fail to show any significant effect for prewriting on writing performance. Prewriting presupposes that at least the major aspects of discourse planning take place prior to writing. Yet quite a bit of research suggests that a great deal of planning actually takes place during the writing process. Flower and Hayes (1981) and Matsuhashi (1981), for example, point out that writing does not occur in an uninterrupted stream of words but is frequently broken up by pauses. The average length of pauses varies, depending on the writer's skill and the difficulty of the writing task. Thus writers tend to take longer pauses when writing an analytical essay than when writing a narrative.

Flower and Hayes and Matsuhashi suggest that pauses represent planning periods, and a simple comparison of pause lengths indicates that, at least for impromptu writing, more planning takes place during than before writing. We have no similar comparison for out-of-class writing, so we can't really conclude that the emphasis on prewriting is misplaced, but it does begin to appear as though the theoretical connection between prewriting and writing performance is not as clear as it should be.

Additional findings make the connection even more problematic. When, for example, Flower and Hayes examined the differences between good writers and poor ones, they found that not only did the good writers engage in more planning than the poor writers during the composing process, but that the nature of the planning differed between the two groups. The good writers primarily considered rhetorical features such as the nature of the audience, purpose, and intention. The poor writers, on the other hand, primarily considered surface features like spelling, punctuation, and word choice.

This isn't to say that good writers don't also consider surface features when writing, only that rhetorical features are primary. Actually, the writing plans of good writers appear to be multilayered, consisting of global features like purpose and local features like word choice. During pauses, these writers seem to shift back and forth from one layer to another (see Williams, 1983, 1987).

Given such findings, we may begin to understand why research has so far failed to demonstrate any significant connection between prewriting activities as generally conceived and writing performance. The activities themselves may be flawed in terms of content or timing, or both. As a result, they may not facilitate discourse planning in any meaningful way. We see little in them, for example, that leads students to engage in the sort of multilayered planning characteristic of good writers. Furthermore, it seems that too much emphasis may be placed on making prewriting a writing activity, in the form of a systematized outline or cluster, when the emphasis should presumably be on getting the mind to work on the various factors related to the writing task.

Pragmatic Approaches to Planning

In light of the difficulties summarized above, you may want to consider alternatives to the common prewriting activities of free writing, clustering, and outlining. The classroom workshop, mentioned briefly in the first chapter, provides an effective environment for helping students with planning during the actual composing process, when it appears to be most crucial to success. With students working on drafts of papers during class time, it is possible to monitor their progress and to provide periodic input that will enable them to modify and elaborate their plans. Students themselves can also help in this regard, reading and commenting on one another's papers in collaborations that not only improve planning but serve to emphasize the social nature of composing.

For teachers concerned that prewriting activities can encourage students to discover things to write, a reasonable goal may be to take the writing out of prewriting. Class discussions of topics before any writing takes place represent perhaps the best-known activity that doesn't involve writing. The problem with class discussions, however, is that they are generally dominated by teachers, which results in students merely regurgitating someone else's ideas, not generating their own (see Goodlad, 1984). Furthermore, such discussions seldom include an entire class. Quiet students, shy students, and uninterested students just don't participate.

A viable modification may lie in a "talk/write" program proposed 20 years ago by Robert Zoellner (1969). He based his proposal on the idea that when students develop an "oral essay" and then write that essay, their performance improves.

In Zoellner's proposal, students are required to meet with their teacher for brief talk/write sessions. In these sessions the students essentially put the essay together orally, or, if the writing assignment calls for a long paper, they put together parts of the essay. In these sessions the teacher functions as, to use Zoellner's term, a "socio-reinforcer" who provides feedback designed to help students achieve a fusion between speech and writing. By linking speech and writing, Zoellner argues, writing teachers can take full advantage of students' existing linguistic and rhetorical competence.

Zoellner's program never caught on in composition studies, perhaps because so many writers and teachers have long been convinced that speech interferes with writing performance (see Dillon, 1981; Hirsch, 1977; Shaughnessy, 1977). Nevertheless, we know that speech reinforces behavior, so we have a model for the program's success (see Crane, 1970). Frank Dance and Carl Larson (1972), for example, explain its success by arguing that speaking acts as a bridge between thought and writing, because it is the discourse mode most familiar to students. There seems to be some element of truth in this claim, at least if we are to give credence to countless teachers who have had the experience of suddenly understanding a difficult topic when forced to present it orally to a class.

The real difficulty in Zoellner's proposal, of course, lies in the time constraints that teachers today must contend with. Meeting with every student for ten minutes, for example, would require five hours for a class of 30. Seeking a compromise that preserves the benefits of the talk/write model, many teachers utilize work groups in which individual students talk through their writing projects before starting them, while the other members listen. At the end of each talk, the group discusses the project and offers suggestions for development. In this setting, the teacher works his or her way around the groups, pausing to listen and offer advice as needed.

The potential success of the talk/write model may perhaps be best understood in terms of discourse planning and *register* (a term used to describe the level of formality of discourse). As already noted, speech is relatively less planned than writing, but there are numerous situations where we are called upon to produce well planned speech. Most of us develop a pragmatic awareness of what constitutes an appropriate register at an early age (Bates, 1976). Dell Hymes (1971) has termed this awareness "communicative competence." It includes not only our knowledge of linguistic or grammatical forms but also our knowledge of language–situation appropriateness. It suggests that with oral discourse, most language users are able to shift from a low level of planning (characteristic, for example, of conversation) to a high level of planning (characteristic, say, of responding to a teacher's question in class). In other words, communicative competence is rhetorical competence. The talk/write model draws on this ability, and students appear to transfer their elaborated speech plan to writing.

Over the last few years interest has been growing among teachers in exploring speaking–writing relationships, as evidenced in the 1984 NCTE publication *Speaking and Writing, K–12*. Nevertheless, the emphasis still tends to be on making distinctions between the two discourse modes, rather than on showing how speech can aid writing development. One hopes that this emphasis will shift in the years ahead as more teachers come to recognize the advantages of applying the pragmatic view of composition.

Rhetoric and Context

One of the major differences between speech and writing is that speech occurs in a context where the audience is visible and where the discourse topic is implicit. Let's suppose for a moment that you are working in your room, typing a term paper on a personal computer. A friend walks in and asks, "How much memory do you have?" Without hesitation you would provide the appropriate response, perhaps "256K." The amount of memory one has in a computer is a fairly important concern, so the question is quite reasonable, as is your response, which indicates the relative storage space your computer has. But both the question and the answer make sense only in a context that includes a computer.

In conversation, the topics of discourse are usually either present or come from a shared body of background information. Moreover, in conversation we are able to draw on a vast range of social or nonverbal cues to help with communication. These range from hand gestures, facial expressions, and other visible points of reference in the context to an understanding of conversational turn-taking and an awareness of appropriateness conditions.

This is not the case in writing. Writing my computer example, for instance, I had to establish a scene to make the question and the response understandable. It was necessary not only to explain the hypothetical situation but to say something about computer memory, in case some readers aren't familiar with personal computers. Writers are required to *create a context* for readers (see Hirsch, 1977; Williams, 1985). If they are successful, writers and readers will share experiences and information that will make the writing comprehensible.

Several researchers have suggested that creating a context for a piece of writing is fundamental to competent discourse (see Bamberg, 1983; Williams, 1985; Witte & Faigley, 1981). In the narrative example of the computer, creating a context consisted simply of setting the scene. In argumentation or analysis, matters are more complex.

Suppose, for example, you ask your class to write an argumentative essay dealing with whether students should be provided smoking areas on campus. Where will they (and you) begin? What must go into creating an appropriate context?

Based on what we know about how people use language in real situations, your students will have to provide background generalizations that establish the topic as one students, parents, and school officials have discussed or may be prepared to discuss. They will also have to establish premises: the value of individual rights, importance of safety from fire hazard, teenagers' personal autonomy, or lack of it, and so on. They will have to identify the topic explicitly, and very important, they will have to offer an acceptable reason for producing the essay. At this point, our discussion of intentionality allows us to recognize that simply fulfilling the assignment should not be deemed an acceptable reason.

Failure to perform any of these tasks may result in incoherent prose (Bamberg, 1983; Witte & Faigley, 1981). It therefore seems that creating a context is another significant by-means-of relation based on an understanding of rhetoric and writing.

Research also suggests that creating a context does not occur spontaneously for student writers, and it is unlikely that it occurs spontaneously for mature, experienced writers, either (see Flower & Hayes, 1981). It requires a plan and an awareness of numerous rhetorical devices related to audience. Writing lacks the social cues that give conversations form and meaning. Creating a context for readers may be thought of as explicitly providing cues that would normally be implicitly available in speech.

In this regard we can imagine the process you would engage in as a teacher if you had to write a note to a student's parents to report poor behavior. The note may be written hours or days after the act that prompted it, and the context of the student's behavior must be re-created for the parents. But the context for such a note would be a relatively easy thing to establish, because you would have a real incident to report, a real audience to report to, and a real purpose in writing. The nonfunctional nature of most student writing, on the other hand, makes it more difficult; it usually lacks reality on all counts, unless one wants to make the dubious claim that the teacher represents a realistic audience.

Sensitive teachers tell students repeatedly to imagine an audience consisting of readers outside the classroom, but as long as the assignment itself remains nonfunctional, such advice doesn't seem to work very well. With little or no experience writing to real audiences with a real purpose, students are inclined to fall back on what experience they do have with real audiences, which is of course speech. Lacking a context for a nonperformative language event, they assume what they consider the normal context or situation for the occurrence of language. With few exceptions, this takes the form of a dialogue where the other participant is internalized as the teacher. Thus student essays are often characterized by conversational features, such as repetition, lack of an identifiable topic, and so forth.

Conclusion

Many people object to the functional view of language and rhetoric presented here. They see language as a tool for reflection and rhetoric as largely a device for the critical evaluation of literature. An emphasis on purpose and plans and intentions is seen as detracting from the role that writing plays in learning and discovery.

In some respects, the discussion of rhetoric in this chapter has implicitly attempted to deal with this point of view. What we currently know about language suggests that we use it to perform actions. One factor that seems to distinguish good writers from poor ones is their awareness that their writing, if successful, will produce an effect on those who read it. This, then, is what rhetoric is about: bringing about a change in an audience. Considering that accomplishing this goal requires knowledge of subject and audience, of sociology and psychology, it seems unlikely that a writer who understands the rhetoric of writing—and it need not be explicit understanding—can produce an essay without learning something.

As teachers, the task we face is devising ways to emphasize the rhetorical aspects of writing in an environment that fosters arhetorical assignments. Admittedly, it's far easier to follow the lessons of those who have come before us and continue asking students to describe their summer vacations. But the reward of seeing students produce readable, interesting essays when they are encouraged to use writing actually to do things seems worth the additional work.

CHAPTER 3

Reading and Writing

Overview

When children grow up in an environment that provides many encounters with written language, most learn to read and write before entering school. Some researchers explain early development of reading and writing ability in terms of pragmatics, suggesting that the functional characteristics of writing help children grasp symbolic correspondences. These characteristics relate context to meaning, as when a child sees her mother remove cookies from a jar labeled "cookies." The child associates the jar and its label with what's inside, arriving at an understanding of the symbol "cookies." Observations like this one have prompted numerous scholars to suggest that meaning is largely context-dependent: We use our understanding of a specific context (understanding based on previous experiences) to construct meaning for the language in that context.

In this account, reading involves much more than simply "decoding" letters and syllables into words. It is a complex activity in which the reader constructs a mental model of meaning and attempts to match this model, on the basis of a set of "instructions" provided in the text, with the one constructed by the writer. These instructions, or *cues*, as they are generally called, include such factors as syntax, context, shared knowledge, and genre. In this model of the psychology of reading, comprehension is the result of what is called a *top-down* process, which indicates that meaning depends largely on global features, such as shared knowledge, rather than on local ones, such as individual words.

Good readers know how to use cues effectively, so they tend to skip over an unfamiliar word encountered in a given passage. They realize that in most instances the meaning will be apparent from the context of the sentence or that its individual meaning is unnecessary to comprehending the whole.

Many beginning reading programs, however, approach reading from the perspective that textual meaning is merely the sum of its visible parts: letters, syllables, and words. They emphasize letter recognition and word accuracy, using a model based on what is generally called a *bottom-up* process. These programs typically attend primarily to form, with repeated error correction as the main pedagogical technique. That this approach has a negative effect on reading seems certain, but often overlooked is the fact that it can also have an adverse influence on writing. Students trained to focus on accuracy and correctness on the surface level of a text when reading will tend to focus on these same factors when writing, failing to consider the rhetorical aspects of composing.

Traditionally, our schools have taught children to read before teaching them to write. Moreover, traditional writing instruction at the beginning level has tended to resemble phonics reading instruction: Students practice writing the alphabet, then words, then sentences, and so on. But over the last several years, increasing numbers of teachers have come to recognize the reciprocal nature of reading and writing. The emphasis on a process approach to composition, with its attention to sharing one's work with others, has made teachers aware that reading what one has written has a positive influence on both activities.

Currently, this awareness is reflected in a growing number of elementary classrooms, where teachers have given up the traditional sequence of instruction. Rather than beginning reading instruction with published texts, children write their own stories and use these as a source of reading materials. Learning how to read is thereby linked intimately with learning how to write, and the children's discourse becomes a vehicle for learning. The availability of microcomputers and printers has facilitated such programs, making it possible for students to "publish" their own texts.

At the junior high and high school levels, the relationship between reading and writing remains largely traditional. For years teachers have used works of literature as models for their students to imitate. The rationale is that by studying a model, students will be able to incorporate the characteristics of professional writing into their own compositions. One of the strongest expressions of this idea is the "reading hypothesis," which maintains that good writers are not only active readers but at some point were *self-motivated, intensive* readers.

There are several problems with this hypothesis, one being the implication that instruction will have little effect on a child who is not a self-motivated reader. For example, Steve Krashen (1981), who developed the reading hypothesis, states that reading "remains the only way of developing competence in writing. . ." (p. 9). Another difficulty is the causal relationship inherent in the hypothesis, suggesting that intensive, self-motivated reading will produce good writers. As we will see, a range of evidence indicates that the reading/writing relationship is far from being as simple as the reading hypothesis suggests. Reading alone may not lead to improved writing performance.

The Psychology of Reading

One of the most fascinating things about children is their ability to grasp complex linguistic relationships without much effort, simply by experiencing them. By the time most children are about three years old, for example, they have made a remarkable discovery: Abstract "pictures" can represent words and convey meaning. With this discovery, they have taken the first step toward reading, and it isn't long before they are able to match individual written words with the things these words designate. When we consider the level of abstraction involved in making the connection between symbols and the world, we recognize that this is indeed no small accomplishment.

A dominant characteristic of children's first efforts with language is that they use it to identify specific objects in their surroundings: "Momma" and "Dadda," of course, but also balls, pets, toys, keys, and so forth. Thus many of their first utterances are names of things.

The special significance of names seems to be related to children's efforts to understand and control their environment. We've already seen how communication requires a background of shared knowledge, and sharing names for things is fundamental to establishing such a background. There's no doubt, certainly, that infants in the pretoddler stage are very good at conveying their wants and needs through gestures, but once they reach the toddler stage parents expect them to begin communicating through speech, and gestures are no longer as readily accepted as communicative acts. Wants and needs also become more complex. Children will use the name of an object to designate the topic of the communicative act and then will use gestures to convey related information (see Foster, 1985a). For example, a child may utter the word *ball* and reach toward it, indicating that she wants the ball.

Moreover, to know the name of something is to give it an existential reality that adults frequently take for granted but that children experience quite profoundly. "I name, therefore it is" doesn't seem too farfetched in light of the fact that a world full of unknown and unidentified objects must appear chaotic. Naming begins to impose order. Most children are therefore excited to discover that names themselves have an existential reality in written form. The visible nature of writing confirms the identity of things in the child's world in a way that speech cannot.

Children are naturally very curious about their own names, and not long after making the connection between words and symbols they take great pleasure in seeing their names in writing. They will frequently ask their parents to write their names for them. Soon, however, they become eager to take up pen and paper themselves and, with a little help initially, will write their name or even the name of a pet or a friend over and over.

Although printing their own name or that of a friend may represent a child's first true act of writing, several investigators have argued that writing begins earlier, in the form of drawing or making squiggles on a piece of paper (see Harste, Burke, & Woodward, 1983; Graves, 1975, 1979; Gundlach, 1981, 1982, 1983; Vygotsky, 1978). Graves (1975), for example, argues that young children use drawing as a rehearsal for writing, and certainly it isn't unusual for preliterate children to combine pictures with scribbles as they "compose" notes for friends and relatives. When asked what a note says, they are quite happy to "read" it aloud, as though they recognize that their writing is not yet at a stage where it can be read by others. Having observed her son engage in this kind of writing activity, Bissex (1980) suggests that he used writing as an extension of both speech and drawing to help himself name and organize his world. She states:

> As a five-year-old he was still absorbed in naming, in knowing his world by naming its parts; through his signs and labels and captions he extended this process in writing. In the next year or two, as his reasoning developed and his need to know and control the world around him [increased] . . . this process was reflected in . . . charts and other organizational writing (p. 101).

Observing young children having their first experiences with the printed word can tell us quite a bit about how reading and writing develop. It appears that the ability to read and the ability to write manifest themselves at about the same time, but usually not at the same pace; language production always seems to lag behind language comprehension, even in adults.

Children have the ability to develop reading and writing skills (admittedly at a rudimentary level) well before starting their formal schooling. Scollon and Scollon (1979) and Heath (1981, 1983) demonstrate that parents in many cultural groups engage their children in reading activities at quite an early age, often as young as one month. They frequently begin with picture-labeling games and bedtime stories, and it isn't unusual for two-year-olds with such experiences to manifest word recognition skills. When working with preschool teachers several years ago, I observed children as young as three reading with both fluency and understanding in preschools that emphasized a functional approach to language.

Based on findings like these, Frank Smith (1983) states that "children do not learn by instruction; they learn by example, and they learn by making sense of what are essentially meaningful situations" (p. 9). It is Smith's belief that if a child cannot read and write by the time he or she begins school, the problem lies not in the child but in the parents, who have failed to provide meaningful reading and writing experiences. He isn't suggesting that parents engage in any of the so-called superbaby programs, which purportedly produce toddler geniuses through intensive stimulation. Smith's "meaningful experiences" consist largely of sharing the printed word with children.

An emphasis on language in meaningful situations reinforces once again our perception of language as a functional activity (see Halliday, 1973). The functional aspects of reading are fairly apparent. Children typically learn to read signs and labels that they encounter on a day-to-day basis before they learn to read books. Being able to distinguish shampoo from conditioner and the boys' restroom from the girls' restroom is important, so children are highly motivated to connect context with print and vice versa. In addition, entertainment seems quite an important function of language, and there is no question that children generally seem to enjoy being read to.

The Nature of Reading

For many years now there has been a debate regarding how people read and thus how children learn to read. The issue is phonics, or the sounds that letters stand for. On one hand are writers like Flesch (1955), Fries (1962), and Mathews (1966), who argue that the best way to teach reading is through the systematic teaching of phonics. In this view, success in reading depends on accurately identifying words and the sound of words. On the other hand are writers like Gibson and Levin (1975), Goodman (1967, 1973), and F. Smith (1972, 1983), who argue that successful reading is more complicated than phonics advocates recognize, and that it entails predicting and synthesizing meaning on the basis of a broad range of cues, such as syntax, context, intention, and purpose, as well as phonics.

The issues in this debate are important to our discussion of writing, because the writer is his or her own first reader. Revisions and editing are inextricably linked to the writer's role as reader. In addition, the phonics approach to reading has much in common with the product view of writing. All these factors suggest that how one reads will therefore affect how one writes (see Beach & Liebman-Kleine, 1986; Self, 1986).

According to advocates of phonics, reading begins with the print on the page. Readers look at individual letters, combine those letters into syllables, the syllables into words, the words into phrases and clauses, and the phrases and clauses into sentences. Meaning in this account is determined from the meaning of individual words; these individual meanings are then summed to form the meaning of an entire sentence.

In addition, individual word meanings are derived on the basis of sound, which is to suggest that there is not only a direct spelling-to-sound correspondence for words but also a direct correspondence between the sound of a word and its meaning. This conceptualization of reading, going from letters to meaning, is usually referred to as an example of a *bottom-up* model of information processing.

There are numerous problems with the phonics view, one of the most obvious being the notion that meaning can be derived simply on the basis of a spelling-to-sound correspondence. The meaning of individual words more often than not depends on syntax and context, not on spelling, as the word *house* in the following sentences illustrates:

(1) The house needs new paint.

(2) The House refused to pass the minimum-wage bill.

(3) The officials asked us to house the refugees.

In addition, there is significant research that suggests that the bottom-up processing model does not correctly depict actual language endeavors (see Abbott, Black, & Smith, 1985; Fodor, Bever, & Garrett, 1974; Kintsch & van Dijk, 1978; Malt, 1985; Schank & Abelson, 1977; Warren & Warren, 1970). Comprehending a sentence like (2), for example, clearly involves knowing not just the meanings of the individual words but also something about how government operates. The meaning of *house* in this case depends on this knowledge. Thus meaning comes not from combining letters into the word (from bottom up) but from applying knowledge of the world to this particular word (from top down). Writers like Johnson-Laird (1983), Sanford and Garrod (1981), and F. Smith (1983) conclude on the basis of sentences like (1)–(3) that reading is primarily a top-down process.

Philip Johnson-Laird suggests that top-down information processing relies on the development of mental models that describe how the world functions. We're able to distinguish the three different meanings of the word *house* in the sentences above, for example, because we're able to construct separate mental models for each sentence. These models, developed from and elaborated through experience, necessarily are relatively general, because the experiences of any two people rarely if ever match exactly. With a sentence like "The house needs new paint," even when the house is visible to the person producing the sentence as well as to the person processing it, their mental models of the house may differ. Consider a scenario in which the house in question is up for sale and a potential buyer tells the owner, "The house needs new paint." The mental models for buyer and seller reasonably would include a component related to "money saved" for the former and "money lost" for the latter.

In spite of the nonspecific nature of mental models—or perhaps because of it—speakers and hearers and writers and readers *can* achieve a match, and then comprehension occurs. But sometimes there is no match. When this happens, the audience will reject its initial mental model and try a different one until a match is achieved or until it gives up and classifies the discourse as incomprehensible.

Frank Smith (1972) calls this process "the reduction of uncertainty" (p. 18), but perhaps a more descriptive and useful expression is *hypothesis testing.* That is, a reader formulates certain hypotheses regarding the meaning of a text and then tests those hypotheses against the text itself. A simple example will illustrate the process. When you looked at the title of this book, *Preparing to Teach Writing,* you automatically formed a hypothesis regarding its content. When you opened the cover and started reading the preface or the table of contents, your hypothesis (that this book is about writing) was confirmed. Your mental model matched the model of the text.

A similar, although more complex, process occurs during the course of reading sentences, paragraphs, chapters, and so forth. For example, when a sentence begins with the subject, readers hypothesize that a verb construction will soon follow. Likewise, the topic sentence of a paragraph prompts readers to formulate hypotheses regarding the content of the rest of the sentences in the paragraph. In the event that a verb construction does not soon follow the subject or the paragraph does not elaborate the topic sentence, readers' modeled expectations are defeated; comprehension is then very difficult.

The concept of hypothesis testing suggests that words, sentences, and longer units of discourse have significance only because readers already know a great deal about what the words and sentences mean. Because children know relatively less about the world than adults, the top-down approach to reading instruction is ideally complemented by phonics instruction, but it seems certain that the emphasis must be on developing knowledge and experience to construct meaning.

In this regard, most of us at one time or another have tried to read a chapter or an article in a subject we know very little about. For some it might be physics or economics, or even something more mundane, like an insurance policy. We know the meanings of the individual words in the individual sentences, but for the life of us we can't figure out what the sentences mean. Drawing on this observation, Sanford and Garrod (1981) conclude that writing consists of supplying "a series of instructions which tell the reader how to utilize the knowledge he already has, and contingently modify this knowledge in light of the literal content of the discourse itself" (p. 8). Thus a successful writer provides appropriate instructions; an unsuccessful writer does not.

Error Correction and Reading

Perhaps an even more significant problem with the phonics approach is its typical emphasis on error. Most beginning reading in the classroom is done aloud, because it allows the teacher to monitor student progress. Such monitoring can be valuable if used properly; the teacher can observe a child's reading strategies and then work individually with him or her to improve comprehension. But what we frequently find in classrooms where teachers stress phonics is that reading becomes merely a process of accurately pronouncing words, with the teacher correcting children when they make mistakes.

To understand the consequences of such error correction, we need to consider that reading strategies fall into only two categories: (1) utilizing the cues provided by syntax, context, purpose, and so forth, and (2) speed. Cues operate in a relatively straightforward fashion. For example, our knowledge of English syntax allows us to predict word functions and meaning. In a sentence that begins "The policeman," we can predict that what immediately follows will probably be a verb.

Speed, however, is often overlooked as a reading strategy, even though it is a very important part of comprehension. If reading proceeds too slowly, comprehension becomes extremely difficult. The reason lies in how the mind processes and stores information.

Cognitive psychologists currently propose that memory consists of three components: short-term memory, working memory, and long-term memory. In regard to reading, short-term memory is where information is stored momentarily while a person decides what to do with it. If one has no need to retain the information, it is discarded after a few seconds, and it cannot be retrieved. If one decides to retain the information, however, it goes into working memory, which is believed to act as a processing buffer between short-term memory and long-term memory. According to most models, one part of working memory stores a limited amount of information for a limited time, while the other part processes the information for meaning. Once processing is completed, meaning is stored in long-term memory, often indefinitely.

Reading speed is therefore crucial to comprehension because it is related to information processing. When proficient readers read a sentence, they break it into phrases that shift very rapidly from short-term memory to working memory. The phrases are held momentarily in working memory, where they are processed into propositions that are stored in long-term memory (see Shankweiler & Crain, 1986). (A proposition may be considered the meaning conveyed in a construction [see Lyons, 1977].)

Because short-term memory has a limited capacity, it is easily overloaded. Few people can hold more than seven bits of information in short-term memory without some deterioration. We can see, then, that if reading proceeds on the basis of words rather than phrases, if attention is on words rather than meaning, each word will be held in short-term memory until its capacity is reached, at which point an incoming word will displace one of those being held. This sort of overload has been demonstrated to severely impair comprehension (see H. Clark & E. Clark, 1977; Malt, 1985).

To prevent an overload, information must be transferred to working memory at a rapid pace, which can be accomplished only if readers process clusters of words (phrases or clauses). Generally speaking, poor readers do not work with phrases, they work with single words. They process words one at a time, soon overloading short-term memory and thus prohibiting integration into sentence or discourse meaning (F. Smith, 1972). We encounter this phenomenon regularly among poor readers. Although they can pronounce every word in a passage, and if queried can provide the meaning of the individual words, they are quite unable to summarize the meaning of what they have just read. They are processing words, not meaning. In this regard, Shankweiler and Crain (1986) argue that reading problems are actually working-memory problems.

Something similar occurs with children reading aloud whom a teacher interrupts in order to correct an error. The child's attention becomes so focused on individual words that comprehension is sacrificed to accuracy. As a result, reading speed slows, making comprehension even less likely because short-term memory becomes overtaxed, which in turn results in working-memory dysfunction.

Reading aloud without practicing the passage in advance is quite difficult. Even experienced readers make errors of various sorts, errors that Goodman (1973) has termed *miscues* (also see Watson, 1985). You can demonstrate for yourself how easy it is to miscue simply by reading the next page aloud. This analysis shouldn't be construed as advocating sloppiness or carelessness, of course. But it does suggest that an overconcern with word accuracy can be damaging.

Miscues can be classified into the following four types, listed in descending order of frequency of occurrence and with corresponding examples:

Type	*Printed Text/Uttered Text*
(1) substitution	the beautiful woman/the pretty woman
(2) omission	a cold, rainy day/a rainy day
(3) insertion	gave her a kiss/gave to her a kiss
(4) scramble	the girls left/they all left

When children read aloud, miscues tend to be seen as evidence of unfamiliarity with a word, so the child is corrected and asked to reread it. Several studies have shown, however, that most such miscues preserve the meaning of the passage, as in (1) above, so such error correction seems of limited value (see Weber, 1968; Gibson & Levin, 1975). Gibson and Levin, for example, report that 90 percent of substitution errors preserve the meaning of the text. If meaning is preserved, there seems no reason to make a correction. In the event that the miscue does not preserve meaning, some evidence suggests that children will stop and reread the passage, making the correction themselves if given the chance (see F. Smith, 1983).

It's difficult to determine to what extent teachers' corrections of reading are influenced by parents' similar error corrections of children's speech. Yet clearly the two are related, not only in their intent but also in their effectiveness, or lack of it. Clark and Clark (1977) offer an example that illustrates the typical result of a parent's attempt at correcting the speech of her child:

CHILD: My teacher holded the baby rabbits and we patted them.

MOTHER: Did you say your teacher held the baby rabbits?

CHILD: Yes.

MOTHER: What did you say she did?

CHILD: She holded the baby rabbits and we patted them.

MOTHER: Did you say she held them tightly?

CHILD: No, she holded them loosely. (p. 333)

Extensive error correction seems to bring an element of fear into the reading process. Students whose mistakes are corrected all the time quickly develop failure anxiety that interferes with learning, because learning involves risk taking. Children who are so afraid of failure that they refuse to take risks will not learn very quickly and most likely will not find learning particularly pleasant (see S. Harter, 1981; S. Harter & Connell, 1981).

When children are trained to read in a way that makes them fear taking risks, they are likely to transfer their failure anxiety to writing. They will also be inclined to concentrate on surface correctness rather than on global features associated with meaning. We can predict not only that these students will find writing unpleasant, but that their writing will lack the rhetorical features essential for comprehension. Their written sentences may not even be "grammatical," because they fail to recognize, and thus to utilize, something as basic as syntactic cues. It appears, then, that reading and reading instruction have a major impact on writing performance, and certainly it isn't surprising to find that poor writers are generally poor readers, and vice versa. Our goal is therefore to provide meaningful contexts for students to engage in reading and writing activities, utilizing a functional, pragmatic approach that links literacy to our students' world.

The Reading Hypothesis

Although teachers have only recently become concerned about the effect of reading instruction on writing performance, they have long speculated on the relationship between people's reading habits and their ability to write, perhaps because classroom experience shows us that good writers are usually good readers.

Various scholars have attempted to explain this relationship, and one of the more interesting efforts comes from Steve Krashen (1981b, 1985). He approaches the question from the perspective that composition skill is similar to second language skill: Mastery requires comprehensible input over an extended time. He bases his argument on our present knowledge of language acquisition.

Let me explain briefly that "acquiring" language is different from "learning" it. Acquisition involves the *unconscious* assimilation *of* language, whereas learning involves the *conscious* mastery of knowledge *about* language (see Chapter 4). In this account, students of a second language acquire that language when surrounded by people who use it daily.

We can further distinguish between acquisition and learning by considering that in the early stages of language development children only occasionally repeat sentences they hear; they tend to generate their own expressions. This phenomenon suggests that children do not learn a particularly large set of expressions or phrases that they repeat back under appropriate conditions. Instead, they seem to internalize the grammar of the language, which enables them to produce unique utterances.

We can't say that they "learn" this grammar. We can't even say that they are *taught* the grammar; in all but a few cases, parents don't have the linguistic background necessary to describe the complex array of grammatical rules that underlies their children's utterances. But because acquisition is based on unconscious assimilation, no such description is needed. What is required is comprehensible and meaningful input, from which a child makes generalizations regarding form, function, intention, and meaning. By way of illustration, we can consider a scenario in which a parent holds out a ball to a child and asks, "Would you like to play with the ball?" and then rolls the ball to the child.

Krashen proposes that writing ability is acquired in a similar manner, through reading rather than through listening. In his view, we gain competence in writing the same way we gain competence in oral language, by comprehending written discourse and by internalizing, after much exposure, the numerous conventions that characterize texts. He states, for example, that "if second language acquisition and the development of writing ability occur in the same way, writing ability is not learned but is acquired via extensive reading in which the focus of the reader is on the message, i.e., reading for genuine interest and/or pleasure" (1985, p. 23).

Krashen (1981b, 1985) calls this proposal the *reading hypothesis,* and he argues the following: (1) "all good writers will have done large amounts of pleasure reading" (1981b, p. 3); (2) "good writers, as a group, read and have read more than poor writers" (1981b, p. 3); (3) "reading remains the only way of developing competence in writing" (1981b, p. 9). Drawing on self-report reading surveys, he further argues that good writers are not only active readers, but self-motivated readers who read intensively during adolescence.

The reading hypothesis is an elegant way of explaining the differences in writing ability that we see in students, and it seems entirely accurate in proposing that reading allows us to internalize the conventions of written discourse as mental models. Nevertheless, the hypothesis may not be valid.

Careful consideration reveals several difficulties. One of the biggest is the notion that writing is the equivalent of a foreign language. This view is quite popular, in part because it reinforces the idea that writing is intrinsically different from speech. Yet we have little or no data to support this position. In fact, a great deal of research indicates that in literate societies writing (at a rudimentary level) and speech manifest themselves at about the same time, which suggests that the two are developmentally linked (Gundlach, 1981, 1982, 1983; Harste, Burke, & Woodward, 1983). If writing is merely another communication mode associated with the primary language and not a separate code, the premise underlying the reading hypothesis is incorrect.

Longitudinal studies of language development like those of Walter Loban (1976) also indicate that language proficiency in general and writing ability in particular begin to manifest themselves very early in life—in the case of Loban's subjects, as early as kindergarten. More important, Loban found that the relative proficiency of subjects remains stable over time: Children with skills rated highly in kindergarten were rated highly in twelfth grade. Similarly, those with skills rated low in kindergarten were rated low in twelfth grade. Clearly more factors are at work than simply self-motivated reading during adolescence. Loban's analysis suggests that socioeconomic status was the variable that best accounted for differences in proficiency (which parallels the findings of Heath [1983] who reports significant differences in pragmatic development of language across socioeconomic and ethnic groups).

Although Krashen uses empirical data to support the reading hypothesis, we may question the validity of conclusions made on the basis of self-reported data such as he reports. Can we truly say that all good writers were intense, self-motivated readers during adolescence, simply because they say they were? Most researchers recognize that questionnaire surveys are generally subject to an affective dimension difficult to control: They often reflect the image respondents would like to have of themselves, or the image they want investigators to have of them.

For example, Irene Clark (1986) conducted a survey at the University of Southern California quite similar to Krashen's, in which she correlated subjects' writing performance with their reading histories. Yet unlike Krashen, Clark found no significant correlation between writing performance and reading history. As she states: "Although students at USC do vary in their writing abilities, at least according to the range of grades given by their instructors and the scores they receive on the [holistically scored] exam, they all claim to have come from remarkably similar home environments . . . and all profess equally similar attitudes and behaviors concerning reading and writing" (p. 9). In attempting to explain these results, she concludes that it is very likely that the subjects "responded not according to what actually occurred [in their reading histories], but according to the way they thought they ought to respond" (p. 11).

Krashen formulates the reading hypothesis as merely a correlation between reading and writing, but he seems unable to avoid shifting to a causal relationship when he discusses reading and writing pedagogy. He states, for example, that "reading is the main 'cause' of writing ability" (1981b, p. 12). In other words, not only do good writers tend to be good readers, but good readers tend to be good writers. Evidence from our own experiences, however, suggests that many people are good readers, self-motivated readers, but terrible writers. Most college students, for example, encounter at least one unreadable textbook during their work toward a degree, and chances are it was written by a professor who has read voluminously.

There is no question that the reading hypothesis offers an attractive explanation of the connection between reading and writing. Careful analysis indicates, however, that it does not adequately deal with the complexities of the relationship. It fails to account for the psychological and social factors that appear to influence writing proficiency. We should therefore be cautious about accepting the reading hypothesis as a valid representation of the reading/writing relationship.

Models and Writing

The study of models to enhance a student's discourse skills is a pedagogical technique that goes back to ancient Greece, where once students in grammar schools had mastered reading, the teacher introduced them to the study of literature. The goal was not only to acquaint students with great works of literature but to give them models to imitate so that their own oratory or writing would reach a higher level of excellence.

Currently, the use of models in writing instruction remains very popular in spite of a shift over the last several years to a process approach that emphasizes students' own writing rather than that of professionals (see T. Johnson & Louis, 1985). The use of models is particularly prevalent in junior and senior high schools. The huge number of anthologies available on the market, a number that increases every year, is one indication of the pervasiveness of modeling pedagogy.

This pedagogy can be divided into two categories. "Passive modeling" consists essentially of literary criticism. Students read published works, write analytical essays about them, and through frequent exposure to the models supposedly acquire the skills of professional writers.

The second category is "active modeling," in which students read an essay or a story and attempt to capture nuances of style or organization in their own work. For example, a teacher may have students read a narrative or descriptive essay about an important event in the writer's life. Students would then be asked to compose a similar essay, reproducing as closely as possible the detail and tone of the original. In another activity, students may be asked to engage in what is frequently referred to as *patterned writing*, in which they are offered a model of language—a poem, for instance—to be used as a framework for their own efforts. The example that follows, written by a third grader, illustrates this technique; the original verse comes from Olive Wadsworth's *Over in the Meadow* (1971):

Original

Over in the meadow, in the sand, in the sun
Lived an old mother turtle and her little turtle one
"Dig!" said the mother
"I dig" said the one
So he dug all day
In the sand, in the sun.

Student version

There in the treetop, on a branch, having fun
Lived a little mother sparrow and her tiny baby son
"Fly!" said the mother
"I fly" said the son
So he flew all day
Through the air, having fun.

Generally speaking, both these approaches require that teacher and students spend a great deal of time reading and then analyzing the models before engaging in any writing activities. As you may have already recognized, there is a similarity between modeling and the product view of writing. In fact, modeling is often considered a component of the product approach. The emphasis is on the surface features of the text and on the finished work.

Several assumptions underlie modeling. One is that reading and writing are interrelated and that the skills involved in each task are mutually transferable. Another assumption is that knowledge of the characteristics of good writing will enable students to produce effective writing on their own. And yet another is that analyzing examples of good writing will provide such knowledge.

Part of the rationale for these assumptions is our intuitive perception that, indeed, one must have at least some genre familiarity in order to manipulate writing's formal conventions. It would, for example, be very difficult to write a sonnet without ever having actually seen and analyzed a sonnet.

In addition, research on mental models supports the idea that performing cognitive tasks relies significantly on internalized models developed generally on the basis of experience (Johnson-Laird, 1983). Thus even if we consider a form less esoteric than the sonnet, the fact remains that many of the formal conventions found in writing, such as explicit cohesive ties like *however* and *therefore*, are rarely found in conversational speech. The models for using these conventions must come from somewhere, and experience with reading appears to be the only reasonable source.

Relatively few studies have thoroughly investigated the reading/ writing relationship, and as a result there is not a vast amount of data to support the idea that studying a professional model will significantly improve writing performance. But Donelson (1967) examined essays from "effective" and "ineffective" tenth-grade writers, comparing evaluations on three of their essays and correlating these with self-reports of reading activity, and he found that the effective writers reported reading more than the ineffective writers. Woodward and Phillips (1967) conducted a similar study using college freshmen; again, the good writers reported reading relatively more than the poor writers. Kimberling, Wingate, Rosser, DiChiara, and Krashen (1978) also used self-reported data and likewise found a significant correlation between reading and writing performance.

Not all studies of the reading/writing relationship have followed this sort of survey approach. Thibodeau (1964), working with sixth graders, Reedy (1966) with ninth graders, and Stefl (1981) with third graders, established treatment and control groups and used brief passages selected to model specific characteristics of good prose. Students in the treatment groups were presented with the models for analysis; students in the control groups were not. In each case, the treatment groups demonstrated significant gains in writing performance over the control groups. Thus it would seem, on the basis of these studies, that the case for modeling is sound. Shortly, however, we will see that this conclusion may be hasty.

Using Models in the Classroom

Certain studies suggest that the role of modeling in writing performance has yet to be described adequately. William Clark (1968), for example, developed a controlled study using one group of college students that analyzed models and a second group that did not. At the end of the study, no significant difference in writing between the groups was found, based on holistic evaluation of pretreatment and posttreatment writing samples. Lareau (1971) and Perry (1980), also working with college students, used similar methods with similar results.

At the elementary and secondary levels, a range of studies using models under controlled conditions failed to demonstrate any significant differences between treatment and control groups (see Caplan & Keech, 1980; Martin, 1981; Pinkham, 1969; Sponsler, 1971; Vinson, 1980; West, 1967). On the basis of findings such as these, it seems that we can conclude only that the empirical results related to using models to improve writing performance are mixed.

Explaining why text modeling is not more effective is difficult and of necessity must be speculative. Krashen (1985) would suggest that time is the significant factor, that students must experience the models over a period of years before their characteristics are internalized. This view, however, is inconsistent with the fact that some models are internalized on the basis of a single experience. A child who watches his father take cookies out a cookie jar once knows forever after where to go for cookies. For concrete linguistic relationships, such as the connection between an object and the word that denotes that object, it also is possible to internalize a model on the basis of a single experience.

It may very well be that the mixed results concerning the effectiveness of writing models can be attributed to the fact that they are so abstract that they are difficult to internalize, through either acquisition or learning. At first glance, one would immediately object to this idea on the grounds that many other aspects of language, such as grammar, are equally abstract and yet are acquired by virtually everyone, regardless of intelligence. We should keep in mind, however, that something like grammar is embedded in a highly meaningful, concrete, functional context. Generally speaking, text models are not.

We begin to see the difficulty the abstract nature of textual models can cause when we consider what Philip Johnson-Laird (1983) calls the "principle of structural identity," which states: "The structures of mental models are identical to the structures of the states of affairs, whether perceived or conceived, that the models represent" (p. 419). If this principle is valid, and there is every reason at this point to believe it is, then we must ask how abstract textual relations, such as tone, audience, purpose, and so forth, are represented in the mind. For that matter, how are they represented in the writing model the student is asked to imitate and ultimately internalize?

This is no trivial issue, because scholars have yet to sharpen their analytical tools sufficiently to be able to identify and describe precisely the various parts of a composition that establish and convey global features (see van Dijk, 1980). Moreover, it seems that in most instances we can't even perceive abstract relations, only the conditions that count as evidence they exist. As a result, transferring mental models of concrete relations to abstract ones is extremely difficult. Thus students given a model essay will be able to recognize that it has a purpose, because in our culture the fact of its being published counts as evidence that some purpose exists. They may even be successful in identifying that purpose. But neither of these occurrences means they will necessarily be able to write a purposeful essay on their own.

What, then, should teachers do with models in the classroom? What should we do with the collections of short stories and the anthologies of essays? On the basis of the preceding analysis, it seems doubtful that text models become internalized to the extent that there is a direct relationship between writing performance and study of a particular rhetorical mode. It isn't a matter of putting something in and getting something similar out. Having students read short stories for a whole semester won't produce a roomful of short story writers.

Nevertheless, if one's aim is to have students write short stories, it seems they do need some familiarity with short story conventions. The same holds true for essays and research papers. Going back to the sonnet example, it would be extremely difficult to write a sonnet without ever having read one. Models, then, may provide a source of genre familiarity.

The question is, how much reading must students do to gain this familiarity? Will one example do, or five, or fifty? Obviously, there is no way to answer this accurately. It will vary from student to student and from class to class. What is important is recognizing that if reading, say, five short stories gives students sufficient genre familiarity to write a story, reading an additional five will *not* have a greater effect on them. For most students, it simply isn't an instance where more is better. Rather than spend time reading another five stories, students are likely to benefit more from writing, practicing what they discovered about narratives on the basis of their reading, with guidance from the teacher.

Finally, one of the things we learn from this discussion of models is that we need to know far more than we currently do before we can reach any definitive conclusions. At this point, for example, we have no idea why the very best writers seem to be people who experienced a novel, a poem, an essay, a film, or a play and said, "I would like to do that; I would like to create something like that." We don't know why they would like to re-create a similar experience for others, but once they decide "I would like to do that," they return to the source of the experience again and again (see Mano, 1986). In such cases, it does indeed seem that more is better, paradoxical as that may be.

It appears, then, that when reading or text models become *meaningful*, they can become sources to imitate. One of the best ways teachers can help students discover meaningful models is to have a continually updated classroom library, with free access and free reading periods, but without pressure to read. Unfortunately, many schools don't have the resources for classroom libraries, and many others insist on a regimented or standardized reading program, so that all students end up reading the same list of materials. Creative teachers, however, usually find ways to start and maintain their own small classroom libraries, and they usually find ways to make these books available to students.

Integrating Reading and Writing

If one were to use a single word to describe literacy instruction in most schools, it would probably be *sequential*. Traditionally, students work on developing oral skills, then go on to reading, which forms the foundation for writing. Following the sequence, beginning writing instruction has tended to resemble phonics reading instruction: Students practice writing the alphabet, then words, then sentences, and so forth.

Although a sequenced approach may be orderly, it may not be pedagogically sound, because it assumes, or at least suggests, that the language modes are distinct and different. Yet all language activities are essentially similar; utterances and texts are alike in a fundamental way. Speech may tend to be interactional and writing may tend to be transactional, but both are actions and both are used to make requests, supply information, make assertions, and ask and answer questions.

Functional similarity suggests that improving students' skills in one area will affect their skills in another. We call this a *reciprocal* relationship. In regard to language, it is indeed the case that students with good oral skills tend to be good readers and writers (see Loban, 1976). But improving skills in one area will have a chance of improving skills in another only if children are given opportunities to practice both skills in conjunction. Separating speech and reading and writing into a sequence greatly limits these opportunities.

As more and more teachers have recognized the importance of an integrated approach to language instruction, there has been a shift—admittedly modest in some districts—away from the traditional language arts sequence. An emphasis on a process approach to composition has made teachers aware that reading what one has written has a positive influence on both activities. In many classrooms, teachers have abandoned language arts sequencing for a more integrated curriculum, where activities draw on students' own experiences and their linguistic and rhetorical knowledge.

Reading and Writing with Computers

Integrated approaches to reading and writing instruction have been enhanced by the growing availability of microcomputers, printers, and the software that makes them function as word processors. Often working in small groups, children develop oral narratives that they then type into a microcomputer or word processor. If the classroom also has a printer, students can "publish" their papers with ease, thereby making it possible to share their writing in a meaningful way. With more sophisticated equipment, students can even add illustrations to their work, a feature that younger children especially appreciate.

Another advantage to computers is that they allow writers to edit their drafts with ease, inserting or deleting words, sentences, and paragraphs at the touch of a button. Word processors also allow writers to reorganize without much effort; any element of the text can be moved and inserted elsewhere. Many software programs even check spelling and tell users if a word is misspelled or incorrectly typed.

When word processors initially became widely available in classrooms, few teachers saw their potential for integrating reading and writing; they were regarded primarily as a means of improving writing through drafting and revision. At the secondary level and the college level, computers continue to be viewed exclusively as a means of making revision less onerous.

By and large, the early expectations teachers had concerning improved revision and improved writing have not been fully realized. There is little doubt that computers have revolutionized the way people produce texts, and when linked with printers in the classroom they seem to offer an effective means of integrating reading and writing. Nevertheless, the research is mixed on the real benefits students derive from computer-assisted instruction when the focus is limited to writing.

For example, Beesley (1986) found no significant effects for word processors in a study of elementary students, and Hammer (1986) found that computer-assisted instruction was less effective in improving writing performance than traditional methods. But Flinn (1986) found that students using computers wrote longer papers and received higher evaluations than students using pen and paper, and Katstra, Tollefson, and Gilbert (1987) and Kurth (1986) found that word processors had significant motivational value for student writers.

Trying to sort through such conflicting data, Gail Hawisher (1987) focused on the revision strategies of 20 college students, half of whom composed on computers. She found that students using pen and paper actually made more revisions than those using word processors, but she found no significant correlation between revision frequency and essay quality. Her interpretation of these results is extremely disquieting, because it raises serious theoretical and methodological questions about current composition pedagogy. She concludes that "one might argue that for many it is not revision that determines [essay] quality. Rather it is whatever writers do in the production of the first draft—that first utterance" (pp. 156–57).

Hawisher's study suggests that the mixed results we see in the research on writing and computers may be associated with the skills students bring to the writing task. Were this the case, teaching revision strategies would appear to have no short-term effect on student writing performance, although it might well have a long-term effect. In each of the studies cited above, the number of students involved was small enough to allow for this possibility. Clearly more research is needed.

In spite of these problematic findings, computer technology appears to be establishing a permanent place in schools. Every year we see an increase in the number of computer programs dedicated to reading and writing. Because you are very likely to be asked to use computers when you teach, it seems important to review some of the software currently available. Any detailed analysis will be out of date by the time you read this, owing to the rapid pace at which educational software is being developed. Still, a brief discussion here will give you some idea of what educational packages can do.

The Writer's Assistant, developed at the University of California in San Diego for high school and college students, keeps track of revisions, giving the teacher further insight into individual writing strategies. When checking spelling, *The Writer's Assistant* gives a definition of possible alternative words and asks students to match their definition and spelling against those offered by the computer, thereby building vocabulary. *HBJ Writer*, developed at the University of California in Los Angeles primarily for college students, will plot sentence variety and paragraph development and will even warn writers when they are using too many abstract words.

More recent packages include the *Writer's Workbench*, developed for high school and college students, which is similar to *HBJ Writer* in that it is designed to help students revise their texts for sentence variety and paragraph development. Packages that offer a greater range of assistance include *Writer's Helper*, which gives students help on prewriting, editing, and revision. *Write*, developed at the University of

North Carolina, Chapel Hill, is an interactive prewriting program designed to help users plan, organize, and draft written work. It encourages inexperienced writers to cultivate the habits of experienced writers.

Continuing to lead the field in educational computing, Apple has a wide array of programs available. *Prose*, for example, is a state-of-the-art interactive program that writing teachers in grades seven and above can use when students compose on a Macintosh. It allows teachers to mark essays that students submit and helps with revision. As students view their work, they can open and read the instructor's remarks and short error explanations. As they do, *Prose* leads them from message to message, in most cases requiring them to make some change in the text before proceeding.

IBM introduced a particularly interesting program a few years ago. *Writing to Read* draws on the proposal that reading and writing have a reciprocal relationship such that children will become better readers and writers if reading instruction is based on texts they write themselves (see C. Chomsky, 1972). Designed for first graders, it requires a special room that serves as a learning center. Here pupils spend an hour a day working at various language stations. After about 15 minutes at one station, they rotate to another.

At the Computer Station, children pair up to work with talking computers that reinforce sound-to-symbol relationships, as well as spelling, and that start them writing complete sentences. At the Work Journal Station, students use audiocassettes and journals to continue the lessons begun on the computer. Activities focus on listening to words on the cassettes and looking at their written form in the journals. They then move on to the Listening Station, where children's stories like *The Three Bears, Make Way for Ducklings, A Tree Is Nice,* and *The Little Red House* are on audiocassettes. Students listen to the stories while simultaneously following the selected story in a book, a task designed to enhance word recognition and sentence pattern skills.

At the Writing Station, students use computers to write their own words, sentences, and stories. These are output on attached printers, giving students a neat, readable copy of their text. Once the narrative has been typed, edited, and revised on the computer, students print a copy that they then read to the entire class. Reading instruction is not tied to professional texts, but to the children's own stories. Learning how to read is thereby linked intimately with learning how to write.

Although to date no thorough studies evaluating the effectiveness of *Writing to Read* have been done, classroom reports and a preliminary evaluation by Educational Testing Service are positive. At this time, however, we have no way of saying whether the success of this program, as well as other computer-assisted instruction programs, is the result of its basic pedagogical efficiency, students' fascination with computer technology, or some combination of both.

Conclusion

Reading and writing enjoy a reciprocal relationship in that one tends to reinforce the other, although we are as yet unable to specify the details of that relationship. It does appear that the phonics approach to reading instruction, which typically concentrates on error correction, is likely to have a negative effect on writing performance, because it reinforces a bottom-up view of discourse that subordinates the global, rhetorical features so important to good writing. We also know that good readers tend to be good writers, and vice versa, but that reading itself doesn't seem to have a significant influence on writing well. Quite simply, it appears that a rich reading history is a necessary condition for good writing, but not a sufficient one. In other words, we won't produce competent writers just by giving students a stack of books to read. And finally, we know that text models, by their very nature, emphasize a product approach to writing. Students and teachers alike are inclined to focus their attention on the most visible features of a model, which generally are surface features.

Nevertheless, there is something to be said for using models in the classroom to help students develop not only their reading skills but also a familiarity with different genres and with the formal conventions of written discourse. What seems important is that modeling be subordinated to reading for the sheer enjoyment of it. This isn't to suggest that reading experiences ought not be discussed and even analyzed; after all, sharing such experiences is one of the pleasures of reading. But it does suggest that analysis with the intention of getting students to imitate the masters should be avoided. Based on what we currently know about the reading/writing relationship, this approach simply doesn't work very well.

Admittedly, when discussing reading and writing, we end up with more questions than answers. But by charting what we do know, this chapter should help you better understand some of the factors involved when you ask your students to read an essay or to write one.

CHAPTER 4

Grammar and Writing

Overview

Grammar is a system for describing language, as well as a device for producing the sentences of a language. It also constitutes a *theory* of language. The purpose of this chapter is to provide a brief discussion of some of the characteristics and goals of three different grammars, then to offer an analysis of the relationship between grammar and writing. The aim is to help teachers evaluate the role of grammar instruction in their writing classes. There are two facets to the grammar/writing relationship: the popular belief that teaching writing entails teaching grammar, and research indicating that grammar instruction has no measurable effect on writing performance.

To give you a better understanding of the goals of grammar, the chapter begins by outlining and discussing the features of traditional, phrase-structure, and transformational-generative grammars. The aim is not to attempt a comprehensive analysis of grammar but rather to give you a working familiarity with several important concepts, such as *ambiguity, prescription–description, competence–performance,* and *transformations.* These concepts are extremely useful when talking about language and what we do as teachers.

Traditional grammar, which goes back to the ancient Greeks, is fundamentally prescriptive; that is, its principal concern is the question of *correctness* in language. It operates on the assumption that literary language is better than spoken language, and thus its focus is, and always has been, literature, usually literature from the past that serves as a model against which speech and writing must be judged (see Lehmann, 1983; Leiber, 1975; Lyons, 1970; Scargill & Penner, 1966). Because everyday language differs from the language of literature, traditional grammar necessarily views speech as inherently inferior to writing (Lyons, 1970).

Phrase-structure grammar, on the other hand, has no real ties to a literary tradition but developed out of anthropologists' efforts to record and describe American Indian tribal languages before they disappeared. These languages had no written form, so speech rather than writing was the focus of the anthropologists' attention. Moreover, the complete absence of literary models and the tribal languages' dissimilarity to European languages prohibited any notions of prescription. Phrase-structure grammar is therefore essentially descriptive (see Bloomfield, 1933).

Transformational-generative grammar is also descriptive. It was developed by Noam Chomsky (1957) to describe certain linguistic features that phrase-structure grammar could not easily account for. Transformational-generative grammar has had a significant impact on every facet of language study. The discussion includes the distinction between linguistic *competence* and *performance*, introduces the idea that language is innate, and summarizes the influence transformational-generative grammar has had on language research.

The second part of the chapter provides an evaluation of studies designed to measure the effect of grammar instruction on writing performance. The results have shown that there is no correlation, either positive or negative. Such findings call into question the role grammar currently plays in writing classes, and the chapter concludes by suggesting an alternative to present pedagogy.

Why a Teacher Should Know About Grammar

When approaching the study of grammar on any level, the question teachers and teacher candidates most commonly ask is, "Why do I need to know anything about grammar?" At the risk of annoying many readers, I would say that no one *need* know anything at all about grammar, anymore than one *need* know anything at all about nuclear physics. One can generally get along quite easily without both. After all, when it comes right down to it, there are precious few things anyone "need" know. But there are many things that teachers *should* know. Grammar happens to be one of them.

Again the question "Why?" crops up, of course, and a significant reason is purely practical. Administrators and parents often judge what students are learning about language on the basis of what they consider the basics, which consist of, among other things, the parts of speech: nouns, verbs, prepositions, determiners, and so on.

Grammar is a significant part of writing instruction in most school districts, as the tremendous success of Warriner's *English Grammar and Composition,* a composition series for secondary students, attests. According to the publisher, it has sold about 30 million copies in its several editions. The 1986 edition includes about 100 pages of grammatical analyses (for example, "A *noun* is a word used to name a person, place, thing, or idea" [p. 4]), and 174 pages devoted to proper usage (for example, "Include the word *other* or *else* when comparing one thing with a group of which it is a part" [p. 228]). Thus the fact that those who teach writing are generally expected to teach grammar provides a fairly strong reason for including a chapter on grammar and writing.

Another reason teachers should know something about grammar, though less pragmatic than the expectations of a school district, seems ultimately more important. We often approach our work as though education is made up of discrete pieces of information that come in packages labeled History, Art, English, and Math. There is some truth to this concept, of course, but we should remember that an implicit part of every teacher's task is language instruction. When we teach students to analyze, infer, deduce, and conclude on the basis of their reading, we are teaching them about language. When we ask them to perform the same tasks when they write, whether it be in history, art, or science, we are teaching them about language. That is, we perform at least two instructional actions simultaneously, and the more we ask students to use language, the more we implicitly ask them to explore what language is about. If we are to guide and enrich their exploration, we require tools for finding out more about language ourselves. Grammar provides those tools. It helps us answer a very important and intriguing question: "What is language?"

We need to recognize, however, that the answer to this question doesn't come through knowing the parts of speech and being able to label sentences, which too often is the only view of what grammar is about. It comes through being able to describe relationships between the various components of language, as well as through being able to describe patterns of language use that are different from the norm we find in school. In this broad sense grammar, especially modern grammar, is quite useful.

Those of us who work with students whose first language is not English have a special appreciation for grammar's usefulness in describing relationships. Very often nonnative English speakers find the key to unlocking written discourse in understanding English grammar. For example, when missionaries in the U.S. territories of Micronesia were strongly advocating statehood some years ago, large numbers of college-age students from the island of Truk were sent to the United States to be educated. I taught many of them at a community college in the Northwest. They knew very little English, but they readily grasped the fundamental relationships of English grammar.

We didn't work on terminology, and we didn't concentrate on error correction. Instead, we simply looked at sentence patterns. The subject/verb/object sentence pattern became a kind of word puzzle that they played with daily in their writing. Once they mastered this basic pattern of grammatical relationships, understanding other relationships, such as subordination, enabled them to expand their repertoire of sentences. They weren't masterly writers at the end of the term, or even at the end of the year, but they were beginning to master English.

Grammar or Grammars

When most people think of grammar at all, they think of it as "the parts of speech" or "rules for putting sentences together correctly." Unless they have studied another language, they usually assume that there is only one grammar for all languages. They express great surprise, even disbelief, when told that there are many different grammars, even for a single language like English. For example, three grammars very well known in linguistics, the scholarly field primarily concerned with the study of language, are phrase-structure grammar, transformational-generative grammar, and case grammar.

To understand how it's possible to have multiple grammars for any given language, one must understand the functions of grammar. On a fundamental level, grammar supplies terms for labeling the various components of language, such as *nouns, verbs*, and *adjectives*. This is the categorical level. It also provides a means of describing relations among sentence components, such as *subject, predicate*, and *object*. This is the relational level. One isn't bound by terms like *subject*, however. One could reasonably develop a variety of different grammars with different component labels. Case grammar exemplifies some of the possibilities. Rather than *subject*, it uses the term *agent* to describe one set of relations between a noun that initiates the action of a sentence and the verb. In "Reina ate the sandwich," for example, *Reina* is the agent.

It's from this relational level that we often encounter arguments for "correctness" in language. For example, many years ago when cigarette commercials were allowed on TV, there was a popular one that depicted a ruggedly handsome man putting up a billboard with the slogan "Winston tastes good like a cigarette should." Just as he finishes, a frail, stodgy fellow, wearing a bow tie and supposedly looking a bit like a college English professor, approaches and voices his outrage at the "ungrammatical" slogan.

In a tone of voice that anyone would find intimidating, the "professor" tells the billboard man: "That should be 'Winston tastes good *as* a cigarette should!'" I would wager that the majority of people who watched that commercial didn't have the faintest idea what the grammatical issue was, but the images were nevertheless quite effective as social commentary. We got a clear picture of the sort of man who smokes Winston cigarettes and of the sort who is interested in correcting grammar.

The grammatical aspect of the commercial escaped so many people because informal English dominates most lives. In the slogan, the word *like*, which we classify as a preposition, is used as a subordinating conjunction; in this case, it was substituted for the conjunction *as*. The fellow in the bow tie was faulting the use of a preposition as a subordinating conjunction. This usage generally doesn't occur in formal English, although most of us make this substitution to one degree or another in informal conversations. As the language situation becomes more formal, those who know the distinction between *like* and *as* are inclined to shift to a more formal level, or *register*, of discourse, not because it is better but because under such conditions it is more appropriate. That is, we use prepositions as prepositions and subordinating conjunctions as subordinating conjunctions, without mixing.

Some people, however, do not accept differences in circumstances as being grounds for variation in register. For such people there is a value judgment: "Winston tastes good like a cigarette should" is simply incorrect "grammar" and is a corruption of the language. What we realize from this example, therefore, is that many people see grammar not only as a way to describe relations among sentence components but also as a way to *prescribe* how those components should fit together to form sentences.

The underlying tension between these two views has its source in different perceptions of language and grammar. One who would prescribe, for example, has internalized a standard or model of correctness by which speech and writing (and thus the speaker and the writer) are judged. This standard necessarily is fixed, and the goal is to prevent deviations. By the same token, one who would describe is committed to change and diversity. An absolute standard is replaced with a scale of what we might call "appropriateness conditions," on which a given utterance or a given piece of writing is seen in relation to its context.

What we are dealing with in this simple cigarette commercial, therefore, are actually different theories of language. This, of course, is the most complex level of grammatical functions. We can conclude, then, that grammar reflects the views and assumptions people have about language. In this sense, grammar is a theory of language. And as theories differ, so must the grammar.

But if grammars differ, how are we to know which one to use? The answer lies in how well a given grammar accounts for the various features of language. A grammar should be able to describe all possible grammatical sentences, of course, but it should also be able to determine why some sentences are grammatical and others aren't.

These are difficult criteria to satisfy. Any decision regarding whether one grammar is preferable to another will be based on its descriptive and explanatory power. Of the three grammars discussed in this chapter, each one is progressively more powerful.

It is important to keep at least two points in mind, however. First, each of these grammars builds on the other. Therefore, without a grasp of basic terminology, which comes to us from traditional grammar, linguistically the weakest of the three presented here, one's understanding of what grammar is about is severely handicapped. Second, aside from a brief period during the 1960s, the more powerful phrase-structure and transformational-generative grammars have had only a tangential impact on the teaching of writing. Some of the reasons for this will be discussed in the pages that follow, but by way of preface, it appears that the most significant reason is simply that, as Sue Foster (1985b) says, we have "attempted to apply the wrong research" (p. 1).

Traditional Grammar

The majority of the writing programs that include grammar as a formal part of the curriculum focus on prescription. Grammar is used to separate what is considered "incorrect" English from "correct" English. This situation is unfortunate because it tacitly advocates the idea that there are two inherently incompatible language forms: speech and writing. It also puts teachers in the undesirable position of making students feel that their language is inferior to some preestablished norm. The effect can be devastating, because our sense of self-worth is so closely tied to the language we use.

To understand the prescriptive nature of the grammar taught in most schools and explained in handbooks like Warriner's, one must realize that the focus isn't modern grammar at all but *usage*. For example, when students write "I want to lay down," they have not produced an ungrammatical sentence; it has, after all, a subject and a predicate in the correct positions. They have, however, ignored the difference between *lay* and *lie* (the former requires an object, but the latter doesn't). The result is not a problem of grammar but a problem of usage. As we will see later in this chapter, true grammar problems are rare; most of what prescriptivists describe as "ungrammatical" is really improper usage.

One should also realize that most schools and handbooks teach a grammar with a history that reaches back to classical Greece. In Athens, when young boys were sent to school at age six (girls were kept at home), they learned the alphabet, or *grammata*, and were taught to read and write. Upon reaching proficiency, they began an intensive study of poetry, particularly Homer and the great Athenian writers of the fourth century B.C. They studied other subjects, of course, such as music and math, but a significant part of their early education was devoted to literature, which represented the ideal form of written discourse.

Literary works were analyzed for their moral messages, but students devoted much effort to grammatical analyses as well, because the Greeks were very concerned with correctness in language. Scholars recognized the fact that languages change, yet they strove to preserve the purity of classical Greek from what they considered linguistic decay. Literary language therefore came to be viewed as standard Greek, and deviations from the standard were condemned as solecisms or barbarisms, this latter term originally meaning simply the use of foreign words or expressions. Thus on the basis of literary analysis, grammar was used to separate "correct" Greek from "incorrect" Greek, and students were expected to model their language on that of the great poets (see Bonner, 1977; Kennedy, 1980).

A teacher of these classes was called a *grammatistes,* or "teacher of letters," and those students who mastered their lessons were *grammatikos,* an adjective meaning literate or lettered. Our term *grammar school,* of course, comes directly from these early schools in Athens, and given our own emphasis on the alphabet, reading, and writing, the curriculum appears to have changed very little.

Boys in ancient Greece studied until they were 14. Then, after two years of military service, if they had the means they could attend classes in public speaking, or oratory. Ability as a speaker was highly respected and was influential in democratic cities like Athens. Writing was relatively less important. During the Roman period, however, and the Middle Ages that followed, when there was no opportunity for public debate, attention shifted to writing until it eventually replaced instruction in oratory. Grammatical treatises became manuals on how to write, and the great Latin masters like Virgil were used as models of correctness, because Latin was considered the normative language.

A significant facet of these medieval treatises was the connection between grammar and logic. The aim was to make language more orderly by linking it to the rules and principles established for logic. Violation of these principles was seen as not only incorrect but illogical.

During the 18th century two other factors increasingly influenced work in grammar: prestige and socioeconomic status. This change resulted largely from the spread of education and economic mobility, which brought large numbers of people from the middle class into contact with the upper class. In England, for example, although both upper class and middle class spoke the same language, there were noticeable differences in pronunciation, form, and vocabulary—what we term *dialect*—much like the differences we notice in the United States between speakers from Mississippi and Massachusetts. Because the upper-class dialects identified one with prestige and success, mastering the upper-class speech patterns became very desirable, and notions of grammar became more normative than ever.

Language scholars during this time suffered from a fundamental confusion that clearly has its roots in the notion of linguistic decay first formulated by the Greeks. They noted that well educated people wrote and spoke good Latin, whereas the less educated made many mistakes. Failing to see that reproducing a dead language is essentially an academic exercise, they applied this observation to modern languages and concluded that languages are preserved by the usage of educated people. Those without education and culture corrupt the language with their deviations from the established norm. Accordingly, the discourse forms of books and upper-class conversation represented an older and purer level of language from which the speech of the common people had degenerated (see Lyons, 1970).

From this analysis, we begin to see that a significant part of traditional grammar is the distinction between what some people *do* with language and what they *ought* to do with it. Aside from simply providing labels for words—nouns, verbs, adjectives, and so forth—it is not particularly concerned with the language people use on a daily basis to get things done. Its chief goal appears to be perpetuating a historical model of what supposedly constitutes proper language.

As already suggested, whether one subscribes to this goal or not depends on one's personal assumptions of what language study is about, yet it should be fairly clear that the goal is antithetical to a rhetoric-based writing class.

It's also difficult for most teachers to be consistent when making prescriptions. We can find any number of interesting examples relevant to teaching today. One of the more curious is related to use of the verb form *to be*. Keep in mind for a moment the early ties between logic and grammar. Now, in logic, *to be* is represented by an equals sign. Thus in logic an expression like "All women are mortals" could be expressed symbolically as $x = y$, where x represents *all women* and y represents *mortals*. (If you wonder why logicians would substitute symbols for words, it's because this reduces the ambiguity of natural-language expressions.)

The equals sign indicates equivalence of classification. In "All women are mortals," *women* and *mortals* share the classification of *human beings*. But more important for our analysis here, they also have a common grammatical relationship, or *case*: We could use either one as the subject of a sentence. This idea of case equivalence is fairly straightforward and usually doesn't cause any difficulties. But consider the following examples:

(1) It is me.

(2) It is I.

In terms of the preceding analysis, sentence (1) is not only ungrammatical but is also "illogical" because *me* doesn't have the same case as *It*. *It* has the classification of subject; *me* has the classification of object, or recipient of an action, as in "Vickie gave *me* a rose."

Speakers of the prestige dialect we call Standard English would not generally use *me* as a subject, but the majority nevertheless utter (1) more often than (2). In Latin and related languages like Spanish, this situation doesn't arise, perhaps because case is a more prominent part of the language system. Consider that Latin has six cases, whereas English has only three.

Matters are made more complex by the fact that Standard English allows us to use an object in a subject position under certain circumstances:

(3) The new play developed slowly.

Given that a verb like *developed* requires an agent, as in "*Chris* developed the new play slowly," *The new play* in (3) is actually an object used as a subject.

Many languages are structured this way, such as Basque (see Comrie, 1978, 1981; Lehmann, 1983). In these languages, a sentence like (4) would be ungrammatical:

(4) She bought a new jacket.

The proper structure would be the following:

(5) Her bought a new jacket.

The frequent occurrence in Standard English of sentences like (3) suggests that our language is less rigid than Latin when it comes to grammatical relationships. Whatever appears before the verb is generally taken to be the subject, regardless of case. This situation may help us understand how it is that we find even well educated speakers confusing the case of pronouns in prepositional phrases:

(6) The superintendent said that the checks *for Wanda and I were lost in the mail.*

(7) The superintendent said that the checks *for Wanda and me were lost in the mail.*

Although (7) is correct in the formal sense, we nevertheless encounter (6) on a regular basis, no doubt because so many people experienced (and misunderstood) error correction as children. Told at some point that saying "Wanda and me were lost in the woods" is incorrect, many children will respond simply by using the pronoun *I* in every position.

By the same token, in certain varieties of English, we also find patterns like (5) used regularly, as in:

(8) Him and me went to the park for a game.

(9) Tom and her took me home that night.

What's particularly interesting is that people who are sticklers for correctness have no difficulty with sentences like (3), but they respond very negatively to sentences like (1), (8), and (9), even though each "violates" the same principle. At best, we would have to call such reactions inconsistent. Many of our students will commonly use structures like (1), (8), and (9), so this analysis shows us we should be very careful when we discuss them, or we may end up being "illogical"!

It's clear that we can't encourage students to write "Him and me went to the park for a game." Part of our responsibility as teachers is to give students access to Standard English, which is the key to the many doors of social mobility in the United States. We do have to prescribe in the classroom. One of the points to be learned from this discussion of traditional grammar, however, is that we not only need to understand some of the basis for our prescriptions but to be cautious when making them.

Phrase-Structure Grammar

We've seen instances in which Latin-based traditional grammar does not accurately analyze English, and there are similar inconsistencies between Latin and other European languages. Nevertheless, European languages have been so influenced on the whole by Latin, the Romance languages being derivatives of it, that the grammar works reasonably well, given its aims. For example, even though English does not have a future-tense verb form, we can distinguish future actions from past and present using *will* and forms of *be going to* to designate future time. We recognize that *will* marks the future in a sentence such as "Kim will go to the party." Contact with "exotic" languages like those spoken by American Indians, however, presented insurmountable problems for traditional grammar.

The American Indian tribes were more or less ignored after the period of the great Indian wars, but during the last years of the 19th century, they became the focus of scholarly attention as anthropologists like Franz Boas came to recognize that the cultures and languages of these indigenous people were quickly vanishing. Researchers began intensive efforts to record the details of these cultures and languages.

Some records already existed, of course, made years earlier by missionaries. But it became increasingly clear during the beginning of the 20th century that these early descriptions failed to record the languages adequately. In fact, in his introduction to the *Handbook of American Indian Languages*, Boas (1911) states that the descriptions are actually distorted by the attempt to impose traditional grammar on languages for which it was simply inappropriate.

The issue of tense provides just one illustration. English grammar distinguishes between past tense and present tense, but Eskimo, for example, does not. In Eskimo, "The husky was running" and "The husky is running" would be the same.

As more and more data were collected, the number of such incompatibilities grew. Within a few years, it became apparent that traditional grammar was inadequate for analyzing and recording these indigenous languages. Moreover, the goal of traditional grammar, prescription based on a literary model, was completely out of place in the study of languages that lacked a written form.

Led by Boas, and later by Leonard Bloomfield (1933), anthropologists and linguists abandoned the assumptions of traditional grammar and adopted the view that every language is unique, with its own structure and its own grammar. Known as the *structuralist* view, this new approach to grammar saw as its goal the objective and scientific description of languages. It dominated American language study for many years. Students completing their doctorate in linguistics, for example, commonly spent time on reservations studying aspects of tribal languages as part of their graduate work.

A detailed analysis of the structuralist approach is, of course, beyond the scope of this book. But several features are important for the discussion of the grammar/writing relationship. First, the structuralists' emphasis on description means that questions of correctness are not germane to grammatical analysis. In the speech of many people, for example, we find the past participle *seen* used where Standard English uses *saw*. Rather than

(10) I saw Harry last night,

these speakers would use

(11) I seen Harry last night.

Focusing on description, structuralists would not make value judgments and accuse these speakers of using incorrect grammar; they would simply note that *seen* is substituted for *saw* in the speech of some people and would study how this variant is distributed geographically and economically.

This is not to suggest that "anything goes" in the structuralist framework. One could not utter something like "Over the in park city football is field there" and express a grammatical sentence. People don't speak this way, so such a jumble of words we may justifiably consider "word salad."

Sentences (10) and (11), however, have several things in common. Both are comprehensible and can be recognized as conveying identical meanings. Both follow an identifiable regularity. That is, each reflects the basic subject/predicate pattern characteristic of English.

From the structuralists' point of view, these commonalities are more important than the irregularity of the verb form. The regularity of structure, for example, allows for a generalization on the basis of observable data, following scientific principles: The dominant sentence pattern in English is subject/verb/object. (Other languages have different dominant patterns. Hebrew, for example, follows a verb/subject/object pattern, and Japanese follows subject/object/verb.)

Structural grammar uses a shorthand notation to depict this generalization about sentence structure. Initially, we may think of it in the following way:

S → subject + predicate

S represents *sentence,* and the arrow essentially means *consists of.*

This expression can be made more descriptive, however, if we consider that subjects consist of nouns, often with modifiers attached. The predicate will consist of at least a verb, but more often a verb, with modifiers, plus an object, possibly with modifiers as well. Thus the two main parts of the basic pattern are made up of several words that form a single unit. Because a group of words working together as a component part of a sentence is called a *phrase,* subjects can be viewed as noun phrases, and predicates can be viewed as verb phrases that may have additional components, such as noun-phrase objects, attached.

Structuralists reasoned that analyzing sentences in terms of their component phrases was more descriptive than simply "subject + predicate," so they offered the following alternative notation to the generalization above:

$$S \rightarrow NP + VP$$

where *S* again represents *sentence*, *NP* represents *noun phrase*, and *VP* represents *verb phrase*. Moreover, each phrase could then be analyzed in terms of its component parts.

The resulting analysis would provide a detailed description, or grammar, of the language. For example, noun phrases consist of nouns plus determiners like *the* and any adjectives. Verb phrases consist of verbs plus any modifiers and any noun phrases that represent objects. Given the focus on phrases and the components of phrases, one can understand why structuralist grammar is also called *phrase-structure grammar.*

It is possible to formalize the preceding analysis, which should make it easier to grasp. We can do this for a simple sentence like (12), which follows. Note that because our formalization of (12) describes the structure of the sentence, we are also writing a grammar for the sentence.

(12) The woman kissed the man.

$$S \rightarrow NP + VP$$
$$NP \rightarrow determiner + N$$
$$VP \rightarrow V + NP$$
$$Det \rightarrow the$$
$$N \rightarrow (man, woman)$$
$$V \rightarrow kissed$$

Each level of this analysis is called a *phrase-structure rule.* Keep in mind that this grammar is designed to describe only sentence (12). It will not work for any other sentence. To make it more general so it could describe more sentences, we would have to make changes in the phrase-structure rules. Actually, this is quite easy. We would merely expand our rules to include, say, prepositional phrases, additional determiners, like *a* and *an*, and modifiers. The range of nouns and verbs would include all nouns and all verbs, not just *man, woman,* and *kissed.*

Now we are in a position to reexamine sentences (10) and (11):

(10) I saw Harry last night.

(11) I seen Harry last night.

The phrase-structure analysis of these two sentences would be identical. The only difference between them lies in the form of the verb: *saw* versus *seen*. Both sentences are equally comprehensible, so phrase-structure grammar would recognize both as being grammatical and would include *seen* in the list of words in the verb category.

At this point one could reasonably argue that, although their goals may be quite different, the grammatical analyses of traditional and phrase-structure grammar are very similar. That is, with certain modifications, traditional grammar could analyze "The woman kissed the man" in much the same fashion as phrase-structure grammar, providing the labels of *noun phrase, verb phrase, determiner,* and so on. Aside from its goal of description rather than prescription, what makes phrase-structure grammar preferable?

The answer lies in descriptive power: Phrase-structure grammar developed conventions that make how the various parts of a sentence work together easier to understand. You may be familiar with the way sentences are analyzed in traditional grammar. One constructs an essentially linear diagram where function categories are indicated on the basis of the lines used to separate components. Sentence (12), for example, would be diagrammed as shown in Figure 1.

Figure 1

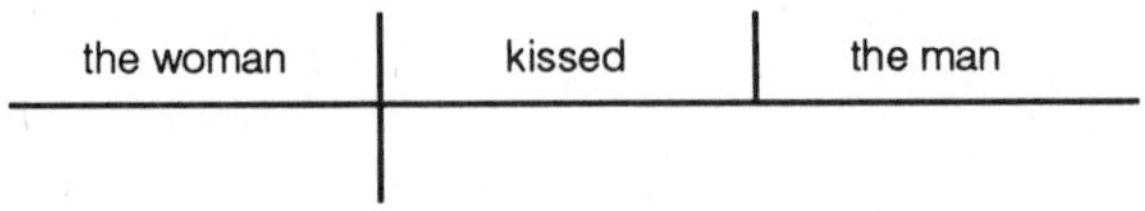

| the woman | kissed | the man |

The vertical line that fully intersects the horizontal line separates subject from verb; the vertical line that does not intersect separates verb from object. Modifiers such as prepositional phrases would be attached beneath the horizontal line on diagonals.

The diagramming convention in phrase-structure grammar draws on the generalization discussed earlier, that the basic sentence pattern in English is noun phrase plus verb phrase. It uses a *tree diagram* to depict how phrases are related within a sentence. Again using (12) as an example, the tree diagram is depicted in Figure 2.

Figure 2

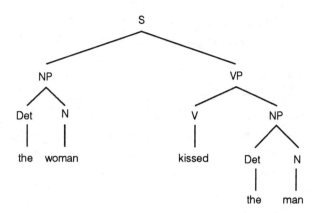

This diagram gives us more information than the traditional diagram. First, we see graphically that the sentence is composed of two constituents, the noun phrase and the verb phrase. We also see which elements make up these constituents. Moreover, the object of the sentence is dominated by the verb phrase that makes up the predicate. Not only is this system more descriptive, most people find it more logical.

Natural languages like English, as opposed to artificial languages like mathematics and symbolic logic, are inherently ambiguous. Note that I'm using *ambiguous* here not in its popular sense of "unclear," but in its technical sense, which is "possessing two or more possible interpretations simultaneously." Sentence (13) illustrates a common ambiguity:

(13) Jim put the toy in the box on the shelf.

There are two possible interpretations of this sentence. In one the toy is *already* in the box; in the other it isn't.

Sentence (14) illustrates another sort of ambiguity:

(14) Old men and women are interesting conversationalists.

In one interpretation, the adjective *old* modifies both *men* and *women;* in the other it modifies only *men.*

In (13) and (14) we have examples of sentences in which the linear sequence of the words does not determine the phrase structure of the constituents. That is, simple word order does not tell us what goes with what, whether the toy is already in the box or not, whether both the men and the women are old or not. Traditional grammar is based on linear order and cannot disambiguate sentences like (13) and (14). Phrase-structure grammar can, however, through what's known as the *bracketing convention.*

Phrase-structure bracketing is based on mathematical bracketing and operates the same way. In the expression $a(b+c)$, for example, we know that the sum of b and c is multiplied by a. That is, a applies equally to both b and c. Using this same principle, we can see that (13) has two bracketed phrase structures, each corresponding to the respective interpretations possible in this sentence:

(13a) (Jim) (put (the toy in the box) (on the shelf.))))

(13b) (Jim) (put (the toy) (in the box on the shelf.))))

This analysis shows us that linear structure, simply categorizing as it does the parts of the sentence, is not necessarily a reflection of phrase structure, which captures relationships important in understanding meaning. Because traditional grammar lacks this ability to disambiguate, we must conclude, as linguists generally have, that phrase-structure grammar is more powerful than traditional grammar.

Transformational-Generative Grammar

Transformational-generative grammar is synonymous with Noam Chomsky, who proposed it as an extension of and an alternative to phrase-structure grammar in his book *Syntactic Structures* (1957). It's difficult to overestimate the influence Chomsky has had on modern language study. His work in linguistics is generally considered as revolutionary as that of Einstein in physics.

As the name suggests, transformational-generative grammar has two related parts. Before taking up the topic of transformations and how they operate, which can become rather technical, it's important to understand the rationale behind a "generative" grammar.

Before *Syntactic Structures*, phrase-structure grammar was based on a body, or corpus, of sentences for a particular language. As already mentioned, during the first half of the 20th century, structuralists would spend time observing the speakers of a language and recording a wide range, though finite number, of its sentences. The emphasis on observation and on methods for compiling a corpus created a specific bias in the grammar: Concentrating on what people do with language tended to exclude what they *might* do with it. Stated another way, the focus was on languages rather than language (see Gazdar et al., 1985, for a significant alternative to the phrase-structure grammar outlined here).

The problem this bias creates is both methodological and theoretical. It's fairly easy to demonstrate that the number of possible sentences in any language is infinite. If we take a given sentence, we can create a new sentence from it simply by adding a word or construction. For example, "The wind was howling" becomes a new sentence through the addition of an adverb: "The wind was howling loudly." Or we may create another new sentence by compounding, as in "The wind was howling and blustering." Either of these processes can be carried out indefinitely without affecting the grammaticality of the sentence, although we would quickly reach a point beyond which it becomes unreadable.

Because the number of possible sentences in any language is infinite, a grammar that concentrates on describing simply a list of attested sentences, even a very long one, will be concerned with only a small portion of the language. The grammar will account for only the sentences in the corpus. Furthermore, it will not account for all the possible sentences a speaker of the language can produce, nor will it describe certain relationships between sentences. For example, phrase-structure grammar would assign different grammatical descriptions to "The wind was howling" and "The wind was howling and blustering," with no account of our intuitive perception that these sentences are closely related. Any such account must be inherently theoretical, but structuralists turned questions of theory into questions of method: "How are the sentences in language related?" became "How should one analyze a given language?"

With an infinity of possible sentences, the likelihood of encountering repetitive sentences other than idiomatic expressions and slogans is very small, which suggests that a grammar should be concerned with the creative aspect of language, with how new sentences are generated, and with how they interrelate. This view of language is quite different from the structuralist view. Moreover, it represents a different view of what an adequate description of a language will involve.

Chomsky argues that an infinity of possible sentences makes listing some of the sentences an inadequate description of the language. What one must do is specify the rules that generate them. The result will be a *generative* grammar applicable to observed and potential sentences alike, a grammar that will reflect relationships between sentences such as "The wind was howling" and "The wind was howling and blustering." In Chomsky's words, such a generative grammar "can be viewed as a device of some sort for producing the sentences of the language under analysis" (1957, p. 11).

Such a device will account for the grammaticality of sentences automatically, because if formulated correctly it will produce only grammatical sentences and no ungrammatical ones. This feature makes the grammar more powerful than phrase-structure grammar, where grammatical description is based on a corpus of attested sentences. Phrase-structure grammar will describe the sentences in the corpus and classify them as grammatical only incidentally, because it must project them onto the infinitely large set of potential sentences that actually makes up the language.

Competence and Performance

In referring to grammar as a device for generating sentences, Chomsky is forced to recognize that in the normal course of speaking we frequently produce utterances that are ungrammatical. Sometimes we are aware of the flaw and will stop in mid-sentence and begin again, repairing the problem. Other times we may not be quite so attentive, and the flaw will slip by us undetected.

As Chomsky formulates the grammar, however, it will not produce ungrammatical sentences under any circumstances. To account for the apparent inconsistency, he distinguishes between the sentences generated by the grammar and the sentences actually produced by language users. The terms he uses to make this distinction are *competence* and *performance*. Linguistic competence may be understood as the inherent ability to make correct grammaticality judgments; Jerry Fodor (1983) suggests that the mechanism involved is basically a reflex. Linguistic performance is what we actually do with the language, which occasionally may result in ungrammatical utterances.

The utterances produced by native speakers (samples of their performance) may be ungrammatical because of such factors as lapses of memory or attention and malfunctions of the psychological mechanisms underlying speech. It therefore follows that we cannot take the corpus of attested utterances at face value as being generated by the grammar. What we must do is propose an "ideal" speaker who is not subject to such things as lapses of attention or slips of the tongue.

This ideal speaker would be able to recognize ungrammatical sentences by virtue of his innate competence, which in effect consists of the rules of the grammar. There is a sense, however, in which we *all* approach the ideal speaker, because we have all internalized the rules of English grammar, as evidenced by our ability to generate endless volumes of essentially grammatical sentences. In this case, we all possess a degree of linguistic competence, though it may not be "perfect" in the way that the ideal speaker has perfect competence. Such an analysis accounts for the occurrence of ungrammatical sentences, and also for the occasional inability of listeners to analyze perfectly grammatical sentences. We say that they are due to errors of performance, errors made in the application of the rules.

Universals and Innateness

Referring to a "device of some sort" for producing sentences also implicitly lays the foundation for a reexamination of *linguistic universals*, an issue that structuralists had abandoned in favor of linguistic uniqueness. Linguistic universals are exactly what the expression suggests: features that are universal to all known languages. For example, although the grammars of, say, English and Eskimo are different, the languages do have several significant features in common. They are easily acquired by children on the basis of relatively little input. Adults use them fluently and efficiently to convey information and ideas. They function as a means of social bonding and cultural dissemination. They make use of implications such as "If I fall into the water I'll get wet." It isn't just English and Eskimo that share these features, of course; all natural languages have all these features in common. Implications, for example, remain the same regardless of language. That is, in all languages, falling into water implies getting wet.

Another topic in linguistics that is closely linked to universals is the idea that human beings are genetically inclined to use language, that it is an innate predisposition (see Caplan, 1987; Chomsky, 1965, 1968). Young children are not taught grammar, yet they manage to produce grammatical sentences at a fairly early age on the basis of often distorted input ("baby talk"). Moreover, their sentences cannot be viewed merely as parroting of adult speech, because their utterances are not repetitions of what they hear. Chomsky maintains that such facility with language would be impossible without some innate "language acquisition device" that generalizes grammatical rules from very little data.

In English, for example, children are able to formulate simple sentences that follow the subject + predicate pattern by about age two, and their facility increases exponentially thereafter. In Chomsky's view, a viable grammar will reflect innateness on some level, and, more specifically, a generative grammar will model the inner workings of the mind as it processes language. If, for example, our intuition tells us that the "wind" sentences used earlier are related, a generative grammar will describe, after a fashion, how our minds structure the relationship.

Over the last two decades, various researchers have explored the controversial question of innateness. Some of the most interesting findings come from studies of people who have suffered brain injuries (see Lenneberg, 1967; Restak, 1979; Wittrock, 1977). The brain is divided into two hemispheres, and mental and physical functions tend to be dominated by one hemisphere or the other. Physical movements on the right side of the body involve primarily the left hemisphere; movements on the left side involve primarily the right hemisphere.

In most people, the left hemisphere controls language, so when adults suffer damage to this part of the brain, language is almost always permanently impaired. This phenomenon suggests that an innate, physiological basis for language exists, that the left hemisphere is genetically programmed to control language function much in the same way that the occipital region of the brain is genetically programmed to control vision.

But in cases of preadolescent children who experience damage to the left hemisphere, the uninjured right hemisphere in most instances somehow manages to take over language function intact without measurable impairment. Although this phenomenon doesn't invalidate the innateness proposal, the effect is to weaken it, because language takes on characteristics of learned behavior. Moreover, we are forced to assume the existence of a critical period during which brain function and language development are plastic and can shift readily from the left hemisphere to the right. The idea of innateness requires evidence that some features of language are specifically and nontransferably located in the left hemisphere.

Such evidence is found in studies of children who at birth were diagnosed as having one diseased hemisphere that would lead to death if left alone. The children were therefore operated on within a few days of birth (see Day & Ulatowska, 1979; Dennis & Kohn, 1975; Dennis & Whitaker, 1976; Kohn, 1980). In some cases the entire left hemisphere was removed; in others the entire right hemisphere was removed. (This procedure does cause some intellectual deficits, but children who undergo the operation develop normally in many ways.)

The children were studied as they matured, with particular attention to language development. Tests of vocabulary and comprehension showed no significant differences between those with right hemisphere or left hemisphere removed. Both also seemed equally able to carry on a normal conversation.

Closer examination, however, revealed several important differences. Dennis and Kohn (1975), for example, found that children with the right hemisphere removed could process negative passive sentences, but those with the left hemisphere removed could not. Dennis and Whitaker (1976) found that children with the right hemisphere removed showed an inability to deviate from subject/verb/object word order. They could not understand or produce what are called *cleft* sentences, such as, "What the teller wanted me to do was deposit more money." Nor could they process sentences that use *by* in any way other than indicating location. Thus they could understand "The book was by the lamp" but not "The cake was made by my sister." On the basis of such evidence, it appears that some grammar-related features of language are indeed exclusively part of left-hemispheric function. Chomsky's intuition about linguistic innateness appears to be substantially correct.

Transformations

Now that we have examined some of the issues involved in a generative grammar, we can address the question of what this grammar looks like. Earlier we saw that a useful generalization about English is that sentences tend to have the form of subject + predicate. Clearly, the generalization would be more powerful if it were universal; that is, if we could say that *all* sentences in English have this form. If we assume for the moment that the generalization *is* universal, we would have to account for many sentences, such as questions and imperatives, that aren't structured subject + predicate.

Imperative sentences, for example, have no subject, as (15) illustrates:

(15) Open your books.

In order to preserve the subject + predicate generalization, grammars, even traditional and phrase-structure grammar, propose that the subject in such sentences is understood to be *you*. In this case, (15) would conform to the generalization and would have the form shown in (15a), where the parentheses around *You* indicate that the subject isn't stated:

(15a) (You) open your books.

If this analysis is correct, it has significant implications for analyses of sentences, because it suggests a generalization every bit as powerful as the familiar S → subject + predicate. To account for one exception to a generalization, we must propose that imperatives have an *underlying structure* (also known as *deep structure*) different from their visible structure, or what we may call their *surface structure*.

To propose, however, that only imperatives have two structures is to establish another exception. It therefore seems we must conclude that all sentences have both an underlying structure and a surface structure. In some instances these will differ, as in (15) and (15a); in other instances, the two structures will be the same. Because both "Open your books" and "You open your books" are grammatical, and both occur in English, either form may be used as the imperative. In an instance where the imperative is "You open your books," the surface structure and the underlying structure are identical.

The following sentences illustrate the relationship between surface structure and underlying structure in imperatives. Again, the parentheses indicate when a subject will be deleted in the surface structure:

Surface structure	*Underlying structure*
Button my dress.	(You) button my dress.
You call me tomorrow.	You call me tomorrow.
Ask her now.	(You) ask her now.
You cook dinner.	You cook dinner.
Wash the car.	(You) wash the car.

The specification of an underlying structure and a surface structure was an important facet of the grammar, because it provided an insight into our intuitive evaluation that some sentences seem to be related. Passives and actives are a case in point. It's easy enough to see that sentences (16) and (17) are related, but neither traditional nor phrase-structure grammar provides an analysis that describes the relationship. Phrase-structure grammar would analyze each sentence independently as distinct entities.

(16) Sue ate the pie. (active)

(17) The pie was eaten by Sue. (passive)

The same holds true for sentences (18) and (19):

(18) A bug was in my soup.

(19) There was a bug in my soup.

By proposing an underlying structure of subject + predicate, we have an analysis similar to that of the imperative. Thus the underlying form of (17) would be "Sue ate the pie"; the underlying form of (19) would be "A bug was in my soup." Chomsky suggested that we get from the underlying structure to the surface structure by means of a mental operation or grammatical rule that transforms the underlying structure into the form we wish. He called these operations *transformation rules.*

Let's take our imperative sentence as an initial example of how these rules operate. Our discussion of underlying structure suggests that all sentences start out in the mind as simply subject + predicate. Thus if you wanted your students to open their books, the beginnings of that desire might be described as an agent (your students), an action (opening), and their books (the recipient of the action).

The verbal form of all this would be "You open your books." Universally, people tend to shorten the forms of their language whenever possible, especially when circumstances restrict the chances for misunderstanding. Thus you would be motivated to use the shorter, and equally correct, "Open your books." Having acquired all the rules of grammar, you tacitly know that the subject of "You open your books" can be deleted, so you apply the appropriate transformation rule and the result is the imperative "Open your books."

Chomsky proposes transformations as an addition to phrase-structure rules, so we can depict this process formally by using phrase-structure notation. The underlying structure consists of:

You open your books
$\quad$ | $\quad$ | $\qquad$ |
NP_1 VP $\quad NP_2$

The transformation rule would consist of deleting NP_1, and would operate optionally on any imperative sentence such that:

$NP_1 + VP + NP_2$ *becomes* $VP + NP_2$

or:

You + open + your books *becomes* Open + your books

We can formulate transformation rules for the other example sentences just as easily. In "The pie was eaten by Sue," for example, the underlying structure is "Sue ate the pie." Again using phrase-structure notation, we have:

Sue ate the pie
$\quad$ | $\quad$ | $\quad$ |
NP_1 VP NP_2

The transformation to turn this sentence into the passive is a bit more complex than the imperative transformation. The first thing we notice is that the order of the two noun phrases has been reversed. Moreover, the verb has been changed to a form of *be* plus the past participle *en*. Finally, the word *by* has been inserted in front of NP_1. We would therefore formulate the transformation as:

$$NP_1 + VP + NP_2 \;\textit{becomes}\; NP_2 + be + en + VP + by + NP_1$$

or:

Sue + ate + the pie *becomes* The pie + was + eaten + by + Sue

We can apply this rule to any sentence with the form $NP_1 + VP + NP_2$. (A separate rule is related to the tense of *be* and to attaching the past participle *en* to the verb.)

Sometimes the transformations are easier to visualize when depicted on tree diagrams. The two diagrams in Figure 3 show how the initial underlying structure is changed into the surface structure for "The pie was eaten by Sue."

Figure 3

Underlying Structure

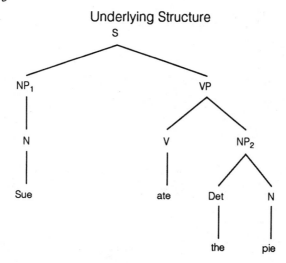

Surface Structure

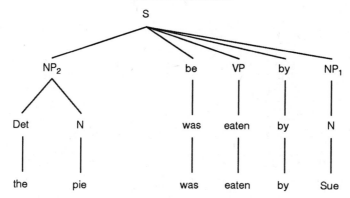

The transformation for "There was a bug in my soup" can of course be formulated in the same way as the imperative and the passive transformations. One difference here is that we are working with a prepositional phrase (PP) for the first time. But it should present no problem. The underlying structure would be "A bug was in my soup":

A bug was in my soup
 | | |
NP₁   VP   PP

The transformation reverses the order of NP_1 and VP, and then inserts the word *there* at the beginning of the sentence. In fact, this is often called the "there-insertion" transformation:

NP_1 + VP + PP *becomes* there + VP + NP_1 + PP

or:

A bug was in my soup *becomes* There was a bug in my soup

Once more, it may help to visualize the transformation if we depict it on a tree diagram (see Figure 4).

Figure 4

Underlying Structure

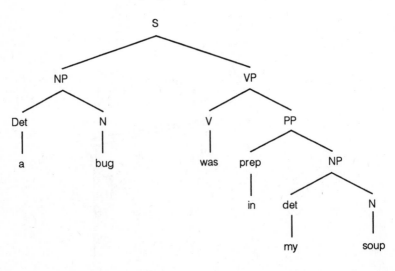

Surface Structure

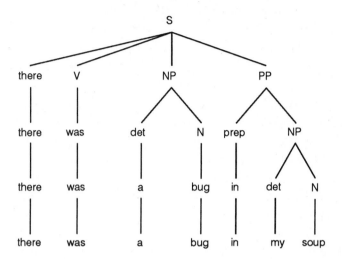

Obviously, much more could be said about transformations. There are, for example, numerous transformation rules that allow for generation of a wide range of sentences. Only three have been discussed because the goal is to provide a sense of what transformational-generative grammar is about, not to offer a full account of the grammar.

Moreover, significant developments in grammatical analyses have taken place since Chomsky proposed the concepts summarized here. Scholars are trying to make their grammars more precise, more descriptive, more comprehensive. Nevertheless, these scholars all work within the transformational-generative framework to some extent. Even those who disagree with the grammar acknowledge its influence in the act of arguing for some alternative.

The Influence of Transformational-Generative Grammar

Although Chomsky developed transformational-generative grammar originally as a tool for language analysis, in later works he began to strongly advocate the view that linguistics is a branch of cognitive psychology and that a generative grammar can reveal the organizational structure of the human mind (Chomsky, 1975). Even before Chomsky explicitly drew attention to possible connections between grammar and psychology, however, the formulation of transformational-generative grammar offered researchers numerous reasons to look at language study in a new light.

The proposal that we can separate linguistic competence from linguistic performance, as well as the proposal that sentences have both an underlying structure and a surface structure, led to interesting studies that attempted to determine the "psychological reality" of grammaticality judgments and of transformations. If language users actually apply transformation rules to underlying structures, for example, then one could reasonably expect transformed sentences to take longer to process than untransformed sentences (Miller, 1962; Miller & McKean, 1964). The findings suggest that such is indeed the case.

Work along these lines led to questions concerning the way sentences, and language, are represented in the mind. How do we comprehend language? How do we produce sentences? How are words stored in memory? How do language and grammar develop in children? How does language differ by sex, by economic group, by age? Each question leads naturally to several more, and whole disciplines concerned with answering these and related questions have developed over the years. *Psycholinguistics* addresses the connection between psychology and language; *sociolinguistics* addresses the social aspects of language. The roots of these disciplines of course antedate Chomsky, but it is fair to say that his work contributed significantly to their growth and development.

Scholars and teachers interested in writing have also been influenced by transformational-generative grammar. During the 1960s, many people reasoned that the competence–performance distinction could be turned into an instructional agenda: One need simply provide students with the means for turning tacit knowledge on the level of competence into explicit knowledge on the level of performance. Numerous efforts were therefore made at teaching transformational-generative grammar to raise performance to the level of competence (see Gale, 1968; Mellon, 1969; O'Hare, 1973; R. White, 1965). Although not terribly successful in a direct sense, these efforts had an indirect and substantial impact on studies of *style* (see Bateman & Zidonis, 1966; Mellon, 1969; O'Hare, 1973; Winterowd, 1975). In fact, the most successful stylistic device over the last two decades, known as *sentence combining*, arose out of attempts to increase writing maturity by teaching students transformational-generative grammar (see Chapter 5).

On a negative note, many people were confused by the notions of competence and performance. From the late 1960s through the mid-1970s, the education section of local newspapers frequently ran articles about how transformational grammar had essentially warped the minds of educators. Students already know everything about language, the writers proclaimed mockingly, so teachers have decided there's nothing to teach. A barrage of criticism followed.

The problem was—and is—that *competence* is a slippery term. In everyday language it refers to *skill level* or *potential ability*. In the first sense you may be a competent swimmer if you don't sink or inhale water when you get into a pool. In the second sense you are competent to play the piano if you have arms, hands, fingers, legs, and feet. You may not be able to play at all, but you are competent to do so, should you decide to try, because you can work the keyboard and the pedals. Of course, we have to assume that lessons of some kind would be involved in your deciding to try; it's highly unlikely that you could simply sit down and play Chopin without training, and even with training there is no assurance that you will ever be competent in the first sense (Foster, 1985b).

Neither of these senses approximates the definition of *competence* given in this chapter, which you will recall is "the inherent ability to make correct grammaticality judgments." This is a technical definition used throughout linguistics. At best it can be broadened, as Chapter 2 does tacitly, to include our unconscious knowledge of how to use language in context, what Dell Hymes (1971) calls "communicative competence."

When composition studies adopted the competence–performance distinction, the tendency was to ignore the technical definition of *competence* in favor of the popular one related to potential ability. Matters were confused further by notions of innateness, until "writing competence" has come to mean for many teachers something along the lines of "the innate ability to write." And writing is usually taken to mean the complete act, not just applying pen to paper. So for many teachers, *competence* suggests a classroom environment where students have ample opportunities to write, where they have the chance to practice what they *already know how to do* (see, for example, Berthoff, 1981, 1983; Elbow, 1973; Graves, 1981; Murray, 1982; Parker, 1979).

Now, even though we may say that people have the innate ability to learn *language*, that they have the innate ability to determine rather consistently whether a given sentence is *grammatical*, and that they have the innate ability to learn how to use language in *context*, there is nothing in linguistics, psychology, or grammar to suggest that people have the innate ability to write. To make this claim is roughly equivalent to claiming that each of us knows innately how to play Chopin—all we have to do is sit at the piano long enough and it will come out.

In spite of this confusion, the overall impact of transformational-generative grammar has been positive, even though it hasn't been direct. That is, the grammar itself hasn't revolutionized writing instruction, for reasons that will become clear in the next part of this chapter. No, the impact has largely been indirect, influencing *how* we study composition and *how* we look at writing performance. It has, for example, stimulated most serious researchers to adopt a formal, rigorous approach to language study. As George Hillocks (1986) tells us, increasing formalization signaled the end of the subjective evaluations of the factors related to writing performance that had long dominated the field.

For teachers, the formalization of research means we can better understand the problems our students encounter when we ask them to write. The distinction between competence and performance, for example, allows us to credit students with being able to use language effectively in a wide range of contexts, while recognizing that their experience with the formal context of writing may be limited. Thus we can acknowledge that the difficulty some students have with writing isn't necessarily a reflection of their intelligence but is more likely a reflection of their unfamiliarity with the formal conventions of writing. Direct instruction that augments what the students already know will be helpful and effective.

By the same token, we can credit students with the ability to perform well in most contexts, while simultaneously expecting them to produce errors related to lapses in attention, to a set of false "rules" related to writing, and to variations in background and experience. As Sue Foster (1985b) says, "Consideration of these possibilities can help the writing instructor diagnose the causes of many of a writer's problems" (p. 8).

Grammar and Writing

It is against this background that we now consider the specific relationship between grammar and writing. One of the difficulties writing teachers face is that writing doesn't really seem to be *about* anything. We ask students to produce a descriptive essay or an analytic essay, we discuss examples of effective writing with them, and then we put them to work. If we confer with them during the rough-draft stages, we may ask them about supplying more details or more examples, or we may say something about organization, but even really experienced teachers find that the comments they give to students tend to be abstract.

In most instances, they simply can't be very concrete. If one tells a student, for example, "You may want to add more details so the reader gets a clearer picture of what you are describing," the student is likely to ask, "What kind of details?" If one succumbs to temptation and actually responds with some concrete details, the student isn't writing the paper, the teacher is. It takes time and patience to follow up the students' questions with questions of one's own that will lead students to discover for themselves just what sort of details are called for.

In any event, it's hard to see how assignments, discussions, writing, and more discussions can be considered learning. After all, there is little in this process that visibly resembles what goes on in other classes. No dates to remember. No numbers to manipulate to get a correct answer. Nothing much that can be tested in any satisfying way. In fact, there seems to be no measurable content at all.

So it's easy to understand why students and teachers alike become frustrated. It may be the lack of content in writing instruction that prompts teachers as well as students to crave work on spelling, punctuation, and, most significantly, grammar. Over the years, numerous students in my writing classes have actually complained about the lack of any grammar instruction. Grammar is something teachable and testable. If at the end of a semester students can analyze a list of sentences and name the parts of speech, they have tangible evidence that they have learned something. Both teacher and student have done their jobs.

In Chapter 7 we'll examine the effect writing and discussing writing have on learning and cognitive processing, but at this point the question to be asked is whether grammar instruction is related to writing skill. One method of answering it is to set up two groups of writing classes, making them as identical as possible in the way they are taught and the material they study. In one group grammar is part of the curriculum; in the other group it is not.

Given that grammar has been taught to generations of writing students, and continues to be taught, it may be surprising to discover that reliable evaluations of the connection between studying grammar and writing performance are fairly recent. This fact offers testimony to the strength of traditional assumptions about language, but it also indicates the impact of modern approaches to language study not only on the research questions we ask but on the way we ask them. Before summarizing several of the more important studies conducted over the last few years, I'll state at the outset that no evidence has been found that shows grammar study has any significant effect on writing performance.

As early as 1963, Braddock, Lloyd-Jones, and Schoer stated:

[I]n view of the widespread agreement of research studies based upon many types of students and teachers, the conclusion can be stated in strong and unqualified terms: the teaching of formal [traditional] grammar has a negligible or, because it usually displaces some instruction and practice in actual composition, even a harmful effect on the improvement of writing (pp. 37–38).

But because the assumed connection between grammar and writing is so strong and permeates every level of public education, various researchers have continued to search for possible relationships since the Braddock et al. report. Each of the three grammars presented in this chapter has been examined and compared in this regard, with consistent results. Whitehead (1966), for example, compared a group of high school students that received no grammar instruction in writing classes with one that received instruction in traditional grammar, with an emphasis on sentence diagramming. The results showed no significant difference in writing performance between the two groups.

As the greater sophistication and power of phrase-structure and transformational-generative grammar came to be appreciated, several researchers developed more complex studies to investigate the effects of no grammar instruction versus instruction in traditional grammar, phrase-structure grammar, or transformational-generative grammar. R. White (1965), for example, worked with three classes of seventh graders. Two of the classes studied grammar, one traditional, the other transformational; the third class spent the same amount of time reading popular novels. At the end of the study, no significant difference was found between groups in terms of their writing.

In a similar investigation, Gale (1968) worked with fifth graders who were divided into four groups: One received instruction in traditional grammar, one in phrase-structure grammar, one in transformational-generative grammar, and one received no grammar instruction. The students who studied phrase-structure and transformational-generative grammar ended up being able to write slightly more complex sentences than students in the other two groups, but no measurable differences in overall writing ability were found.

In a much longer investigation, Bateman and Zidonis (1966) conducted a two-year study that started when the students were in ninth grade. Some of the students received instruction in transformational-generative grammar during this period; the rest received no grammar instruction. Once again, students who studied transformational grammar were able to write more complex sentences than those in the no-grammar group, but no significant difference in overall writing performance was found.

An even more detailed investigation was conducted by Elley, Barham, Lamb, and Wyllie (1976), who began with a relatively large pool of subjects (248) and were particularly careful to control variation in teaching styles. Moreover, their study lasted three years, making it the most comprehensive in the field to date.

The students were divided into three groups. The first group, composed of three classes, studied transformational-generative grammar, various organizational modes (narration, argumentation, analysis, and so on), and literature. The second group, also of three classes, studied the same organizational modes and literature as the first group but not transformational-generative grammar; instead, they studied creative writing and were given the chance to do additional literature reading. The two classes in the third group studied traditional grammar and engaged in reading popular fiction.

At the end of each year of the investigation, students were evaluated on a range of measures to determine comparative growth. These measures included vocabulary, reading comprehension, sentence complexity, usage, spelling, and punctuation. Furthermore, students wrote four essays at the end of the first year and three at the end of the second and third years, which were scored for content, style, organization, and mechanics. The students were also asked to respond anonymously to questionnaires designed to assess their attitudes toward the various parts of their English courses.

No significant differences on any measures were found among the three groups at the end of the first year, with one notable exception. The students who had studied transformational-generative grammar seemed to like writing less than students in the other two groups.

At the end of the second year, the students who had studied traditional grammar produced essays that were judged to have better content than the students who had not studied any grammar, but the raters found no significant difference between the traditional-grammar and the transformational-grammar groups. In addition, other factors, such as mechanics and sentence complexity, were judged similar for all groups.

The results of the attitude questionnaire at the end of the second year indicated that the students who had studied transformational-generative grammar not only continued to like writing less overall than their counterparts but also felt English as a whole was more difficult. Nevertheless, in regard to expository writing and persuasive writing, the students who had studied transformational-generative grammar and those who had studied no grammar had a significantly more positive attitude than the traditional-grammar students. They also seemed to enjoy literature more.

At the end of the third year, the various factors related to writing were evaluated a final time. A series of standardized measures showed that the students who had studied grammar performed better on the usage test than those who hadn't. No significant differences on the other measures were found. On the final attitude survey the transformational-grammar students indicated that they found English "repetitive," which is understandable considering that each year they studied the same grammatical principles. The traditional-grammar group indicated that they found their English program less "interesting and useful" than the other two groups.

More significant, however, is the fact that even after three years of work and effort, the actual writing of the students who had studied traditional grammar or transformational-generative grammar showed no significant differences in overall quality from that of the students who had studied no grammar. Evaluations of the three groups' essays failed to reveal *any* measurable differences at all. Frequency of error in spelling, punctuation, sentence structure, and other mechanical measures did not vary from group to group. As far as their writing was concerned, studying grammar or not studying grammar simply made no difference.

Teaching Grammar

What are we to conclude from these studies? One point seems clear: Grammar instruction has no demonstrated positive effect on the quality of students' writing. This is not to suggest, of course, that it has a negative effect, nor should we dismiss the possibility that grammar instruction may have some as yet unspecified effect on students' general language skills. But the data do suggest that teaching students grammar has no measurable effect on writing performance.

The mandate for grammar instruction seems unlikely to disappear. But if one considers grammar as a tool for understanding language, there is little reason that teachers in the classroom should feel compelled to link it to writing instruction, especially in view of the research noted in the preceding section. The real issue is *how* grammar should be taught, not *whether* it should be taught.

We must be sure to distinguish between grammar and usage. Grammar describes language, it does not prescribe language. Issues of correctness are important and should not be neglected, but they have little or nothing to do with grammar instruction (see Finegan, 1980). Most of the problems with usage for native English speakers are problems of register; that is, being informal when they should be formal. More often than not, the key to solving usage difficulties lies in making students more aware of how audiences can differ, then making them more aware in general of writing for an audience, not for themselves. That is, we can use a bit of descriptive investigation to help analyze the source of students' problems and then prescribe a solution appropriate for academic writing.

Perhaps a more important point, however, regardless of whether one teaches traditional grammar or transformational-generative grammar, is that the instruction should be incidental. Rather than drills on the parts of speech, followed up with sentence diagramming, students should learn grammar as an integral part of some other subject of study, as an integral part of their daily activities. Reading, of any variety, seems to be the most appropriate.

The rationale for this suggestion is straightforward. Discussions of reading inevitably involve questions of meaning as students and teacher explore what a given author is saying in a text; questions of "what" lead quite naturally to questions of "how," which is where issues of structure and usage come in.

In this way grammar instruction becomes part of an overall analysis of how writers achieve the particular effects they do. Such analyses are important from any number of different perspectives, beginning with attention to detail and craftsmanship. Drills and diagramming may be easier, because one simply hands out the exercise books and puts students to work, but they are the stuff that puts bright, curious minds to sleep. Perhaps you can recall situations where you were asked by a teacher to perform busywork. Did you resent the waste of time? Did you find the experience frustrating and annoying? Did you really learn anything?

It seems that one of the things successful teachers do is keep in mind what sort of learning activities they enjoy and then try to translate these to their classes. We find a great deal of consistency. Most of us, for example, don't do well on rote exercises. We don't do well when we fail to see a purpose for a task. We learn best when new information is presented in a familiar context and when we are actually engaged or involved in that context.

As an example of this sort of positive learning environment, I recall visiting a classroom where a teacher was leading a group of seventh graders in a discussion of a poem by the Chilean poet Pablo Neruda. Most of the comments focused on what it feels like to be a stranger in a strange place, something most of the students could relate to. The teacher read a few lines aloud to the class and then paused to repeat a key phrase. "What an interesting adjective!" she exclaimed, and, having their attention drawn to it, many of the students spoke the line softly to themselves and agreed that it was indeed so. They had learned two very important lessons in that moment.

Conclusion

The study of grammar has been linked to writing skill for hundreds of years, based on the assumption that understanding grammar will lead to improved writing ability. The discussion presented in this chapter indicates that this assumption is wrong. Studying grammar does not seem to improve students' writing.

The way grammar is taught in most schools is also problematic. It tends to focus on training students to distinguish between standard and nonstandard usage and on diagramming sentences, as though writers frequently are called upon to parse their work. Although it is very important for students to be able to use Standard English, and although correctness in terms of spelling, punctuation, subject–verb agreement, and so on is important in writing, these features are not part of what writing ability is really about. They have little to do with clarity and depth of ideas, organization, and persuasiveness. Moreover, mechanics are best addressed through direct instruction at the time difficulties arise—that is, during the composing process.

In light of these realities, we need to reevaluate why and how we teach grammar. I would suggest that grammar instruction should give students the tools for discovering language, because language is at the center of all we do. Not only does grammar allow us to describe language, but the particular grammar we adopt reflects our personal theory of what language is about. Grammar therefore should have an important role in the language arts, although it should have an insignificant role in writing instruction.

CHAPTER 5

Stylistics

Overview

Questions of style have long dominated writing pedagogy, even though our understanding of just what style is has only recently emerged from murky subjectivity. Now closely tied to grammatical analysis, style is generally viewed as the linguistic choices a writer makes in the course of producing a written text.

The study of style, *stylistics*, gained great impetus during the 1960s, when scholars adopted a quantitative approach to discourse. Of special interest were differences between speech and writing, because literacy was deemed a reflection of cognitive development. In this case, not only writing but stylistic maturity was seen as a manifestation of reasoning ability. This presumed connection between style and mind formed part of the rationale for several studies in the mid-1960s that attempted to identify the characteristics of sentence or syntactic maturity. Kellogg Hunt (1965) pioneered this work, determining that as writers mature they produce sentences with longer clauses.

On the basis of such research, theorists proposed that syntactic maturity could be increased through direct instruction. The result came to be widely known as *sentence combining*, which consists of exercises that require students to manipulate combinations of sentences, a technique that helps develop syntactic fluency. Sentence combining has had a major impact on writing instruction, and currently it is the most widespread stylistic component in all writing classes. Substantial evidence suggests that it is effective in helping students produce longer and more varied sentences, and some evidence indicates it has a positive effect on overall writing quality. At the same time, however, several studies suggest that the effects of sentence combining are transient, and still others indicate that the gains attributed to the technique may actually be the result of underlying rhetorical factors.

In light of the conflicting data, and owing to its association with the product view of writing, teachers might want to consider alternatives to a pedagogy that emphasizes style. Style, involving as it does work at the sentence level exclusively, is best left to the final moments of essay production. That is, questions of style should be addressed after the whole essay is completed.

The Problem of Defining Style

Language has many features that we all use in common, but nuances of vocabulary, sentence patterns, and organization vary from person to person, giving each his or her own individual linguistic signature. We all tend to use language slightly differently, in speech as well as writing; it's unusual to find two people who speak or write exactly alike. When discussing writing, we usually use the term *style* to refer to this individual and identifiable pattern of language.

The topic of style has dominated writing instruction in this country since the 19th century, when Alexander Bain (1866) argued that, because composition has no real subject matter, style is all one can possibly teach.

It's easy to confuse style with *register*, so you should keep in mind that the two words don't mean exactly the same thing. Register is generally used to describe the level of formality a speaker adopts with a given audience. Word choice, sentence structure, and the like are important, but the focus is on whether the language is at an appropriate level of formality for that audience. For example, the language you use when having dinner with your best friends would be much less formal than the language you would use in a job interview.

Style, on the other hand, tends to be more concerned with word choice, punctuation, and sentence structure in written discourse. We don't find quite as much emphasis on matching language's level of formality to the context in which it's used. Style is generally subject to genre, so different kinds of writing call for application of different stylistic conventions. Indeed, this fact is a central part of most writing-across-the-curriculum programs, in which students are taught how to adapt to the varying conventions of a range of disciplines. For example, writing in the social sciences usually follows the convention of passive-voice constructions, whereas writing in the humanities does not.

Mature readers usually have some awareness of stylistic features in discourse, even if only on a tacit level. They recognize, for example, that the writing of Harold Robbins or Jackie Collins is different from the writing of Keri Hulme or John Steinbeck, not just in subject matter but in expression. Each writer has a different quality of prose, a different style. If one were to ask just what that style is, however, most people would have a hard time describing it. The typical response might be "Robbins has a manly style," or "Collins has a titillating style," or "Hulme has a confused style," or "Steinbeck has a talkative style." The problem with these descriptions, of course, is that they are so subjective as to be almost useless. They are essentially metaphors that reveal more about the person offering the description than they do about the writer's style.

We see, then, that it's possible to notice the style of a piece of discourse without being able to describe the style in any concrete way. In fact, many of the definitions of style over the centuries have been metaphors. For example, in "A Letter to a Young Gentleman Lately Entered into Holy Orders," Jonathan Swift (1712) tells us style is "proper words in proper places," without making it clear whether this means using words in some proper sequence, as in subject/verb/object, or using language appropriate to a given social context. Buffon (1769), in his *Natural History*, takes a more sweeping view: "Style is the man himself." Equally problematic is Puttenham's (1589) observation: "Style is a constant and continual phrase or tenour of speaking and writing."

Impressionism of this sort dominated discussions of style until the 1960s. Then, as noted in Chapter 4, Chomsky's work in linguistics brought about a change in perspective for many people concerned with language. Its operational framework stresses precision and exactness, especially in regard to linguistic description. In other words, it is about as opposite to impressionism as can be. Various scholars, influenced by Chomsky and utilizing the transformational-generative framework, began considering style in a new light, essentially abandoning the qualitative approach characteristic of literary studies (see Love & Payne, 1969; Turner, 1973). Qualitative analyses of texts, which previously had gone relatively unquestioned, were increasingly deemed simply unacceptable (Ohmann, 1969).

In the first formulation of transformational-generative grammar, any given sentence was reducible to its underlying structure, which was generally a shorter, simpler version of the surface structure. This underlying form was often referred to as a *kernel sentence*, which always existed as an active declarative, as in "Dogs bark" and "Mary kissed Juan." Scholars reasoned that because just about all writing has a variety of surface structures and is not limited to active declaratives, a writer achieves stylistic effects by performing transformations on kernel sentences, thereby creating the structural diversity that we recognize in discourse.

Chomsky (1957) had argued vigorously that grammar was unrelated to semantics and that transformations did not affect meaning. Thus it was deemed possible to apply alternative transformations to any given kernel without significantly affecting its meaning, while nevertheless generating different surface structures. And although there are many different transformations, they perform only four different functions on kernels: (1) they *add* words or structures; (2) they *delete* words or structures; (3) they *substitute* one word or structure for another; and (4) they *reorder* words or structures.

From a linguistic perspective, therefore, style seemed to be a matter of the choices a given writer makes on a consistent basis in regard to the transformations applied to kernels. Thinking of style in this way, as being a writer's linguistic choices, may not make for a less problematic definition, but it is at least more concrete than Swift's "proper words in proper places."

Scholars during the 1960s saw that if a writer had only four stylistic options—addition, deletion, substitution, and reordering—it was possible to *quantify* style. One need only analyze a piece of discourse carefully, determine what transformations were applied, add them up, and calculate how two or more writers differed. Style becomes a matter of statistics, not metaphor.

The quantification of style had two very important consequences. First, the study of style became the study of grammar, or at least of grammatical relationships, and indeed, grammatical analysis is now a fundamental characteristic of modern stylistics. One of the more popular composition texts during the 1970s, for example, was Tufte's (1971) *Grammar as Style*. Second, the serious investigation of style, which in the past had largely been the province of literary scholars, was no longer limited to literature; it became a viable research question for scholars investigating student writing.

We now understand that various social and genre conventions severely limit the writer's options regarding how a discourse is structured. For example, scientific writing, in spite of occasional efforts at reform, uses the passive voice extensively because it lends an air of objectivity. Most people who engage in scientific writing are, because of the convention, expected to use the passive. They therefore lack the freedom of stylistic choice afforded, say, a novelist. Similarly, social pressures to avoid sexist language have led most writers to drop the exclusive use of the generic pronoun *he* when referring to people in general, adopting instead *he/she* or *they*. It seems, therefore, that when discussing style and the constraints writers must work under, constraints that significantly influence stylistic choices, we are dealing with perhaps one of the more tangible psychosocial aspects of writing.

This insight does not reduce the importance of the linguistic perception of style. The notion that style is a matter of linguistic choices remains both powerful and elegant. It does suggest, however, that, like one's relationship to a particular grammar, one's perception of the role style plays in writing instruction may reflect a personal theory of language. The fact that issues of style have tended to dominate composition studies for the past 25 years may in this light be a reflection of the literary training most writing teachers receive. The emphasis on style remains strong today, even though during this same period we have witnessed a shift away from concern for product to a concern for process.

The Sociology of Stylistics

We begin to understand the psychosocial nature of style when we consider certain historical factors. For example, the study of style during the 1960s appears to have been closely linked to significant changes in college demographics at that time, and it has ramifications even today. Although some democratization had occurred after World War II, higher education had generally remained until the 1960s the domain of the elite. The civil rights movement and its subsequent legislation, however, mandated equal educational opportunities; more important, it provided the funds to make the mandate real.

Those who benefited were not just blacks. Suddenly the universities were inundated by a flood of internal refugees: various minority groups who, by virtue of previously unobtainable financial aid, entered higher education for the first time; working-class students who, faced with the choice between carrying a rifle to Vietnam or a book to class, enrolled in colleges by the tens of thousands (see Jencks, 1972; Shayer, 1972).

Generally, these students were unprepared for college, and colleges were largely unprepared for them. Faculty were faced with varieties of English that had long been associated with ghettos and the working class, neither of which fit into the cultivated image of ivory towerism on most campuses. The students' language was unacceptable by academic criteria, and given the lack of preparedness on the part of so many, it was relatively easy to equate nonstandard English with failure and stupidity.

One of the biggest problems nontraditional students had was expressing themselves in writing. Their speech was described as barely adequate, though sometimes colorful, but at least it was comprehensible. Their writing, however, was described as totally *incomprehensible*. This observation led to two widespread conclusions: First, the nation's public schools were not doing much in regard to literacy; second, spoken language is intrinsically different from written language. Educators and theorists proposed, for example, that "utterance is spontaneous" and "text is planned" (Dillon, 1981).

You may think these conclusions seem unrelated, but they were connected by a model describing the interaction of language and mind that attempted to explain why certain segments of the population did so poorly in school (see Chapter 7). This "cognitive deficiency" model was based on research conducted by a number of anthropologists who investigated the cognitive development and reasoning abilities of nonliterate tribespeople during the late 1950s and early 1960s (see Goody, 1977; Goody & Watt, 1968; Greenfield, 1972; Greenfield & Bruner, 1966; Levy-Bruhl, 1975). They determined that the literate people in their studies significantly outperformed the nonliterate people on tests of reasoning ability. On the strength of these findings, many researchers concluded that cognitive development is shaped by the acquisition of literacy (see, for example, Bruner & Olson, 1979).

The principal component of this model in U.S. education is the idea that black children who speak what is known as Black English Vernacular, or simply Black English, come from impoverished cultural environments and have underdeveloped language skills. Because their experiential and linguistic backgrounds are assumed to be basic to their learning, and because both are deficient, their cognitive abilities must also be underdeveloped (see Chapter 6). The educational impact of this model is most clearly seen in the charter of the Head Start programs during the 1960s, which was to aid cognitive development and increase IQ levels among minorities.

In regard to mastering written discourse, proponents of the cognitive deficiency model maintained—and continue to maintain—that learning how to write consists of acquiring the conventions of text and shedding the conventions of utterance (see Dillon, 1981; Olson, 1977; Ong, 1978, 1982). This view is essentially a version of *linguistic relativism* (see Whorf, 1956), which claims that language influences the nature of thought. Dillon (1981) and Shaughnessy (1977), for example, argue that the source of most difficulties in writing lies in students' failure to make a complete shift from one set of conventions to the other. Underlying this proposition is the notion that the ability to write well is linked to the ability to think well. Thus poor writers are simply poor thinkers. For minorities, the educational implications are harsh indeed: By this account their written discourse will be deficient in both form *and* content.

The cognitive deficiency model has been repudiated by psychologists since the early 1970s for a number of reasons (see Cattel, 1971; Epstein, 1978; J. Hunt, 1975; Jensen, 1969). For example, the anthropological studies that led to its formulation are flawed: The investigators failed to develop adequate controls and ended up comparing fundamentally dissimilar groups of subjects (see Scribner & Cole, 1981). Nevertheless, it continues to find favor among many educators because it provides a facile explanation for the traditionally low academic performance of minorities.

A full analysis of the connection between literacy and thought will be offered in Chapter 7. We can see even in this barest of outlines, however, that if writing reflects cognitive development, mental maturity can be evaluated on the basis of writing maturity. It was this assumed relationship that gave impetus and validity to the study of style. Stylistics promised to provide the long-term benefit of better understanding the mind and the short-term benefit of understanding why minorities did poorly in school.

If one were to accept the premise of the cognitive deficiency model, it would seem reasonable that studying surface features, or style, could provide insight into mature cognitive functioning. In addition, the notion of linguistic relativism (language affects thought) would predict that teachers could have students work on style and thereby directly influence mental processes and content (see Christensen, 1967; Ong, 1978). During the late 1960s and early 1970s, numerous teachers and scholars in fact accepted not only the cognitive deficiency model but also the idea that stylistic exercises led to heightened reasoning abilities. Thus, when we consider the sociology of stylistics we begin to perceive a seldom articulated rationale for viewing utterance and text as distinct forms of language, and for making style the focus of writing and writing pedagogy: A theory of composition should be based on style because style has a direct impact on the way the mind operates.

There is no evidence at all, however, that links style to cognitive ability. We simply have no valid reasons for believing that style has any effect whatsoever on either the way the mind operates or on the content of an essay. Nevertheless, this assumed connection has had a major impact on writing research and instruction; this impact is the topic of the next section.

Style and Sentence Combining

Kellogg Hunt (1965) was one of the first researchers to use the transformational-generative framework to examine the relationship between stylistic maturity and cognitive maturity. He studied maturation by comparing student writing at three grade levels to the writing of "superior" adults who published regularly in magazines and journals. Before Hunt's work, stylistic maturity had been measured in terms of sentence length. He immediately found that sentence length was a poor standard for defining a mature style and that a much better indicator was clause length, or what he called a "minimal-terminal unit," or simply *T-unit*, the shortest grammatical construction that can be punctuated as a sentence.

Underlying Hunt's research is a hypothesized linear relationship between age and style (which has prompted Witte & Cherry [1986] to ask whether we should predict such a thing as "syntactic senility"). Within limits, such a relationship does exist. The older and more experienced writers in Hunt's study produced sentences with longer T-units, which prompted him to link *syntactic maturity* with *developmental maturity*.

Sentences (1)–(3), which follow, illustrate this finding. A third-grade student, for example, would use two sentences to express two propositions, as in (1) and (2), producing two short T-units, whereas the adult would embed one proposition in the other in a single sentence, creating a single T-unit, as in (3):

(1) The woman had red hair.

(2) The woman laughed.

(3) The woman who laughed had red hair.

Based on what you now know about competence and performance, you can perhaps see that Hunt's study suggests a goal of composition instruction would be to raise students' linguistic competence to the level of performance. In other words, we know that third graders, for instance, can understand sentences with embedded subordinate clauses, like (3), even though they themselves don't produce such sentences as often as adults. Hunt's study suggested that at least one factor involved in moving from competence to performance in writing was to get students to produce longer T-units by embedding dependent clauses. That is, instruction could increase the *rate* of syntactic maturation.

Mellon (1969), drawing extensively on Hunt's findings, recognized these embeddings as having a transformational basis, and he hypothesized that teaching students how to perform grammatical transformations would have a significant effect on T-unit length. He gave a group of seventh-grade students intensive training in applying transformations over a period of nine weeks and then presented them with sentences like (1) and (2) above, with a relative-clause marker indicating the appropriate transformation. Pretest–posttest analysis of T-units indicated a significant increase in length, from 9.98 to 11.25 words. Unfortunately, although the subjects managed to produce longer T-units, trained readers did not judge their writing to be particularly better overall.

Despite these problematic results, the theory underlying the technique of combining short sentences into longer ones seemed flawless. Then O'Hare (1973) saw a difficulty in Mellon's methodology. He reasoned that subjects did not need any formal instruction in grammar to perform transformations, because such transformations were already part of their linguistic competence: That is, students did not need to know the formal aspects of, say, the relative-clause transformation in order to form a sentence with a relative clause.

Using 95 percent of the sentences from Mellon's study, O'Hare simply had students manipulate them to form the combinations, which they were able to do quite easily. His results showed an increase in T-unit length 5 times greater than what Mellon reported, and 23 times greater than the "normal" increase reported by Hunt. Moreover, trained readers rated the quality of the subjects' posttreatment writing as better than the writing of the control group.

One result of these studies, particularly O'Hare's, has come to be known as the "sentence-combining movement." Another was dozens of sentence-combining textbooks and the subsequent development of sentence-combining methodology as a major feature of composition pedagogy.

We should note at this point that many teachers were asking students to combine sentences long before the studies summarized here were published. The technique was not really "new." We must also recognize, however, that the work by Hunt, Mellon, and O'Hare achieved nationwide attention. In this regard it is significantly different from earlier combining experiences.

Additional examples of typical sentence-combining exercises follow, with the underlined sentences being those students would be expected to generate on the basis of the shorter ones:

(4) The ship left port rapidly.

(5) It was two days behind schedule.

(6) <u>The ship left port rapidly because it was two days behind schedule.</u>

(7) Paula filled her pockets with cookies.

(8) Her mother watched from the doorway.

(9) <u>Paula filled her pockets with cookies while her mother watched from the doorway.</u>

(10) The cake looked delicious.

(11) Thomas baked the cake.

(12) <u>The cake that Thomas baked looked delicious.</u>

(13) Cece studies three hours a day.

(14) Cece always receives good grades.

(15) <u>Because she studies three hours a day, Cece always receives good grades.</u>

(16) The skies rumbled.

(17) The rain poured down.

(18) <u>The skies rumbled before the rain poured down.</u>

(19) The book was on the table.

(20) Elmer wanted the book.

(21) <u>The book that Elmer wanted was on the table.</u>

Francis Christensen (1967) took a somewhat different approach to syntactic maturity. After studying the work of professional writers, he determined that they used short base (or independent) clauses to which they attached modifying phrases that add detail and depth. The following student sentences illustrate this technique. The underlined portion of the sentences is the base clause:

(22) <u>I danced with excitement</u>, winding myself around my nana's legs, balling my hands in her apron, tugging at her dress, step ping on her toes, until finally she gave me a swat across the bottom and told me to go play.

(23) <u>I dragged a chair to the counter and climbed up</u>, grasping the counter edge with my hands, stretching my body, pulling up with my arms until my head was above the tiles.

Unlike other sentence-combining techniques, this one emphasizes having students start out with short base clauses, then asking them to supply modifying detail on the basis of close observation. Modifying constructions are usually added to the end of the base clauses, producing what Christensen refers to as a "cumulative sentence." These sentences, found with great frequency in narration and description, have an ebb-and-flow movement from the general to the specific, what Christensen calls changes in "levels of generality." His approach focuses on helping students shift from one level of generality to another.

Both methodologies were instantly popular, in part because sentence combining fit neatly into the already established focus on style in student writing. In addition, it was noted that many students find an element of fun in figuring out different ways to join sentences together. The task has a puzzlelike fascination. Even more important, teachers began to see that sentence combining seemed to improve writing performance. Students who practiced it gained greater control over their sentences and were able to develop more variety in sentence types.

These classroom observations have been supported by many studies showing that students who engage in regular sentence-combining exercises increase the length of their T-units and improve overall composition quality (see Combs, 1977; Daiker, Kerek, & Morenberg, 1978; Howie, 1979; Pedersen, 1978). For example, after reviewing the major investigations related to sentence combining, Kerek, Daiker, and Morenberg (1980) state that sentence combining "has been proven again and again to be an effective means of fostering growth in syntactic maturity" (p. 1067).

One of the major attractions of sentence combining is that it can be used effectively by students at all grade and ability levels (O'Hare, 1973;

Sullivan, 1978; Waterfall, 1978). If anything, in fact, poor writers seem to benefit most from this technique.

Part of the explanation appears to be that sentence combining offers an algorithmic approach to teaching writing that many teachers and most students are very comfortable with, owing to composition instruction's lack of content. The perception is that if writing is a skill, it should be reducible to a series of steps that can be articulated by teachers and followed by students. And certainly sentence combining satisfies these desires, because students are given a series of short sentences and asked to combine them into longer ones. Occasional difficulties arise with older students who have generally been told to perform just the opposite task, taking long sentences and reducing them to short ones, but these are certainly not insurmountable.

As positive as this review of sentence combining sounds, however, several questions are associated with the technique. Various studies have suggested that over time, the gains in sentence length and writing quality attributed to sentence combining disappear (Callaghan, 1978; Green, 1973; Sullivan, 1978). Kerek, Daiker, and Morenberg (1980), for example, in the same study that comments on the positive effects of the technique, found that two years after instruction, no measurable differences were perceived between the writing of students who had practiced sentence combining and of students who had not. The control group had completely caught up with the treatment group, which over the two-year period had made no further gains. If the results are transient or mitigated by time, teachers must carefully evaluate the energy and effort involved in using the technique.

In addition, it should be noted that rhetorical mode may affect measures of syntactic maturity. Studies by Perron (1977) and Crowhurst and Piche (1979) suggest that narration and description result in the shortest T-units, whereas analysis and argumentation result in the longest. Furthermore, having students write regularly in the argumentative mode seems to produce gains in T-unit length and writing quality equal to those related to sentence-combining exercises.

Ample data indicate the reality of what we might think of as a "complexity continuum" for rhetorical modes (see Britton et al., 1975; Williams, 1983). At least in regard to classroom compositions, analysis and argumentation are cognitively more demanding than description, so the frequently noted correlation between complexity of thought and syntactic maturity would serve to explain the effect of mode on perform-ance (see Williams, 1983, 1987). (This isn't to suggest, of course, that we don't find complex constructions in description; we do. But generally these constructions consist of short T-units with attached modifying phrases [see Christensen, 1967]).

Along these lines, Kinneavy (1979) and Witte (1980) argue that the gains in T-unit length and writing quality attributed to sentence combin-ing may actually be the result of teaching rhetorical principles like analysis and synthesis inductively, principles that are inherent in the process of combining. If this is the case, teaching these principles directly, no doubt through the associated rhetorical modes, would probably be more efficient. In other words, it may well be that teachers can have a significant effect on syntactic maturity and writing perform-ance simply by focusing more attention on more demanding writing tasks, such as analysis and argument.

This suggestion is an important one, because it raises a serious question not only for sentence combining but for any approach to writing instruction that emphasizes style. The issue is this: Will students benefit more from working on isolated sentences or on whole essays?

Over the last few years, as composition pedagogy and theory have increasingly adopted a position that advocates an emphasis on the process of writing rather than the finished product, many teachers have come down solidly on the side of the whole essay. Writing, like reading, has come to be viewed as primarily a top-down process rather than bottom-up. In this view, to focus on style is to deal with the surface features of discourse, with matters of form. As we have already seen in our discussion of the phonics approach to reading, an emphasis on surface features tends to lead to error correction that slights the rhetori-cal, functional nature of discourse. Content, meaning, and purpose too often get ignored in such a learning environment, and an emphasis on style in general and sentence combining in particular may not be conducive to successful writing instruction over the long term.

But in spite of these significant theoretical difficulties, style remains a powerful force in most writing classes and in many of the discussions about teaching writing. Proponents of sentence combining, for ex-ample, have frequently skirted the theoretical problem by falling back on the flawed work of those writers who claim that mastery of surface features and the conventions of written discourse are linked to cognitive development.

On this basis, sentence combining is seen as a comprehensive model for constructing texts, its advocates maintaining that increasing "syntactic fluency" affects global discourse skills. Christensen (1967), for example, claims that work on sentences will provide a discovery procedure that will enable students to find things to say about a topic. To date, however, there is no solid evidence to support the idea that teaching students to write better sentences will lead to their writing a better essay.

Conclusion

Ultimately, style's appeal for those concerned with teaching writing may lie in the way it lends itself to an algorithmic method of instruction. When working with sentences, teachers and students have a limited and easily identifiable range of operations that can be performed, and the results are almost immediately visible. After all, we can see the effect of turning two short sentences into a single longer one. When working with an entire essay, however, matters are usually not so simple, nor are gains quite so readily measured.

Nevertheless, the research we've reviewed in this chapter and preceding ones suggests that we should focus our instructional efforts on the whole essay, not on isolated parts of it. It seems reasonable to suggest, therefore, that teachers should embed sentence work, or style, in the context of writing complete essays.

CHAPTER 6

English as a Second Language and Nonstandard English

Overview

In an increasingly pluralistic society, teachers face a major change in classroom demographics. More and more students in the public schools do not have English as their native language. To meet the challenge these students present, bilingual education programs have been established across the United States with federal support. The goal of these programs is to help nonnative speakers master English while simultaneously providing core curricula in the students' first language.

Outside the United States, most school systems approach bilingual education through what are referred to as *language immersion* programs. Nonnative speakers are placed in classes with native speakers and are treated as though that particular language is their own. Experiments in the United States with immersion programs (designed to exclude native English speakers) have not been particularly successful with minority students, especially Hispanics.

Currently, two major alternatives to immersion are being used in the U.S. Some districts offer programs in English as a second language, or ESL–transition. (These are sometimes referred to as *language shift* programs.) This approach concentrates on providing special English classes for non–English speakers. These classes are not linked to content courses such as math or history; they concentrate exclusively on English skills. Students simultaneously are enrolled in content courses conducted in English.

Many school districts have shifted from ESL–transition to *transition–maintenance* programs. (These are sometimes referred to as *language retention* programs.) In this approach, teachers work with largely homogeneous language groups. They provide instruction in students' native language, or, where there is a shortage of bilingual faculty, schools use bilingual aides to translate for the monolingual English-speaking teacher. Usually, there are no designated English-instruction classes. General English skills are viewed as acquirable from contact with the English-speaking community.

The "maintenance" aspect of such programs aims at preserving the status of the native language (Garcia, 1983). Lessons frequently focus on students' native culture in order to emphasize the idea that the English language need not diminish a student's own heritage. Instruction continues in the native language until students meet district-established criteria for reclassification as "English proficient." The students we find in writing classes will generally have been reclassified, and the discussion in this chapter assumes that teachers will be working with students who have been properly reclassified.

In addition to nonnative English speakers, today's classrooms have large numbers of *nonstandard* English speakers. Most come from ethnic minorities, particularly black and Hispanic, but significant numbers are white students from lower socioeconomic backgrounds. The combination of various language groups in individual classrooms suggests that we need to see our classes as being both multilingual and multidialectical.

A *dialect* is a variety of a language, distinguished in terms of either geography or socioeconomic status, not race. In fact, if we could remove the influence of socioeconomic status, we would find that dialect is independent of race (see Peck, 1982). Nevertheless, the most widely dispersed nonstandard dialect is Black English Vernacular, or Black English. This dialect, with roots in various African languages, has its own grammar and rhetorical conventions. It is not, as is sometimes thought, a degenerate version of Standard English.

A dialect of growing importance is Chicano English, used by millions of Mexican-Americans. As yet we have little research exploring anything but the fundamental characteristics of this dialect, but even understanding these basic features is of consequence to teachers, because it is their task to help the children who speak it become literate in Standard English.

English as a Second Language

As this book is being written, the United States is experiencing one of the largest waves of immigration in its history. Fleeing poverty that most people in this country probably can't even imagine, millions of Mexicans and Central and South Americans are crossing the border to find a better life. Frustrated by limited economic opportunities in Korea, Hong Kong, and Taiwan, hundreds of thousands of Asians are crossing the Pacific to America.

The social consequences of this mass immigration are difficult to define, but the linguistic consequences are already being felt from one end of the nation to the other. Quite simply, the place English has enjoyed since World War I as the dominant language in American society is no longer as secure as it once was.

We can readily see that the sheer number of Spanish speakers now in the United States (estimated by census authorities to be anywhere from 20 million to 40 million), the majority of whom speak little or no English, is reshaping the linguistic characteristics of the nation. For example, there are now about 250 Spanish-language newspapers in the United States, almost 300 radio stations, and two television networks. Some analysts predict that in 20 years, Spanish will be the first language of the majority of the population in the Southwest, which includes California, Arizona, Colorado, New Mexico, and Texas. Native English speakers in Los Angeles, San Antonio, and Miami already know the advantage, in some cases the necessity, of being able to speak Spanish.

The nation's public schools started feeling the effects of immigration some years ago. Whether parents have come to this country legally or illegally, one of the first things they do is enroll their children in school. Florida and the Western border states began noting significant increases in Hispanic students in the early 1960s. They responded by establishing programs in English as a second language (ESL) and bilingual education, both designed to ease these children—classified generally as "Limited English Proficient," or LEP—into the mainstream English-speaking society as gently as possible. In 1963, for example, the Ford Foundation helped establish a bilingual education program in Dade County, Florida, that taught students in both Spanish and English (Hakuta, 1986).

Against this background, we have the critical need for improved literacy skills nationwide. The need for such skills among immigrants and other language minority groups is especially acute, because without these skills, assimilation into mainstream America—and the economic benefits that go with it—become an empty hope. Yet how do we help nonnative English speakers master written English? What theoretical and practical factors are involved? The following sections attempt to answer these and related questions.

What Is Bilingual Education?

Before we begin examining the principles related to writing instruction for nonnative speakers, some understanding of what bilingual education is about is necessary. Bilingual programs in this country differ from region to region, sometimes from district to district, but they all have essentially the same goal: helping nonnative speakers master English while simultaneously remedying the low achievement levels and high dropout rates among language-minority students. We occasionally find these programs in middle and high schools, but the majority are offered at the elementary level, because this is deemed the age of greatest need.

Until relatively recently, the approach used in the United States was one in which non–English speakers were simply placed in classes with English speakers and were treated as though English were their native language. This approach, called *language immersion*, has been used quite successfully in several countries, particularly Canada, which has for years used a dual-track immersion program in both English and French (see Garcia, 1983; Lambert & Tucker, 1972; Swain & Lapkin, 1982). In Quebec Province, for example, the language of instruction is the child's second language: Native English speakers are enrolled in courses taught in French; native French speakers are enrolled in courses taught in English.

The single-track immersion programs in the United States are designed to exclude native English speakers. Some educators suggest that the term *immersion* is therefore misapplied in American programs. They prefer to describe the American approach as one of language *submersion* (Snipper, 1985).

Whatever we call the approach, it has proven stubbornly unsuccessful with Spanish-speaking students. Why this is so is the topic of much debate. Some scholars attribute the failure to the proximity of Mexico and the widespread belief among many Mexican-Americans, even second and third generation, that they will someday return permanently to Mexico (Griswold del Castillo, 1984; R. Sanchez, 1983). Others attribute it to the size of the Hispanic community; with their own subculture of shops, newspapers, radio stations, businesses, and so on, native Spanish speakers experience less socioeconomic pressure to master English than, for example, an immigrant from Iran would feel. Because socioeconomic factors are the principal motivators in mastering another language, in this case English, the lack of such pressure would significantly diminish efforts at second-language acquisition.

Still others argue that Spanish speakers have been systematically excluded from America's mainstream economic community, kept at the lowest end of the socioeconomic scale for so long that they lack hope of entry and therefore lack motivation to master English (Griswold del Castillo, 1984; Penalosa, 1980; R. Sanchez, 1983). Additional explanations abound, which means that at this point we really don't have an answer to why immersion has not worked with Spanish-speaking children, although there does seem to be a correlation with socioeconomic status. In any event, as a result of its failure, we find immersion/submersion programs only occasionally in larger districts.

In some schools, programs in English as a second language, or *ESL–transition* programs, are used extensively. (These are sometimes referred to as *language shift* programs.) This approach concentrates on providing special English classes for non–English speakers. These classes are not linked to content courses such as math or history; they concentrate exclusively on English skills. Students simultaneously are enrolled in content courses conducted in English.

Over the last several years, increasing numbers of schools have shifted from ESL–transition to *transition–maintenance* programs. (These are sometimes referred to as *language retention* programs.) In this approach, there are no special classes for teaching English to nonnative speakers. General English skills are viewed as acquirable from contact with the English-speaking community. Working with largely homogeneous language groups, teachers provide instruction in students' native language, or, where there is a shortage of bilingual faculty, schools use bilingual aides to translate for the monolingual English-speaking teacher.

The "transition" aspect of such programs focuses on teaching specific skills in students' first language (L_1) that will transfer to their second language (L_2). The "maintenance" aspect of such programs aims at preserving the status of the native language. Lessons frequently focus on students' native culture in order to emphasize the idea that the English language and Euro-American culture need not diminish a student's own heritage (Garcia, 1983).

Instruction continues in the native language until students meet district-established criteria for reclassification as "English proficient." Upon being reclassified, the nonnative English speakers are placed in classes where the lessons are conducted in English. This process of English acquisition takes about two years in most cases, but it isn't uncommon to find students being inappropriately reclassified in as little as six months by teachers overly anxious to "mainstream" them (Snipper, 1985).

The Need for Bilingual Education

Bilingual education programs have come under fire since the very beginning from several groups. Some people believe these programs pose a threat to the dominance of English and undermine the European heritage of the nation. Others believe they remove any incentive for LEP students to learn English. And still others believe they ultimately foster a linguistic and cultural segregation that will prevent immigrants from fully participating in American society, keeping them always at the bottom of the socioeconomic ladder.

Such criticism, however, has not stemmed the growth of bilingual education, even though program administration is often less than ideal. There is no need here to delve into a detailed description of the troubles that beset many schools; suffice it to say that some administrators and teachers, like society at large, tend to feel ambivalent about bilingualism. As a result, programs in many schools receive only token support. Students are frequently reclassified as English proficient before they are ready, and they begin falling behind in academic achievement almost at once (Snipper, 1985). In numerous districts around the country, between 50 and 75 percent of Hispanic students drop out of school before they reach 11th grade, and it is likely that hasty reclassification contributes to these numbers.

Yet even though a significant percentage of teachers and administrators may personally dislike bilingual education, the majority seem to agree that some such approach is the most humane way to mainstream immigrant children into American culture. When in 1986 California passed legislation establishing English as the official language of the state, educators were among the first to voice fears that bilingual programs would be adversely affected. Careful reading of the legislation, however, showed that these programs were explicitly protected from legislative tampering. Thus, aside from setting forth a cultural principle, decreeing English to be California's official language has had no impact at all. Similar bills elsewhere around the country are also likely to have minimal effects on bilingual education.

Part of the explanation, of course, is that literally millions of students nationwide are at issue. To ignore the educational needs of such vast numbers for the two to three years they need to master the language is simply deemed unconscionable. Moreover, bilingual education has received federal support since the mid-1960s, when schools around the country were beginning to see enrollment increases for nonnative English speakers that paralleled those in Florida, Texas, and California. The result was passage of the federal Bilingual Education Act of 1968. This legislation, which has been renewed regularly, was designed to make school districts more responsive to the "special educational needs of children of limited English-speaking ability" (Bilingual Education Act, 1968).

Even with this federal mandate, however, over the last 20 years bilingual programs have generally failed to keep pace with the influx of non–English speaking and limited-proficiency students. The apparatus has been overwhelmed.

In the school yards of the nation's larger districts, one hears a potpourri of different languages, many unrecognizable to the lay observer. In Los Angeles, for example, more than a hundred languages are currently represented among students. Smaller districts are experiencing the same phenomenon; schools in Wyoming, Illinois, and Indiana now report LEP enrollments approaching 20 percent, with few instructors qualified to teach them.

Finding qualified bilingual teachers is extremely problematic; for some languages it is outright impossible. Though most teachers have studied some foreign language, they are far from being bilingual. Moreover, if the language they studied was French, Italian, or German, for example, it is essentially useless in the classroom. The languages of our newest immigrants tend not to fall into the major European categories, with the obvious exception of Spanish, but are more likely to be Cambodian, Vietnamese, Korean, Farsi, Hindi, varieties of Amerind, or some dialect of Chinese.

The number of teachers who can speak those languages is understandably very small, but consider how much smaller it must be for Hanunoo, a language used in the Philippines, or Huichol or Nahautl, languages spoken among the Indians of Central America. Yet each of these languages is represented among our students. The situation is so extreme, in fact, that most districts are unable to hire enough teachers who speak the most widely distributed language, Spanish, because the demand exceeds the supply. Many schools in the Los Angeles area, for example, are 60, 70, in some cases even 80 percent native Spanish speakers. There just aren't enough bilingual teachers to go around.

The consequences of this situation are felt by almost every teacher at the elementary and secondary level, whether one is teaching a designated bilingual class or not. Increasingly, we must view our classes as being *multilingual.* Today's teachers are increasingly likely to work with nonnative English speaking students at some point, regardless of what part of the country they teach in. The tendency to reclassify these students as English proficient before they are ready adds to the teacher's problems, because it usually places LEP students in classes with native English speakers, making uniform assignments and grading difficult at best. In addition, the writing teacher will be confronted with linguistic patterns that he or she has not been adequately trained to handle.

Becoming a qualified bilingual teacher takes a great deal of time, for it involves mastering another language. It is possible, however, to gain fairly quickly both sensitivity to and understanding of the educational issues involved in teaching LEP students in a multilingual classroom. To teach writing to language-minority students, sensitivity and under-standing precede all other requirements for success.

Instructors who are committed to effective teaching must begin to develop an awareness not only of how nonnative speakers use language but how they acquire it. That is, the distinction between performance and competence already made in connection with native speakers is equally important here. The need for this awareness will grow in the years ahead: Enrollment of nonnative speakers is predicted to increase by 35 to 50 percent over the next 12 years (Hakuta, 1986).

Bilingualism and Intelligence

The problems all teachers face when working with nonnative English speakers are major, but they are especially acute for writing teachers, because surface errors can so easily render an essay unreadable by most standards. Making the situation even more difficult is the very human inclination to equate intelligence with how one speaks (and writes) the language. Most of us make judgments regularly about people on the basis of how they use English. Even in regard to different dialects or accents of English we encounter tremendous biases (see Farr & Daniels, 1986; Hudson, 1980; Trudgill, 1974).

Many people from the West Coast, for example, when hearing a New York or a Southern accent, will automatically form a negative view of the speaker, assuming that he or she is, if not stupid, at least less intelligent than someone with a Midwestern or West Coast accent (see Trudgill, 1974). Our judgments of nonnative English speakers as they struggle with the language can be even more severe, especially if the speaker is from a national group demeaned by unkind stereotypes. French- or Scandinavian-accented English is usually viewed as having an air of romance, whereas Asian- or Hispanic-accented English is viewed far less favorably.

Perhaps the most effective way to appreciate the position of LEP students is to imagine going to school in Italy or China or Mexico with only a modest knowledge of the native language. You might be very intelligent, yet a poor command of the language would make your thoughts seem awkward and confused to others, no matter how cogently they would sound in English.

This popular misconception about intelligence and nonnative English is potentially very harmful, particularly if it finds its way into the classroom, because it inhibits the educational process. Teachers who share this misconception will have lower expectations for LEP students, and, in the peculiar self-fulfilling dynamic that exists between teacher expectations and student achievement, these students will indeed perform at a low level.

In their four-year study of writing teachers, Perl and Wilson (1986) found that what most distinguished successful from unsuccessful instructors was their attitudes toward students. The successful teachers viewed students as possessing considerable linguistic and rhetorical knowledge, as possessing language competence, and held corresponding expectations. The unsuccessful teachers viewed students as having little or no competence, as being, in fact, linguistically deficient. Perl and Wilson report that in classrooms where this latter view was evident, even the most sound instructional methods failed to produce significant gains in performance. Clearly, the lesson to be learned is that negative linguistic biases that influence teacher expectations and performance have no place in the classroom.

There is another view of the relationship between intelligence and bilingualism, however, that is more difficult to dismiss because it is supported by numerous studies performed by reputable researchers. It maintains that bilingualism is inherently "bad" because it leads to a form of intellectual confusion whereby children become handicapped in both their first language and their second.

The tendency of bilingual children to mix vocabularies, using words and expressions from both languages in their speech, is often pointed to as evidence of such confusion. More compelling evidence comes from investigations of bilingualism and intellectual performance where bilinguals consistently were outperformed by monolinguals on language tasks as well as intelligence tests (see Anastasi, 1980; Christiansen & Livermore, 1970; Killian, 1971; M. Smith, 1939; Yoshioka, 1929).

Killian, for example, administered a battery of tests to compare intelligence and language abilities among English monolinguals, Spanish monolinguals, and English–Spanish bilinguals. The bilinguals performed significantly lower on both measures than the monolinguals.

In another study, Anastasi and Cordova (1953) evaluated Spanish–English bilinguals from Puerto Rico. Thinking that the language used in presenting tests to bilingual subjects might influence results, these researchers gave one administration in Spanish, a second in English. Yet the language of administration seemed to make no difference in the results: The subjects performed significantly below the norms for monolingual subjects in both test conditions.

The researchers conclude that one of the major factors involved in the poor performance was the subjects' bilingualism, "which makes them deficient in both languages. . . . In so far as this maladjustment itself appears to have arisen from the children's severe language handicap during their initial school experiences, a solution of the language problem would seem to be a necessary first step for the effective education of migrant Puerto Rican children" (p. 17).

Over the last several years, studies like these that suggest intellectual and cognitive deficits in bilingual children have been severely criticized (see Peal & Lambert, 1962; Swain & Cummins, 1979). Peal and Lambert, for example, after a close analysis of many early investigations, determined that researchers who found monolinguals outperformed bilinguals were actually testing dissimilar groups. The bilinguals were not true, or "balanced," bilinguals, proficient in both languages. Their lack of fluency in both languages resulted in lower performance scores.

When researchers ensured that similar groups were being compared, the bilinguals performed just as well on intelligence tests as the monolinguals, and in some cases performed better (see Bruck, Lambert, & Tucker, 1974; Cummins, 1976; Duncan & De Avila, 1979; Lambert, 1977, 1978). Other investigators have argued that the performance differences are the result of using subjects from dissimilar socioeconomic groups, with the monolinguals coming from the middle class and the bilinguals from the lower class (see Christiansen & Livermore, 1970; Garcia, 1983). Socioeconomic status, of course, has consistently been related to IQ scores; poor people tend to have lower scores than wealthier ones.

These conflicting results are vexing, because as teachers we often feel the need for clear-cut answers to questions about how our students learn and achieve. Parents who speak a language other than English at home may be truly concerned about the effects of bilingualism, and if they ask a teacher how two languages may affect school performance and achievement, it just won't do to say that the evidence is inconclusive. In addition, these equivocal results seem to fuel the politicization of bilingual education, making it easier for essentially research–pedagogical questions to degenerate into language policy issues.

In *Mirror of Language*, Kenji Hakuta (1986) casts an interesting light on the problem when he notes that the majority of the negative findings have come from the United States, where bilingualism has historically been linked to racial and ethnic groups on the periphery of mainstream America. The positive findings, on the other hand, have generally come from Canada, which has a long tradition of French–English bilingualism, with the French-speaking community a vital social force in Quebec Province.

The equivocal results, in other words, may reflect different sociopolitical climates: The American studies were interpreted in a context that looked for negative findings, whereas the Canadian ones were interpreted in the opposite context. But the real problem, Hakuta suggests, may lie in trying to compare inherently dissimilar groups, monolinguals and bilinguals, which leads to distorted results.

In an effort to overcome this potential limitation, Hakuta and Diaz (1984) and Hakuta (1984) evaluated intelligence and linguistic skills in 300 bilingual Puerto Rican children without comparing them to monolinguals. The hypothesis was that bilingualism is a performance continuum, with some individuals being more bilingual than others. Thus if bilingualism affects cognitive ability and overall linguistic performance, it should be possible to evaluate these variables *within* a group of bilingual subjects without reference to a monolingual group. The investigation evaluated subjects' level of bilingualism, their intelligence, and their degree of language awareness. Values were then correlated to determine how the variables interacted.

A modest, but nonsignificant, correlation was found between intelligence and bilingualism, but none at all was found between bilingualism and language awareness. In other words, the results were just as inconclusive as those we have already examined. After evaluating the findings, Hakuta (1986) suggests that his study and all the others in this area may have a fundamental flaw. For years investigators have been measuring intelligence and correlating IQ scores with bilingualism, yet what gets overlooked is that correlations do not measure cause–effect relations. For example, it would be possible to find a very high correlation between gender and hair length, but gender itself is not a causal factor in this case; one's sex does not *determine* the length of scalp hair.

By the same token, bilingualism is not a casual factor in intelligence; all other things being equal, the bilingual children who scored low on IQ tests would probably have achieved the same score had they been monolingual. Hakuta (1986) therefore concludes that "bilingualism . . . bears little relationship to performance on these measures [intelligence and linguistic performance]" (p. 40). Given the success of bilingual education in various countries, such as Canada, India, and Denmark, it's difficult to reasonably dispute that conclusion.

What we need to recognize, therefore, is that bilingualism itself does not seem to be significantly related to intelligence. With this point in mind, we cannot, and certainly should not, view the various errors that characterize the writing of LEP students as indicative of low intelligence.

That a student is not very adept at writing in a second language does not mean he or she is mentally deficient. Considering the difficulties related to writing in general, even a modest success in a second language should be viewed as an accomplishment. As for the errors in syntax and vocabulary that plague language-minority compositions, careful analysis shows that most surface problems fall into categories of error that are closely related to the level of developing competence in English, not to intelligence (see Edelsky, 1986; Farr & Daniels, 1986). Beneath those surface problems, one often discovers a thoughtful composition. As the student gains greater competence, the number of errors will decrease.

First-Language Acquisition

On a day-to-day basis, the question of bilingualism and intelligence, and indeed of nonstandard English and intelligence, is ever present as a pedagogical issue in the bilingual or multilingual classroom. It is especially pressing for writing teachers, because grammatical, or surface, correctness is the criterion by which society generally evaluates the success of written discourse. Elimination of errors therefore takes on a sense of urgency for both students and teachers.

With nonnative and nonstandard speakers alike, however, instruction proceeds with great difficulty. Lessons that have taken long preparation and that have been taught with diligence and care frequently seem to make no difference. The Hispanic child, for example, who uses Spanish grammar in designating the negative and produces "Marie no have her homework" may continue to do so even after work with the English verb form *do* ("Marie *doesn't* have her homework"). Many teachers find this lack of change extremely puzzling, and even the most conscientious may begin to doubt the intellectual ability of their non-mainstream students.

We need to recognize that in the process of language acquisition, linguistic patterns become deeply ingrained and therefore difficult to alter. Moreover, gains in linguistic competence do not appear to be related closely to direct instruction, a point that can lead to limitless frustration for teachers if not accepted fully. Composition instruction that focuses on surface errors occurs on the level of linguistic perform-ance—and second-language performance at that. It will have little or no effect on competence.

Lessons and activities that affect students' competence and that then have an impact on their writing require some awareness of the prin-ciples involved in acquisition. We can begin to understand how in-grained acquired linguistic patterns are if we consider that language acquisition begins shortly after birth. Halliday (1979), for example, reports that a one-day-old child will stop crying to attend to his mother's voice; this response is generally viewed as a precursor to actual language.

Because the infant's response is not yet language, a more flexible term to describe its behavior is *communicative competence*, which specifies, among other things, the ability to make clear a topic of interest, the ability to produce a series of relevant propositions, and the ability to express ideas in a way that is sensitive to what the speaker knows about the hearer (Foster, 1985b).

The development of competence seems to be a fundamental com-ponent of the parent–child relationship, as Halliday (1979) indicates when he states that, just as a child will stop crying to listen to his or her mother's voice, a mother, "for her part, will stop doing almost anything, including sleeping, to attend to the voice of her child. Each is predis-posed to listen to the sounds of the other" (p. 171). This predisposition can be thought of as a reflection of the innateness of language, and so we can say that early parent–child interactions will have a deep and powerful influence on language development.

We begin to see the complexity of these interactions within a few weeks of birth. A mother and her child will actively engage in an early form of conversational turn taking that consists of ongoing exchanges of attention. The child attends carefully to the sounds and the movements of his or her mother, moving with her in a dance of body language. To capture this turn taking, Trevarthen (1974) used video cameras to record mother–child interactions. The videos show mother and child in animated mutual address. The child moves its entire body in a way that is clearly directed toward the mother; in addition, it moves its face, lips, tongue, arms, and hands, in what seems best described as incipient communication.

At the same time, the mother is addressing the child with sounds and gestures of her own that mirror her baby's actions. The two do not appear to imitate each other; rather, the gestures and vocalizations appear to be communicative (though nonlinguistic) initiation and response. When viewed in slow motion, the movements of the child are slightly ahead of the mother's, suggesting that he or she is the initiator, not the mother. (In those cases where a child is raised by an adult other than his or her parents, a similar situation obtains.)

This is not yet language, and the amount of "meaning" conveyed in such exchanges is open to argument. But these gestures and movements are clearly important precursors to recognizable words and expressions that begin to emerge typically between 12 and 20 months. Prespeech exchanges may not have a propositional meaning, but they are meaningful from the standpoint of communicating attention and developing pragmatic (for example, turn taking) competence. As a result, when children do begin to produce language, they have already been engaged in meaningful communication for a long time.

Most of a young child's preverbal communication is related directly to his or her world, composed of toys, pets, parents, and so forth. Children work at communicating particular needs and desires within the context of their environment. Their first communicative efforts are highly pragmatic and functional, bound tightly to their immediate surroundings and their parents, as evidenced by the fact that parents seem to interpret their children's preverbal vocalizations rather accurately, whereas a stranger cannot.

By the age of one, and perhaps even earlier, children have a broad range of knowledge about the way the world operates. They know, for example, that cups are for drinking, knives and forks are for eating, beds are for sleeping, that cars take them places, that knobs turn on TV sets, and so on. Moreover, their pragmatic awareness gives them an understanding that includes knowing that their environment can be manipulated. For example, a reaching gesture made to a parent will result in being lifted and held; crying attracts attention and usually results in the elimination of some unpleasantness, such as a wet diaper, hunger, or the need for a hug (see Clark & Clark, 1977). Such pragmatic knowledge appears to be universal across cultures and languages; we can observe essentially identical behavior in children everywhere.

It should come as no surprise, therefore, that the first verbal vocalizations children make are about the world around them, regardless of the native language involved. Animals, food, and toys were the three categories referred to most frequently in the first ten words of 18 children studied by Nelson (1973). The people they named most often were "momma," "dadda," and "baby."

By age 18 months, children typically have a vocabulary of only 40 or 50 words, but they are able to use single-word utterances to accomplish a great deal of communication by assigning them different operational roles, depending on the communicative context and the relevant function. "Cookie," for example, uttered in the context of a market (where the child knows, apparently, that cookies can be obtained), can mean "I want some cookies." Uttered in a high chair with a cookie on the child's plate, the same word can simply be an act of identification. Uttered in the act of tossing the cookie on the floor, it can mean "I don't want a cookie," and so on.

Within a few months of their first single-word utterances, children begin combining words into two-word utterances, such as "Jenny cup" ("This is Jenny's cup") or "Car go" ("I want to ride in the car"). In each case these two-word phrases seem to represent a natural progression toward more complete verbal expressions. Language acquisition, therefore, can be thought of as a continuum, with children moving from preverbal gestures to single words, two-word utterances, and finally complete expressions.

The source of children's initial utterances is the family, but as noted in Chapter 4, children do not engage explicitly in imitating the language of those around them. The majority of their utterances are novel, not mere repetitions of heard expressions, and they characteristically are designed to manipulate and organize the children's environment. Infants spend their first 12 months, approximately, listening to language and experimenting with sounds before producing recognizable utterances, but all research in this area indicates that first words cannot be linked to specific input provided by parents (see Clark & Clark, 1977; Hudson, 1980; Slobin & Welsh, 1973). Instead, they are linked to the whole universe of discourse uttered in the baby's immediate environment and directed toward the baby, which explains why we encounter initial utterances like "kitty" and "dadda," but not "taxes," "groceries," and "furniture."

The absence of direct imitation suggests that during their first years of life, children are involved in mastering the grammatical and pragmatic rules that govern language use. Because parents just don't go about giving their children explicit lessons in grammar, and children obviously produce grammatical utterances, we have to conclude that they master linguistic patterns more or less on their own through a process of observation and hypothesis testing.

Evidence comes from a number of sources, but one of the more impressive involves irregular verb forms and tense. During one stage of their language development, English-speaking children between three and a half and four will correctly apply the past tense to irregular verbs like *run* and *eat*. They will produce sentences such as "I ran home" or "I ate my sandwich." They then go on to another stage in which they overgeneralize the past-tense rule for regular verbs to include the irregular form. Irregular verbs that they once used correctly they now use incorrectly, producing utterances such as "I runned home" and "I eated my sandwich."

Contrary to what parents may want to believe, direct instruction has no effect on children's overgeneralization, because during this period they lack the linguistic competence to make sense of the explicit input (see the example on page 61). But over time, children make the correction on their own as their competence grows and as they modify their internalized grammar to include the category of irregular verbs. On the basis of such behavior, we can conclude that language competence grows in the presence of general, meaningful input, defined as functional language directed toward the child, from which children derive the underlying grammatical and pragmatic principles that govern language.

The ineffectiveness of direct instruction in regard to verb forms raises some interesting questions and is of course part of our central concern as teachers. It suggests not only that certain elements of language development proceed at their own pace in spite of our efforts but that teachers as well as parents do not play as big a role in children's emerging language as we usually imagine. For example, although parents provide a source of meaningful input, they do not specifically teach their children how to speak any more than they teach them how to walk. Here lies the source of the distinction between learning and acquisition. For this reason, most scholars consider language acquisition to be primarily a matter of mastering linguistic patterns through what is essentially an unconscious process. It is the development of language competence.

Steve Krashen (1982) argues that direct instruction in later years provides a "monitor" that helps bridge the gap between competence and performance. For example, a child who has grown up using *lay* ("I want to lay down") when Standard English usage calls for *lie* ("I want to lie down") can potentially benefit from direct instruction. The teacher can point out that *lay* is a transitive verb in Standard English and therefore is always followed by a noun, as in "I will lay the book on the table." *Lie*, on the other hand, is an intransitive verb and is not followed by a noun, as in "I will lie down for a nap." With this rule at their disposal, students can monitor their speech and writing to avoid the nonstandard intransitive use of *lay*.

Of course, this shift in usage can be accomplished only through the *conscious* application of the monitor. If one is distracted for any reason, or if one tries to apply so many rules that the language production system becomes overloaded, the monitor fails. Because the monitor operates on the level of performance, not on the level of competence, we begin to understand why direct instruction proceeds so slowly: We are asking students to apply conscious procedures to unconscious processes.

This is not to suggest, however, that teachers and parents have no influence on children's language. Teachers are largely responsible for helping students develop monitors. Parents, for their part, seem to be responsible for children's development of psychosocial patterns related to how language is used to interact with the world.

For native English speakers, William Labov (1964, 1970, 1972a) and Shirley Heath (1983) have laid the groundwork in the parental area. Their research suggests that different cultural–social groups learn to use language in quite different ways, as determined by variations in parent–child interaction. Heath, for example, notes that the ways lower-class black children learn to use language are fundamentally different from the ways upper-middle-class white children learn to use it. The determining factor is how parents interact with their children.

In the community she studied, Heath observed that black children were rarely spoken to and that little of the prelinguistic interaction between mothers and offspring described in the Trevarthen (1974) investigation took place. One result was that the black children appeared to place more reliance on contextual cues for comprehension than the white children.

This factor proved to be extremely problematic for them in school, where the emphasis is on language use that has no immediate audience, feedback, intention, or purpose. Another result, Heath tells us, is:

> [The black children] . . . never volunteer to list the attributes which are similar in two objects and add up to make one thing like another. They seem, instead, to have a gestalt, a highly contextualized view, of objects which they compare without sorting out the particular single features of the object itself. They seem to become sensitive to the shape of arrays of stimuli in a scene, but not to how individual discrete elements in the scene contribute to making two wholes alike. If asked why or how one thing is like another, they do not answer; similarly, they do not respond appropriately to tasks in which they are asked to distinguish one thing as different from another (pp. 107–8).

The reliance on context would inevitably lead to difficulties in composition, because writers must step outside the language event to avoid producing an essay that sounds like a conversation with the second party missing. They must create a context by explicitly providing some of the very factors that make conversations successful, such as audience, purpose, intention, and so on.

In addition, a holistic view of the world that is largely unconcerned with attributes and detail is one that seems fundamentally at odds with the kinds of tasks children are frequently asked to perform in school, where describing objects by listing their attributes is a common activity.

It should be clear, however, that both the reliance on context and the holistic view are part of these children's linguistic competence. This is how they understand language and how they use it. Asking them to focus on attributes or to decontextualize is therefore somewhat akin to asking a person to change the natural word order of sentences, shifting from subject/verb/object to, say, object/verb/subject. People *can* talk backward, but only with great difficulty.

Although more research is needed, there is some evidence to suggest that Mexican-American children manifest many of the characteristics just described (see Buriel, 1975; Kagan & Buriel, 1977; Kagan & Zahn, 1975; Ramirez & Castaneda, 1974; Ramirez & Price-Williams, 1974). In this case, writing instruction for Hispanic children that does not attempt to place the task in a meaningful context may be extremely problematic.

If the influence parents exert on language development lies primarily in the realm of pragmatic competence, what are the sources of significant influence on *performance?* Many people assume that it is schools, but, unfortunately, this turns out not to be the case. Based on what we currently know, the most powerful influence on a child's language performance is his or her peer group. (In fact, peer groups even shape adult language.) Labov and Harris (1983), for example, tell us that "our basic language system is not acquired from schoolteachers or from radio announcers, but from friends and competitors: those who we admire, and those we have to be good enough to beat" (p. 22).

The common phenomenon of accent shift illustrates this point. If a family native to Boston, for example, moves to Oregon, the children will quickly lose their Boston accent, until their speech is indistinguishable from the native Oregonians'. The parents' accent will soften measurably, though it may not disappear entirely. The linguistic explanation is that it is more important for children to identify with a specific peer group than it is for the parents. Another illustration is slang. Slang is characteristically adolescent, for it serves as a bonding device. As people grow older, their usage of slang begins to disappear, until by middle age it occurs only rarely in most speech.

On the basis of such observations, we can say that first-language acquisition involves mastering numerous linguistic features and principles that are universal across all languages, but that even within a single language, such as English, there will be features that are particular to specific social and cultural groups. For example, a lower-class child and an upper-class child will both possess functional competence, but the pragmatic details may differ in terms of, among other things, reliance on context. In a bilingual or multilingual classroom, the universals form the foundation for instruction within the framework of "linguistic transfer," where the teacher draws on what a child already knows about language in L_1 to aid the child with what he or she needs to learn in L_2 (see Thonis, 1983).

This topic is of great interest to those working in bilingual education, because it allows students to build second-language skills on knowledge they already have. In many respects this process is very similar to rhetorical competence (Chapter 2) and the psychology of reading (Chapter 3). That is, it operates on a top-down basis.

Unfortunately, the equivalent of Shirley Heath's (1983) important study has yet to be conducted for Chicano English or any of the other nonblack-minority variants. As a result, it is difficult to determine which psychosocial factors influence communicative competence among these groups. But given the serious problems we encounter with such students, it seems reasonable to suggest that their competence differs significantly from what we take to be the norm among speakers of Standard English.

If this is the case, then what we know about first-language acquisition would appear to call for a pedagogy that has as its main components effecting changes in how students perceive the world around them, background and foreground, the abstract and the concrete, and showing them ways to evaluate the difference. Its focus would be primarily on critical thinking and secondarily on writing; writing performance would become a product of cognitive performance. That is, phenomena of psychosocial development must be viewed as influencing language use in general and writing in particular. For language-minority students, such a pedagogy would include activities to engage writers in the mainstream culture, providing opportunities to interact significantly with the social context needed for making meaning in Standard English.

Second-Language Acquisition in Children

There is significant evidence that suggests second-language acquisition proceeds along the same lines as first-language acquisition (see Gardner, 1980, 1983; Hakuta, 1986; Hatch, 1978; Krashen, 1981a, 1982).

Hakuta offers a case study that typifies the process for children who are immersed in an L_2 environment: Uguisu, the five-year-old daughter of Japanese parents who moved to the United States for a two-year stay. Both parents knew English, but they talked to their daughter exclusively in Japanese. When Uguisu was enrolled in kindergarten shortly after the family's arrival, she spoke no English.

Over the next several months, Uguisu continued to speak Japanese. Although she did pick up a few words of English from her playmates, these were generally imitations of expressions the playmates uttered, such as "I'm the leader." We can safely assume that the kindergarten teacher knew no Japanese and therefore would not readily be in a position to provide formal language instruction, so it appears that, with the exception of classroom activities, Uguisu's exposure to English was largely informal and consisted of playtime with peers. That is, it resembled a child's exposure to his or her first language, except for the obvious lack of parental input.

Seven months after arriving in this country, Uguisu began to use English suddenly and almost effortlessly. Over the next six months, English became her dominant language. She used it when talking to her parents, who continued to respond in Japanese, and when playing by herself. Hakuta states that "within eighteen months after her initial exposure to English, only a trained ear would have been able to distinguish her from a native speaker" (p. 108).

It appears that during her initial months in the United States, Uguisu was unconsciously sorting through the linguistic data she received on a daily basis, using her innate language abilities to master the grammatical, lexical, and pragmatic patterns that govern English. Once she had grasped these patterns, she was able to begin using the language. English input from her parents was unnecessary in this case because Uguisu was, like all other five-year-olds, linguistically mature and had already developed a high level of communicative competence in her first language.

We can conclude from this example that second-language acquisition, like first-language acquisition, relies on meaningful input, not formal instruction. The primary difference between the two lies in the role of parental input: It is crucial in L_1, but largely incidental in L_2, because children can draw on their already developed L_1 competence.

The role of peers or playmates is powerful, perhaps even more so than for the child's first language.

Contact with English-speaking peers is an important underlying assumption in bilingual education. The model of second-language acquisition is similar to the one just outlined: The children are expected to participate in the larger English-speaking community and acquire the language on their own outside the classroom.

But many nonnative English-speaking children live in neighborhoods where their primary language dominates and English is heard rarely. Schools in these neighborhoods will be linguistically dominated by the "minority" language, so they provide little or no opportunity for children to interact with English-speaking peers. Busing is often viewed as one means of alleviating the problem, but unfortunately, in the majority of schools where students are bused in from other neighborhoods the children segregate themselves outside the classroom along racial, linguistic, or socioeconomic lines, again leaving little chance for natural acquisition to occur.

Linguistic Transfer: A Rhetorical Approach

In light of such difficulties, many teachers understandably despair when asked to teach writing to LEP students. Too much of the available research suggests that teachers will have little success in developing competence and that students will never achieve proficiency.

Krashen (1982, 1984), however, argues that language instruction does in fact have a positive effect on second-language acquisition when it is the major source of meaningful input, as is true in many schools. We shouldn't be surprised if this is indeed the case, for even the most conservative, xenophobic linguistic analysis contains a great deal of social pressure for children to master English. They will respond to this pressure by using whatever sources are readily available to improve their command of Standard English, thereby creating conditions that increase the significance of teachers' roles in second-language acquisition.

Given the general scarcity of relevant research, it isn't possible to determine the extent of our impact, but this may be more of a policy issue than an instructional one, anyway. On a day-to-day basis, our first concern as teachers is the *potential* for influencing children's language development. We have to recognize that the extent of our influence not only will vary from child to child but will always be difficult to measure accurately.

Considering the potential evident in multilingual classrooms, it is extremely disheartening to observe how writing classes for nonnative English speakers are generally conducted. The concern with surface errors that so often dominates writing instruction for native English speakers becomes an outright mania when the students are from a language minority. Even teachers who utilize a process approach with mainstream students may abandon it in favor of grammar drills, vocabulary lessons, and spelling exercises, as though the techniques that fail to improve the writing of native speakers will somehow work with the nonnative (see Diaz, 1986; Richards, 1985).

This peculiar notion remains quite strong in some areas of bilingual education. Mary Finocchiaro (1986), for example, tells future teachers that they should deduct "points" on compositions for errors in spelling, punctuation, and vocabulary. Although accuracy is an important goal for bilingual children to strive for, and although negative reinforcement is one way for teachers to approach it, there is some question as to the long-term benefits to be derived from punishing children's mistakes. For any student struggling with a rough draft that attempts to capture an idea, such deductions will inevitably be defeating. But they will no doubt be particularly so for the LEP student, who is likely to be painfully self-conscious about surface accuracy.

Of course, some teachers may believe that the ability to develop ideas has a lower priority than the ability to write error-free sentences. It's a question of preferred methodology that perhaps is rooted in one's theory of language. Finocchiaro, for example, goes on to advise readers that "if ideas are important . . ., give two points for ideas. If you think four ideas are necessary, give $1/2$ a point for each" (p. 88). Were we to follow such a plan, most nonnative speakers would end up with negative scores on their papers. In fact, most native English speakers probably would too.

Approaches to teaching writing that focus on correcting errors and punishing mistakes fail to recognize that the majority of the surface errors we find in the English compositions of LEP students are developmental. That is, they are quite similar in nature to those we find in children acquiring a first language (see Diaz, 1986; LoCoco, 1975; L. White, 1977). From this perspective, we not only should expect a high number of errors as students work on initial drafts but should indirectly encourage them by urging students to take linguistic risks. Pushing LEP writers to experiment with new words, sentence structures, and organizational patterns as they work at making meaning will result in more mistakes while at the same time it expands their repertoire of skills. Risk taking is an important part of language growth, yet language-minority students are generally risk-adverse because of previous school experiences that have punished error.

In fact, what we generally see in writing classes for LEP students is a pedagogy antithetical to current research and theory concerning how people use language and how they develop writing competence (Diaz, 1986). Strategies and techniques for the classroom will be discussed in detail in Part Two, but it should be clear at this point that effective teaching will establish a meaningful context for student writing and will draw on students' existing communicative competence.

LEP students understand the performative nature of language, although their skill lies in L_1 rather than L_2. Communicative functions, however, remain the same regardless of language; requests, assertions, and argumentation are fundamentally universal. It therefore seems reasonable to suggest that two significant strategies are available for teachers in a bilingual or multilingual setting. The first consists of providing opportunities for LEP children to interact in a meaningful way with the mainstream social context, while the second consists of transferring skills in L_1 to L_2.

Developing a methodology on the basis of the first strategy seems fairly straightforward. Considering the position of nonnative English speakers as persons on the threshold of mainstream America, the bilingual writing class should be a rich source of meaningful writing activities. For example, questions dealing with similarities and differences of culture and language can lead not only to interesting writing assignments but, when shared with the class, to better understanding of the backgrounds of individual students. Group writing activities can emphasize the social nature of written discourse.

One of my former credential candidates took advantage of the multicultural mix of her high school writing class by having students formally introduce themselves at the beginning of the semester and describe their country, culture, or neighborhood. This latter category, of course, was for native English speakers in the class. A writing assignment that followed asked students to provide a much more detailed description. This assignment was then followed by one that asked students to trace their family tree as far back as possible, using whatever sources were available, including interviews with kin, and to develop a narrative that related the family history.

It usually turned out that many of the native English-speaking students had grandparents who were immigrants, and sharing these essays had a positive effect on student interactions. Group work sessions, in which students discussed drafts in progress, provided opportunities to use English to talk about writing, aiding the development of metalinguistic knowledge. Moreover, students actually enjoyed the assignments.

The second strategy, linguistic transfer, requires that the writing teacher recognize LEP students indeed have communicative competence in their native language, a fact too frequently ignored. In addition, it requires an instructional agenda focusing on global features of discourse: organization, development, detail, purpose, intention, and so on. In other words, helping LEP students learn to write better involves the same strategies we should use with native English speakers: We show them ways to perceive and reason more cogently.

From this perspective, commonplace tasks take on new meaning. For example, the Christensen method of sentence combining discussed in Chapter 5 becomes more than merely a device for increasing T-unit length. You will recall that this method consists of adding modifying constructions to a short base clause, as in the following, where the base clause is underlined:

(1) <u>The pilgrims come in dusty mobs,</u> long peregrinations that wind their way down into the valley of Tenochtitlan from the high mountains, from Cholula, Atlixco, and Otlaltepec, villages as much as thirty miles away.

Such sentences move writers toward a blend of the general (the short base clause) and the specific (the concrete modifiers). The algorithmic structure of this type of combining requires students to distinguish between the concrete and the abstract and to focus on explicitness.

A similar result can be obtained through the use of oral discourse as a focus for writing assignments. Tape recordings of conversations, interviews, and oral presentations can form the basis for tasks that call for re-creating the gist of the discourse with an altered context. The question for students becomes: What must be added or subtracted from a taped conversation, for example, to communicate the same message in writing? In sum, the teacher draws on what the students already know about language to develop tasks that will have a positive effect on writing performance.

Writing and the Nonnative Speaker

In order to carry out the methodology suggested in the preceding section, teachers have to overcome the very strong temptation to spend hours marking and correcting surface errors on students' essays. The best way to read papers is without a pen or pencil nearby. Once we stop this futile editing, we can get on to matters like the students' purposes in writing an essay, the context of the assignment, their intentions, essay organization, the levels of abstraction and concreteness, the aptness of examples, and so on, which are much more amenable to direct instruction. Correcting spelling, vocabulary, and sentence structure can be reserved for class sessions where students help each other edit. This approach not only enables them to learn by doing, it gives you back many evening and weekend hours you would otherwise have spent editing the students' work for them.

It's important to note, however, that even the most successful teacher in the most successful class may encounter compositions that are measurably different from those of native English speakers. Students more or less fluent in English may produce essays that seem off topic, incoherent, or out of focus. The problem appears to be one of rhetorical differences that are thought to be inherent in individual cultures and languages. We saw in Chapter 2 that the term *rhetoric* has meant different things at different times. Experience with students from diverse national backgrounds suggests that the term also means somewhat different things in different cultures. This isn't to suggest that there are functional differences such that argumentation, for example, ceases to be argumentation. It does suggest, however, that the form of argumentation may vary from culture to culture.

The following example illustrates a few of the rhetorical differences we find in the essays of nonnative English speakers. It comes from a high school student we will call Jon, whose first language is Chinese. The assignment asked students to compare the American ideal of individual freedom with the degree of personal freedom they have as teenagers. During discussions prior to work on initial drafts, the class talked about feeling that they have too many restrictions, as well as about the idea that freedom entails a significant amount of responsibility:

> When I first arrive in America I was impressed by the clean, well-built freeways. They seem symbolic of America's great strength and freedom. Freedom is what has make America great, and it was our quest for freedom that brought my family to this country.
>
> The ideal of freedom in America is known to all the world. In America people may travel where they wish when they wish. If they wish to own a business and to become rich, they may do so as long as they are willing to work very hard.
>
> In my country, there is not freedom. One must do what the government tells and must think like the government. One can not operate a business and only the politicians have the opportunity to become rich. My family have much more freedom in America.
>
> This much freedom carries great responsibility. Everyone must work very hard. It is as though everyone accepts Mr. Ben Franklin's advice that "Idleness is the devil's hand mistress."
>
> In a communism society people only work hard if they fear punishment. Everyone get paid the same, except the politicians, so it doesn't matter. Work much, work little, everyone is the same standard of living.
>
> Some teenagers in America do not appreciate this freedom. They do not know what is like to live under communism or dictatorship. Perhaps American teenagers should appreciate their freedom more and watch less MTV. Then they could work hard to keep America strong and to become rich.

To most native English speakers, this essay is off topic, incoherent, perhaps even rambling. The opening paragraph doesn't establish the topic, nor does it state the problem or provide a rationale for the composition—characteristics we find in essays by proficient native English speakers. The reference to Franklin seems thrown in to offer proof of the writer's knowledge. The mention of communism seems designed simply to introduce the rhetorical device of comparison/contrast. The final paragraph seems grandiose, a kind of big-bang conclusion.

In trying to explain the composition's inadequacy, some teachers might attribute it to the surface errors or to the student's failure to understand the assignment. In either case, they would be wrong. Close analysis, for example, shows that the surface errors in this essay are neither serious nor frequent. As for understanding the assignment, it's hard to convey the student's qualities through the medium of this text, so I ask you to take on faith my evaluation that five minutes' worth of conversation with Jon would demonstrate that he is bright, dedicated, eager to learn, and fully aware of what the assignment asked for. What, then, is the problem?

Robert Kaplan (1972) suggests that the form of Jon's essay reflects the rhetorical patterns characteristic of Chinese, patterns we just don't find in English. He notes that whereas in English we have the "five-paragraph essay," in Chinese there is the "eight-legged essay," in which the beginning and end are largely flourishes that complement the center, or "fourth part," which contains the author's thesis or position. As Kaplan states: "This approach is typical of the solution by indirection which marks much Oriental writing. The careful attention to the balance of the essay and to the fulfillment of the pattern also eliminates any real concern with the kind of logic considered so significant in western analytic writing" (p. 53). In his analysis, other cultural groups have their own distinct rhetorical patterns. Semitic languages are characterized by parallel structures; Romance languages, like Spanish, are characterized by digressions.

Kaplan's analysis carries no value judgment; each rhetorical pattern is valid within its particular culture. Thus we cannot object to the digressions of the Spanish pattern, for example; to do so would be the equivalent of objecting to the Mexican fondness for spicy foods. We can only note that the pattern is different from what we find in English.

If we accept Kaplan's analysis, Jon's essay would probably be very successful—were it written for an audience whose first language is Chinese. The fact that it has six parts rather than the traditional eight suggests a "Westernizing" influence, perhaps, but we note that the third paragraph is nevertheless the central one, where we recognize some attempt at establishing a thesis. Moreover, Asian cultures tend to subordinate individual concerns to family ones, so we should not be overly surprised to find that Jon says little about himself but focuses instead on his family.

Although many more investigations are needed in this area, Kaplan's work has received support from several research studies. Jones (1982) and Jones and Tetroe (1983), for example, examined the writing of bilingual students in Canada and established that syntactic, rhetorical, and planning skills in students' first language transferred, with little change, to their second language. Harder (1984), also studying bilingual students in Canada, obtained similar findings. He concluded that complex communication difficulties of the sort evident in Jon's essay "cannot be explained as merely insufficient knowledge of English grammar, diction, or idiom. Such problems do not involve linguistic differences in the native (NL) and target language (TL) but encompass different stylistic habits, different ways of thinking, and different cultural values" (p. 115).

We can derive important benefits from recognizing that our students may be applying a rhetorical model that is correct and appropriate in their first language but not in English. Being able to identify organizational patterns, for example, allows us to show students how their essays compare with those written by native English speakers. No stigma is involved, because we can also point out that the pattern is characteristic of the students' cultures. In other words, we can emphasize the fact that the students are *successful* in the writing context they know best, and we can then go on to teach them how to modify their rhetorical patterns to match more closely those used in English. The result is a more positive classroom environment, one in which students are eager to follow up on their success in their native language with one in their second.

Nonstandard English

In addition to students whose first language is one other than English, we regularly have students in our classes whose native language is English but who do not speak the variety known as Standard English. Much of the previous discussion is extremely relevant to our work with nonstandard-English speakers. Up to this point, *Standard English* has been used loosely to describe the prestige dialect in the United States, without any real effort to be more specific. A closer analysis will perhaps make our students' linguistic diversity easier to understand.

Defining Standard English in a precise way is rather difficult, and even an imprecise definition requires a clearer understanding of *dialect.* In one sense, a dialect may be thought of as a spoken variety of a language; that is, it isn't used in formal writing. In another sense, it seems more worthwhile to think of dialects in geographical and social terms. We begin with the broad category of "language" and divide it into subcategories on the basis of variations associated with where people live and what socioeconomic status they have (see Haugen, 1966; Hudson, 1980; Trudgill, 1974). A "standard dialect" in this analysis will be the one with the largest number of users and the one with the greatest prestige owing to the socioeconomic success of those users.

Standard English meets both criteria. It is the dialect of government, science, business, technology, and education. It is the dialect associated with success, as evidenced in part by the number of young actors and actresses in Los Angeles who take voice lessons to lose their regional dialects. It is also the language of the airwaves. Radio DJs and television news anchors universally communicate with us in Standard English. In the case of Dan Rather at CBS, the long vowels of his native Texan accent have been carefully polished away to avoid any suggestion of nonstandard dialect.

The United States doesn't have a monopoly on a prestige or "standard" dialect. Countries like France, Germany, and Mexico have their own standard versions of their respective languages. Moreover, there is nothing inherently "better" about a standard dialect. After all, where people are born and how much money they make involves a certain element of luck.

In most cases, sheer historical accident led to the dominance of one variety of a language rather than another. If the South had won the Civil War, had then developed a vigorous and influential economy and a strong educational system, and had become the focal point for art and ideas, some Southern dialect might be the standard in the United States rather than the current Western–Midwestern dialect.

Haugen (1966) suggests that all standard dialects undergo similar processes that solidify their position in a society. The first step, and the one apparently most influenced by chance, is *selection.* That is, a society will select, usually on the basis of users' socioeconomic success, a particular variety of the language to be the standard. At some point, the chosen variety will be *codified* by teachers and scholars who write grammar books and dictionaries for it. The effect is to stabilize the dialect by reaching some sort of agreement regarding what is correct and what isn't. Next, the dialect must be *functionally elaborated* so that it can be used in government, law, education, technology, and in all forms of writing. Finally, the dialect has to be *accepted* by all segments of the society as the standard, particularly by those who speak some other variety (also see Hall, 1972; Macaulay, 1973; Trudgill, 1974).

If we are distinguishing language varieties geographically, we will speak of a New England dialect, a Midwestern dialect, a Southern dialect, and so on. But if we are distinguishing language varieties socially, we will speak in economic terms. The majority of nonstandard-dialect speakers are poor and undereducated, and they also tend to come from our ethnic minorities, whether black, Hispanic, or Asian (see Ferguson, 1977; Hudson, 1980; Labov, 1966, 1972a, 1972b). We should be careful with this generalization, of course. Large numbers of white Americans speak a nonstandard dialect, just as large numbers of nonwhite Americans speak Standard English. As we have noted, if we could remove the influence of socioeconomic status, we would find that dialect is independent of race (see Peck, 1982).

Language Variation and Code-Switching

It's common for different dialects to use different sets of grammatical rules for generating the language. In certain dialects we would find a sentence like (2) regularly, but not one like (3):

(2) I seen Harry last night.

(3) I saw Harry last night.

By the same token, in other dialects we are more likely to find (4) than (5):

(4) Rosie be workin at Ralph's.

(5) Rosie is working at Ralph's.

In the discussion of grammar in Chapter 4, we noted that speakers of Standard English may use certain linguistic forms that in the strict sense fall into the category of nonstandard usage. For example, people who otherwise use Standard English may say "It is me" rather than "It is I." Other examples abound, such as the general confusion regarding *lay* and *lie* and the widespread disappearance of the relative pronoun *whom*, even in much formal, academic writing.

Two factors account for these occurrences. The first is simply that languages change, in spite of often vigorous efforts to prevent it, as in schoolteachers' prescriptive admonitions about what constitutes "correct" speech and writing. In this analysis, "It is me" will eventually have to be accepted as standard to reflect changes in usage. The second is that linguistic variation exists not only across dialects but within them. We have already discussed one source of variation within dialects in regard to register, or the level of formality language users adopt in relation to a specific audience. Other sources of variation include age, occupation, and gender. Women, for example, tend to be much more conscientious about language than men. As a result, in a family whose dialect is nonstandard, the woman's language will come closer to Standard English than the man's (Trudgill, 1974).

The phenomenon of linguistic variation has led William Labov (1969) to suggest that every dialect is subject to "inherent variability." That is, speakers of a particular dialect fail to use all the features of that dialect all the time. For example, we can occasionally hear Standard English speakers reducing a sentence like (6) to one like (7):

(6) I've been working hard.

(7) I been working hard.

More common, however, is variation of nonstandard features to standard features. This frequently occurs in formal and semiformal situations, such as a classroom. A student who uses a nonstandard dialect, for example, might write (7), but if asked to read his or her composition aloud might read (6). In the course of reading an entire essay, a student is likely to change many of the nonstandard features, but not all of them.

These observations suggest that "dialect" is far from a discrete entity. Instead, it may be thought of as a continuum influenced by the social context in which language is used. People move back and forth on the continuum as context demands and as their linguistic skills allow.

The term used to describe this back-and-forth movement is *code-switching*. In its broadest sense it refers to the act of using different language varieties at different times. Code-switching can also occur within a single language event, as the following exchange illustrates (Gumperz, 1982):

> Following an informal graduate seminar at a major university, a black student approached the instructor, who was about to leave the room accompanied by several other black and white students, and said:
>> a. Could I talk to you for a minute? I'm gonna apply for a fellowship and I was wondering if I could get a recommendation?
>
> The instructor replied:
>> b. O.K. Come along to the office and tell me what you want to do.
>
> As the instructor and the rest of the group left the room, the black student said, turning his head ever so slightly to the other students:
>> c. Ahma git me a gig! (Rough gloss: "I'm going to get myself some support.") (p. 30).

In Hispanic English or Asian English, the switching can and often does occur across languages. In other words, we will find a mixture of, say, Spanish and English. Labov (1971) observed code-switching within single sentences or utterances when studying Puerto Rican English in New York, as the following example shows. The brackets enclose the translation of the Spanish phrases:

> Por eso cada [therefore each . . .], you know it's nothing to be proud of, porque yo no estoy [because I'm not] proud of it, as a matter of fact I hate it, pero viene Vierne y Sabado yo estoy, tu me ve hacia me, sola [but come (?) Friday and Saturday I am, you see me, you look at me, alone] with a, aquí solita, a veces que Frankie me deja [here alone sometimes Frankie leaves me], you know a stick or something. . . . (p. 450)

Some people who encounter code-switching see it as evidence of "linguistic laziness" (see, for example, N. Sanchez, 1987). Witnessing code-switching on a daily basis, many teachers have often assumed that black students who speak the dialect known as Black English Vernacular (BEV) are simply being perverse when they fail to modify their speech and writing to Standard English on a permanent basis. If these children can "correct" their nonstandard features to standard ones on some occasions, as when reading a composition aloud, then they must "know" Standard English and are simply too lazy to use it, or so the reasoning goes. The situation for children who speak Chicano English is perhaps even more difficult, because they may be ridiculed by members of the Hispanic community who speak Standard Spanish as well as by members of the mainstream community who speak Standard English.

Most of the studies in this area suggest, however, that code-switching is acquired behavior rather than learned (see Baugh, 1983; Genishi, 1981; Labov, 1971, 1972a, 1972b; McClure, 1981; Peck, 1982; Wald, 1985). Wald, for example, examined the language of 46 bilingual (Spanish–English) fifth and sixth graders. The spontaneous speech of the students was sampled when they were interviewed in peer groups of 4 by a bilingual male investigator, when the peer groups were alone but observed surreptitiously by the investigator, and in individual sessions with a bilingual female investigator.

The subjects not only switched from Spanish to English with ease, but, more important, preserved syntactic and semantic grammaticality in both cases, as in the following: "There's *una silla así, y como sillas de fierro . . . no, si, para de que se usan en de-para* backyard" (There's a seat like this, and like metal seats . . . no, yes, that you use in the backyard). We note that *There's* is followed by a noun phrase, *una silla así,* just as it would be in English. Given the spontaneity of the responses and the ambiguous results of grammar instruction, it seems unlikely that the subjects were applying learned grammatical rules through an internal monitor.

If code-switching is indeed acquired, it is largely an unconscious process. This suggests that the nonstandard speakers who change nonstandard forms to standard ones are probably unaware of the changes they make. These speakers may change standard features to nonstandard ones as well, and they will be equally unaware of what they are doing. Experience in the classroom tends to bear this point out. If you have a student who speaks Black English Vernacular, for example, and who writes "Rosie be workin at Ralph's" but reads "Rosie is working at Ralph's," there is only a slight chance that he or she will be able to change the sentence during essay revision or editing. As Farr and Daniels (1986) note, "Many students do not know how to correct nonstandard features in their writing and, even when highly motivated to learn to write standard English, are quite puzzled about which features in their writing to change" (p. 20).

Recent research by Edelsky (1986) and Farr and Janda (1985), however, suggests that code-switching in writing is not as significant a problem as many people seem to believe. In these studies, both LEP and BEV students' writing was only modestly affected by switching to the primary language or dialect. The use of first-language expressions, for example, did not disrupt the coherence of the text overall. In those instances where switching did occur, it seemed to be used to fill in a linguistic or rhetorical gap in the writer's second-language or second-dialect repertoire of skills. For example, the appearance of double negatives among writers whose primary language is Spanish indicates that they have not fully mastered the use of the verb *do* in English. They have a gap in their skills that will close as their proficiency in English continues to develop. These students are in about the same position as the child who overgeneralizes past-tense verb forms and says, "We holded the rabbits and petted them": Further language development eliminates the improper form. Such findings suggest that writing instruction for non-mainstream students (LEP or BEV) should focus on developing global skills rather than on surface errors.

Black English

For many decades, serious study of Black English was impeded by myths and misconceptions. J. L. Dillard (1973) summarizes many of these misconceptions quite succinctly. He reports, for example, that until the 1960s it was often argued that Black English was a vestige of a British dialect with origins in East Anglia (see also McCrum, Cran, & MacNeil, 1986). The idea was that American blacks had somehow managed to avoid significant linguistic change for centuries. There was also the physiological theory, which held that Black English was the result of "thick lips" that rendered blacks incapable of producing Standard English. More imaginative was H. L. Mencken's (1936) notion that Black English was the invention of playwrights:

> The Negro dialect, as we know it today, seems to have been formulated by the song-writers for the minstrel shows; it did not appear in literature until the time of the Civil War; before that, as George P. Krapp shows . . . , it was a vague and artificial lingo which had little relation to the actual speech of Southern blacks (p. 71).

No mention is made of how blacks were supposed to have gone to the minstrel shows so that they might pick up the new "lingo," nor of why in the world they would be motivated to do so.

Today, most linguists support the view that Black English developed from the pidgin versions of English, Spanish, and Portuguese used during the slave era. A *pidgin* is a "contact vernacular," a mixture of two (or possibly more) separate languages that has been modified to eliminate the more difficult features, such as irregular verb forms (see Kay & Sankoff, 1974; Slobin, 1977). Function words like determiners (*the, a, an*) and prepositions (*in, on, across*) are often dropped. Function markers like case are eliminated, as are tense and plurals. Thus we might translate the sentence "Melanie is at Jack's house" to "Melanie be Jack's house."

Pidgins seem to arise spontaneously whenever two people lack a common language; in fact, you may have actually developed a pidgin yourself if you have ever tried to communicate with someone who didn't speak English and whose language you didn't know.

In this view, the European slavers developed a variety of pidgins with their West African cohorts to facilitate trade. The result must have been a potpourri of sounds. The slavers came not just from England but from France, Spain, Portugal, and Holland. Their human cargo came from a huge area of western Africa, including what is now Gambia, the Ivory Coast, Ghana, Nigeria, and Zaïre, and spoke dozens of mutually unintelligible tribal languages. McCrum, Cran, and MacNeil (1986) suggest that the pidgins began developing shortly after the slaves were captured, because the traders separated those who spoke the same language to prevent collaboration that might lead to rebellion. Chained in the holds of the slave ships, the captives had every incentive to use pidgin to establish a linguistic community.

When a pidgin acquires native speakers, it is termed a *creole*. It then can be deemed a full language in the technical sense, with its own grammar, vocabulary, and pragmatic conventions. The creole that developed into Black English was for generations thought to be merely a degenerate version of Standard English, and speakers were believed to violate grammatical rules every time they used the language. We now know, however, that Black English has its own grammar, which is a blend of Standard English and a variety of West African languages.

We find a strong similarity between Black English and the English used by white Southerners, because blacks and whites lived in close-knit communities in the South for generations, slavery notwithstanding, and the whites were the minority. White children played with black children, who exerted a powerful influence on the white-minority dialect. As Slobin (1977) indicates, language change occurs primarily in the speech of children. Over the years, the slave owners' language conformed more and more to that of the slaves. But in spite of the many similarities, Southern white dialect is not identical to Black English. The two dialects are governed by different grammars.

Black English Grammar

A detailed analysis of this grammar is beyond the scope of this book, but it is important for teachers to be aware of some of its more significant features. Knowing them will, for example, enable you to better determine when a nonstandard speaker is having a real writing problem or is having difficulty switching to the standard code. In other words, you will be better prepared to distinguish between students' competence and their performance.

Black English normally omits the *s* suffix on present-tense verbs ("He run pretty fast"), except in those instances where the speaker overcorrects in an effort to approximate standard patterns ("I goes to the market"). It drops the *g* from participles ("He goin home"), and it also uses four separate negators: *dit'n, not, don', and ain'.* Consider the following sentences:

(8) Vickie dit'n call yesterday.

(9) She not comin.

(10) Steve don' go.

(11) Steve don' be goin.

(12) She ain' call.

(13) She ain' be callin.

The last four sentences illustrate one of the more significant differences between Standard English and Black English, which is called *aspect.* In Standard English we regularly mark verb tenses as past or present, but we have the option of indicating the static or ongoing nature of an action.

Black English grammar, on the other hand, allows for optional tense marking but requires that the action be marked as momentary or continuous. Sentences (10) and (12) indicate a momentary action, whether or not it is in the past, whereas (11) and (13) indicate progressive action, whether or not it is in the past.

Another feature of aspect is the ability to stretch out the time of a verb, and Black English uses the verb form *be* to accomplish this. Sentences (14) and (15), for example, have quite different meanings:

(14) Nancy lookin for a job.

(15) Nancy be lookin for a job.

In (14), Nancy may be looking for a job today, at this moment, but she hasn't been looking long, and there's the suggestion that she hasn't been looking very hard. In (15), on the other hand, Nancy has been conscientiously looking for a job for a long time. We see similar examples in the following:

(16) Jake studyin right now.

(17) Jake be studyin every afternoon.

Studyin agrees in aspect with *right now*, and *be studyin* agrees in aspect with *every afternoon*. It would therefore be ungrammatical in Black English to say or write "Jake studyin every afternoon" or "Jake be studyin right now" (see Baugh, 1983; Fasold, 1972; Wolfram, 1969).

Been, the participial form of *be*, is used in Black English as a past-perfect marker: It signals that an action occurred in the distant past or that it was completed totally (Rickford, 1975). In this sense it is similar to the past-perfect form *have + verb* and *have + been* in Standard English. For example, compare the following sentences:

(18) They had told us to leave. (standard)

(19) They been told us to leave. (black)

(20) Kerri had eaten all the cake. (standard)

(20) Kerri been eat all the cake. (black)

(22) She had been hurt. (standard)

(23) She been been hurt. (black)

Been is also used, however, to assert that an action initiated in the past is still in effect, as in the following:

(24) I have known Vickie over three months now. (standard)

(25) I been been knowin Vickie over three months now. (black)

Black English and Written Discourse

The essays that follow were written by two students in Los Angeles who speak Black English. The first comes from a sixth-grade writer, Marcy. The second comes from a twelfth-grade writer, Bud. At the time these samples were taken, the students were attending predominantly black schools in southeast Los Angeles, an area at the lower end of the socioeconomic scale. Marcy and her class had visited the Aerospace Museum several days before the writing assignment, which asked students to describe what they liked best about the field trip. Bud and his class were approaching graduation, and their teacher asked them to write an essay describing their plans once they were out of high school.

(1)
My feel Trip

Lass weak we went to the natual histry museum. We seed the air Planes an they be big. If you be standin next to one of them Planes you be lookin real Small. they could be goin real fast if they be flyin. I think it be real nice to be flyin one of them planes. Maybe to hawae or some-place like that. When I grow up I think I be a pilot an fly one of them big planes.

(2)

I know most good job needs a college education. I would like to go to college to git me a degree. but my grades isn't the best. It would be fun to be a docktor or a lawyer or something like that because then I have me a big fine car. May be a Benz. But like a says my grades isn't so good and I don't think I could be going to college. They is some good jobs in electonics that don't take that much training. And I think that I could maybe go into that. the important thing is to think positive. I know I can do good work. I can work hard when I wants to. My brother got him a job doing construction and it pays real good. The trouble is that it isn't all year long work. They git laid off alot. That might be good in a way though. Because then you could have more time to enjoy life. I know that no matter what kind of job I git after schools out I wants to be enjoying my self.

There is little question that Black-English speakers have a difficult time with school writing, but the exact causes of their difficulty are subject to debate. We simply haven't had an intensive effort to research the writing of Black-English students, and as a result our understanding of the factors related to their composing is extremely sketchy.

As we saw in Chapter 5, a number of writers in composition studies have attempted to explain the writing problems of Black-English speakers by arguing they experience "oral language interference." In other words, these students fail as writers because their composing becomes an act of transcribing their nonstandard speech (see Dillon, 1981; Olson, 1977; Ong, 1978, 1982; Shaughnessy, 1977). In this view, the failure can be accounted for on two levels. First, the writing displays the lexical and grammatical features characteristic of BEV. Second, the lack of organization and the paucity of content is the result of linguistic deprivation and its associated cognitive deficiency.

No evidence has been found, however, to support this second position on either linguistic or psychological grounds. Labov (1972a), for example, shows rather convincingly that Black English is just as rich as any other dialect and that children whose dominant dialect is Black English cannot be classified as "linguistically deprived." Writers like Dillon (1981) and Ong (1978) would perhaps claim that the problem is more accurately one of "literacy deprivation," arguing that facility with the written word develops cognitive abilities related to abstract reasoning. But in the most detailed study published to date on the effect literacy has on cognitive abilities, Scribner and Cole (1981) found *no* significant correlation between literacy and cognition. They state, for example: "Our results are in direct conflict with persistent claims that 'deep pyschological differences' divide literate and nonliterate populations . . . . On no task—logic, abstraction, memory, communication— did we find all non literates performing at lower levels than all literates" (p. 251).

The relatively few reliable studies of the effects of speech on writing indicate that the influence is trivial. Tannen (1982), for example, shows that speech and writing share each other's "typical characteristics," even though they differ in terms of level of abstraction, sentence length, sentence patterns, and vocabulary. Speech tends to have shorter sentences, to use less subordination and more coordination, and to use a simpler vocabulary than writing. From a pragmatic perspective, these differences are insignificant. As noted in Chapter 2, what speech and writing share is the functional, rhetorical aspect of social actions. And in this regard, Tannen concludes that how the discourse is being used is more important than what are ultimately superficial differences.

Erickson (1984), studying the speech patterns of black teenagers, reports that the organizational pattern of Black English has its own structure, different from that of Standard English. He found, for example, that shifts from one topic to another were not explicitly stated but were implied through concrete anecdotes. He tells us that close analysis of Black-English speech patterns shows a "rigorous logic and a systematic coherence of the particular, whose internal system is organized not by literate style linear sequentiality but by audience/speaker interaction" (p. 152).

In an effort to look more closely at the possible influence of speech on the writing of BEV students, Farr Whitemann (1981) correlated the speech of a group of Black-English speakers with their writing. She found that oral language patterns were present in the students' written language, but that these patterns did not reflect an attempt at transcribing speech. The most dominant characteristic of the subjects' compositions was the presence of BEV grammatical patterns, specifically the omission of *s* suffixes and of past-tense *ed* suffixes.

In a related study, Farr and Janda (1985) analyzed a 45-minute, 3,021-word interview with an 18-year-old BEV speaker, Joseph, from a lower socioeconomic background. His oral discourse was compared with essays he had written during a 10-week basic composition course. The total written sample consisted of 2,841 words. Although his oral discourse manifested features typical of Black English, Farr and Janda report an almost total absence of these features in Joseph's writing.

Of equal importance was the finding that Joseph's oral discourse was characterized by literate features, reinforcing Tannen's conclusion that speech and writing share important characteristics and also reinforcing the position outlined in this book that the two discourse modes are interrelated. Farr and Janda state that Joseph's

> utterances flow from one to another in clear organizational patterns . . . ; he seemed to determine not only topic, but how long he would stay on that topic and when he would conclude it. He explicitly signalled each introduction of a new topic, elaborated on that topic in various ways, and then always returned to the original topic to "wrap it up" before moving on to another explicitly signalled topic . . . (p. 78).

On the basis of their analysis, Farr and Janda conclude that the real problem with Joseph's writing was that it was not elaborated, with inexplicit and therefore ineffectual logical relationships. But we find unelaborated content and weak logical relationships in poor writing generally (see Williams, 1985), which suggests that at issue is something other than the influence of Black English, perhaps the lack of a truly functional perspective for writing tasks. It seems, therefore, that when working with students who speak BEV, we must be extremely careful not to ascribe possible writing difficulties to the students' dialect. The presence of dialect features, although more visible, may be unrelated to deeper rhetorical deficiencies that render their compositions inadequate.

Chicano English

Chicano English is the term used to describe the nonstandard dialect spoken by many second- and third-generation Mexican-Americans, many of whom do not speak Spanish, although they may understand it slightly (see Garcia, 1983). It is also used to describe the dialect spoken by first-generation immigrants who have lived in the United States long enough to have acquired sufficient mastery of English to be able to carry on a conversation exclusively in it (see Baugh, 1984). The fact that measurable differences can be found between the language of relatively recent immigrants and the language of Hispanics who have lived in the United States for generations is one indication of the difficulty involved in making a concrete assessment of Chicano English.

The dialect is in many ways more complex than Black English because it is influenced by monolingual Spanish speakers, monolingual English speakers, and bilingual Spanish–English speakers, all of whom we generally find in a single linguistic community. The number of influences appears to further complicate children's acquisition of Standard English (see Penfield & Ornstein-Galicia, 1985).

On the level of phonology (the sound of words), Spanish uses a *ch* pronunciation where English uses *sh*. Thus Chicano English speakers often pronounce a word like *shoes* as *choose*. In the classroom, we see the effect of Spanish phonology in how students spell English words. For example, students will perceive the short *i* sound in the verb *live* to be a long *e* sound, producing sentences like the following in their writing:

> (26) I used to leave in Burbank but now I leave in North Hollywood.

> (27) Seens I been in L.A. I ain' found no job.

Other phonological differences produce additional difficulties, as the student samples below illustrate:

> (28) I try to safe as much money as I can.

> (29) When I'm a mother, I won't be as strick as my parents.

The Spanish influence is also evident on the grammatical level. Spanish, for example, uses the double negative, whereas English doesn't. As a result, we encounter written statements like "I didn't learn nothing in this class." Other syntactic influences abound, as the following sentences illustrate:

> (30) I asked Mary where did she live. (Chicano)

> (31) I asked Mary where she lived. (standard)

> (32) My parents were raise old-fashion, and so they don't let me date or nothing. (Chicano)

> (33) My parents were raised old-fashioned, and so they don't let me date or anything. (standard)

Chicano English and Writing

The few studies that have examined the writing of Chicano English speakers are not particularly satisfying, because they tend to focus on the sentence level rather than on the whole essay. Jon Amastae (1981, 1984), for example, evaluated writing samples collected from students at Pan American University in Texas over a four-year period to determine (1) the range of surface errors and (2) the degree of sentence elaboration as measured by students' use of subordination. Amastae (1981) found that Spanish interference didn't seem to be a major source of error in the compositions, but that the students used very little subordination (also see Edelsky, 1986; Hoffer, 1975). Because subordination is generally viewed as a measure of writing maturity (see K. Hunt, 1965), its absence in the essays of Chicano English speakers could adversely affect how teachers judge their writing ability.

The problem with such studies, of course, is that they fail to examine rhetorical features like topic, purpose, and audience. On the basis of Kaplan's (1972) work, referred to earlier, we would expect Chicano English speakers to manifest rhetorical characteristics measurably different from the Standard English norm. This topic is so new, however, that currently no reliable research is available on rhetorical features in Chicano English.

The closest approximation to such research appears in Edelsky's (1986) study of bilingual, elementary-age Spanish-speaking students. She found that when her LEP subjects wrote in English, their compositions manifested rhetorical features similar to those we encounter among weak writers whose first language is English; that is, the rhetorical problems were largely developmental. Her students appeared to be in the process of transferring their L_1 rhetorical competence to L_2. During the transfer period, the students' rhetorical skills in English, like their surface feature skills, contained identifiable gaps that continuing development of English proficiency is likely to eliminate.

Conclusion

This discussion of nonnative English speakers and nonstandard-English speakers outlines one of the most significant challenges we teachers face over the next decade: helping children who are not part of the mainstream become literate in Standard English. Although the factors affecting these students' writing are complex, three points of direction are relatively clear.

First, we must be sensitive to the difficulties these students face. The errors they make when they work with Standard English are often developmental, indicating the growth of increased language competence. These errors also exist on the level of linguistic competence and are therefore not readily influenced by direct instruction. They are part of the language patterns acquired over years of exposure.

Second, our sensitivity and our awareness of how children acquire language should motivate us to use students' first-language or first-dialect competence to develop skills in Standard English. Students come to school with an inherent knowledge of rhetorical devices, and we can use that knowledge to structure assignments that are functionally meaningful. Moreover, we will be more reluctant to associate failures to master Standard English with intelligence or basic language competence.

Finally, we must expect progress to be slow. Many of our nonstandard English–speaking students will be reluctant to adopt Standard English because it is likely to sever social bonds. The terms "Uncle Tom" and "Tio Taco" are used, in part, to deride members of ethnic communities who have abandoned the nonstandard dialect. Social bonds are vital for everyone, but they are particularly important to young people. As advocates of Standard English, we need to recognize that many nonmainstream children will not see what we offer them as a gift.

CHAPTER 7

Writing as a Psychosocial Action

Overview

The idea that writing is related to cognitive abilities pervades composition studies and is especially evident in the rationale for the traditional sequencing of assignments. Yet the exact nature of the relationship is not often rigorously examined. Some teachers assume that writing is thinking, whereas others, in a subtle distinction, assume that thinking is writing.

In order to explore the relationship between mind and language, the chapter begins with a summary of the two dominant positions. The first, that cognition influences language, draws significantly on the work of child psychologist Jean Piaget. The second, that language influences cognition, relies on the theories of another child psychologist, Lev Vygotsky, drawing on work in cultural anthropology for empirical support. This position currently appears to prevail in composition studies, where it has led to two related proposals: that writing is inherently superior to speech, and that abstract thought is impossible in the absence of literacy (in this context, the ability to read and write).

A close analysis of these two views shows that both lack sufficient evidence to support their theoretical claims. At best, one can note only that cognitive processes influence *some* aspects of language, while simultaneously language—specifically literacy—influences *some* cognitive processes. An interactive view of the mind–language relationship appears to be the reasonable alternative, and the chapter includes an outline of its chief characteristics. In this view, cognition and language exert a reciprocal influence on each other.

The significance of the interactive model to writing teachers becomes clearer in light of what we know about the nature of the plans writers construct when they compose. Good writers appear to think more than poor ones, and they also appear to think more about rhetorical features such as purpose, intention, and audience. Thus writing can be seen as a psychosocial process. An effective writing teacher will therefore develop activities that encourage interaction between cognitive and social processes. A realizable goal is to enable students to become more reflective as they consider issues and ideas during composing.

Mind and Language

People use language, specifically writing, to interact with one another and the world around them. Part of this interaction is related to learning, for writing can be used in a general way to enhance our knowledge. It provides a kind of rehearsal of information that helps us remember things better. As a vehicle for analysis, it helps us discover a subject's complexities, and it can also help us organize our thoughts. Given these factors, we shouldn't be too surprised to find that many teachers and scholars believe that a strong relationship exists between mind and language.

The nature of this relationship continues to be vigorously debated among scholars. Some believe that the nature of mind influences the nature of language. Based on the work of Jean Piaget, one of the foremost child psychologists, this view proposes that language is part of our capacity to represent ideas and objects mentally (Piaget & Inhelder, 1969). Hence cognition in general has structural parallels to language. Both, for example, are hierarchical as well as linear, and both are temporally ordered.

In Piaget's view, cognitive abilities developmentally precede linguistic abilities; thus the development of linguistic structures depends on cognitive abilities. John Trimbur (1987) suggests that this view finds expression in composition studies as an "inner/outer" dualism, in which "the writer's mind is a kind of box" that we try to pry open "in order to free what is stored inside" (p. 211).

In contrast to this view, writers like Vygotsky (1962) and Whorf (1956) believe that language influences cognition. We encountered this idea briefly in Chapter 5, when examining stylistics. This view is perhaps the more popular in composition studies, and we see its influence not only in an emphasis on style but in the notion that writing is inherently superior to speech. Its chief advocates, among them Dillon (1981), Hirsch (1977), Moffett (1985), and Ong (1978), argue that writing promotes the ability to reason abstractly, and that without the ability to read and write, people are limited to concrete, situational thinking.

The Cognition-Influences-Language View

In composition studies, the proposal that cognition influences language can be seen as a reaction against Chomsky's (1965) argument that some linguistic features are innate, which in its strongest form posits autonomous linguistic mechanisms outside the cognitive domain (see Fodor, 1983). Along these lines, Jerry Fodor suggests that language processes such as grammaticality judgments, parsing sentences into constituents, and comprehension are essentially a *reflex*. Many people who study and teach reading and writing are understandably uncomfortable with this idea.

The influence of cognition on language is inherent in Piaget's (1953, 1955, 1962, 1974) model of children's intellectual development. The goal of his model is to explain children's behavior so as to determine what is common to all of us as a species. According to Piaget (1955), children go through a continuum of three developmental periods that correspond to intellectual growth and reasoning ability. During the *sensorimotor period*, which starts at birth and ends at about 18 months, children are largely governed by reflexes and cannot really think in the sense that an older child or an adult can. They are extremely egocentric and initially have little or no awareness of the world beyond their own sensations of hunger, cold, warmth, and discomfort. Objects initially have no existential reality for them, as evidenced by the observation that children at this age will not reach out for a toy that is suddenly covered by a blanket. This phenomenon is interpreted as indicating that for the child the toy ceases to exist once it is out of sight.

Intellectual ability during this period is viewed as very limited. Children seem able to deal with only one task at a time, in a serial fashion. In addition, they seem concerned only with functional success, with performance, and generally have no abstracting ability.

The *concrete operational period* is from 18 months to about 11 years. Piaget (1955) divides this period into two stages: the *preoperational stage*, which lasts until about age 7, and the *concrete operational stage*. This period is followed by the *formal operational period* beginning in early adolescence, which marks the development of adult reasoning ability.

The preoperational stage is characterized by very limited thinking ability, by an inability to reason abstractly, by an inability to classify appropriately, and by a high degree of egocentricity that makes taking on the point of view or role of another difficult for children. They cannot, in the words of Piaget (1955), "decenter," and as a result they are poor communicators. The concrete operational stage marks a shift in intellectual ability. When children's intellect becomes "operational," they become much better at identifying changes between states and understanding the relationship between those different states. For example, a toy under a blanket is understood to be simply covered up, not to have disappeared.

The relationship between these stages of development and language becomes clear when we observe infant behavior. Infants focus their attention on their immediate surroundings and the people and objects they interact with on a daily basis. Such observations led Piaget (1955) to characterize the first stage of children's cognitive development as being concerned with mental representations of reality.

These interactions begin at birth, yet language typically doesn't appear until children are about a year old, when representations of reality are already well established. And as language does emerge, it is object-related. Most of a child's first words are names of people and objects in the immediate environment (see Bates, 1976; Bates, Camaioni, & Volterra, 1975; Macnamara, 1972; Nelson, 1973). Thus the order of development is essentially the following: Cognition related to people and things in the immediate environment leads to language use about those same people and things. This pattern of cognitive development/ language development appears to be fairly consistent from one culture to another (see Bloom, 1970, 1973; Schlesinger, 1971).

Over the last several years, however, additional research into cognitive and linguistic development has forced a reevaluation of the Piagetian view. Bates (1979), for example, engaged children in cause–effect tasks and symbolic play in order to measure cognitive development. She then compared their performance on these tasks with their performance on language tasks and found that cognitive knowledge did not always precede linguistic performance (also see Corrigan, 1978; J. Miller et al., 1980). After reviewing several of these more recent studies, Rice and Kemper (1984) conclude that

> empirical support for a direct influence on formal linguistic structure in terms of children's emerging grammatical competencies remains to be demonstrated. . . . On a more specific level, the relevance of Piagetian sensorimotor tasks to language performance is questionable (p. 29).

In addition, several researchers have shown that Piaget's analysis of children's intellectual abilities may be flawed, in which case his formulation of the way cognition influences language would have to be seriously questioned (Donaldson, 1978). The claim that children are poor communicators because they are "egocentric" provides an important example. (If language users can't adopt alternative points of view, they will fail to bridge information gaps that exist between themselves and others.)

The idea that preoperational children cannot decenter is based largely on investigations involving the "mountains task" (Piaget & Inhelder, 1969). In this task, children are seated at a table that has a model of three mountains on it. Each mountain is a different color, and each has a different summit: One is covered with "snow," one has a house, and the third has a red cross. The experimenter then introduces a doll, moving it to different positions around the table. The task becomes describing what the doll "sees" in each of the different positions.

Children below the age of eight invariably fail at this task, leading to the conclusion that they cannot adopt the point of view of another. Martin Hughes (1975), however, hypothesized that the children's failure was related to the content of the specific task rather than to undeveloped cognitive abilities. He altered the task first by intersecting two walls to form a cross; he then changed the dolls, introducing a policeman doll and a small boy doll. The policeman doll was situated so that it could "see" two areas of the intersection, as shown in Figure 1.

Figure 1

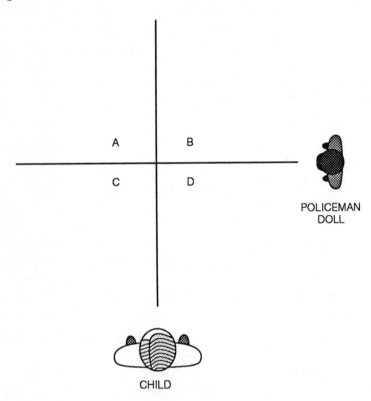

The boy doll was then placed in the various sections made by the intersecting walls, and the subjects were asked whether the policeman doll could "see" him. Few subjects had any difficulty with this. Next, subjects were told to hide the boy doll so that the policeman doll could not see him, and again few errors were made. At this point, Hughes increased the complexity of the task by introducing a second policeman doll and situating him at the top of the intersection, where he has a view of sections A and B, as shown in Figure 2.

Figure 2

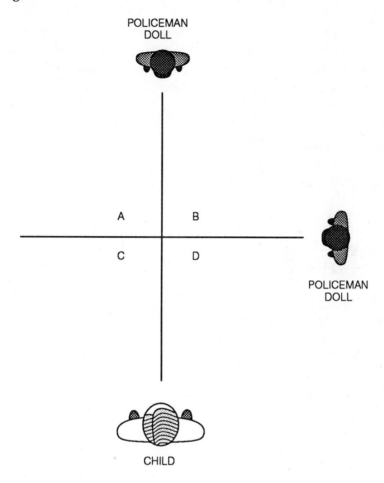

POLICEMAN
DOLL

A   B

C   D

POLICEMAN
DOLL

CHILD

Subjects were again told to hide the boy doll, this time from both policemen, which requires coordination of two different points of view. Ninety percent of the responses were correct. These findings suggest that children as young as age three are as able to reason abstractly as children two to four years older, as long as the task is made understandable to them. Commenting on Hughes's data, Margaret Donaldson (1978) points out that we can "appeal to the generalization of experience: they [the children] know what it is to try to hide. Also they know what it is to be naughty and to want to evade the consequences. So they can easily conceive that a boy might want to hide from a policeman if he had been a bad boy. . ." (p. 24).

Piaget's method apparently failed to test children's cognitive abilities adequately. The tasks he and his associates designed were removed from the world of children, and the young people they studied simply couldn't understand what they were being asked to do. Consequently, Piaget's interpretation of results was significantly confounded. On this basis, it seems reasonable to conclude that the view that cognition influences language, at least in the strong version we see in Piaget's work, does not offer an adequate description of the relationship between mind and language.

The Language-Influences-Cognition View

The theoretical framework for the view that language influences cognition comes primarily from the Russian psychologist Lev Vygotsky, who made his observations of child behavior during the late 1920s and early 1930s. Like his contemporary Piaget, Vygotsky (1962) noted that at about age three young children begin to talk to themselves when doing things, as though giving verbal expression to their actions. Such talk is inherently different from the "conversations" they have been having for some time with others, because it seems to lack a social function. When dressing a doll, for example, children will commonly utter such expressions as: "Now I'm going to put the dress on the dolly, and then I'm going to comb her hair." More often than not, children make these utterances as though no one else can hear them; hence they are often referred to as examples of "egocentric speech."

Vygotsky proposed that these egocentric utterances mark the beginning of thought. Claims, assertions, reasons, examples, counter-examples—the building blocks of logical thought—are inherent in the language we use daily. On this basis, Vygotsky argues that the fundamental pattern of logical thought is evident in "social, collaborative forms of behavior" (p. 19). The emergence of egocentric speech signals the start of an internalization process in which those social patterns of behavior take the form of what Vygotsky terms "inner speech," or thought. This proposal can be interpreted to mean that the very processes of thought are social, which suggests that the quality of the social patterns a child draws on will influence the quality of his or her thought.

Some years ago, David Olson (1977) used Vygotsky's theoretical framework to explain the differences in academic achievement he observed among students from diverse linguistic backgrounds. His paper had a significant effect on many people working in composition studies. He argued that speech is fundamentally different from writing in several important ways. In his view, they don't use similar mechanisms for conveying meaning: In speech, meaning is derived from the shared intentions and context of speaker and hearer, whereas in writing, meaning resides in the text itself at the sentence level and has to be extracted by readers. He states that writing has "no recourse to shared context . . . [because] sentences have to be understood in contexts other than those in which they were written" (p. 272). Olson goes on to suggest that human history has reflected an evolution from utterance to text that has profoundly affected cultural and psychological development.

Olson's view is that writing in general and the essay form in particular account for the development of abstract thought in human beings. According to Olson, people in nonliterate cultures are incapable of abstract thought. Writing is the key to developing abstracting ability because it forces people to comprehend events outside their original context, which alters their perception of the world, which in turn leads to cognitive growth. Following Olson's (1977) lead, Ong (1978) comments that "without writing . . . the mind simply cannot engage in [abstract] . . . thinking . . . . Without writing, the mind cannot even generate concepts such as 'history' or analysis . . . " (p. 39).

These are powerful claims, and many teachers and scholars in the field have embraced them enthusiastically (see, for example, Dillon, 1981; Hirsch, 1977; Ong, 1982; Scinto, 1986; Shaughnessy, 1977), perhaps because they create an "us–them" dichotomy that can be used to explain why some students don't succeed in school. Followed to its logical end, this view suggests that children from backgrounds where written discourse isn't stressed will have culture-specific cognitive deficiencies that make significant academic achievement essentially impossible.

We've already seen in Heath's (1983) research that there is a strong social influence on language development and that this in turn affects school achievement. Indeed, *Preparing to Teach Writing* was developed in part to advocate a social view of language. But to propose that the quality of mind is affected by the quality of language, whether oral or written, is to make a much stronger claim. The educational implications are clear-cut: We would have to characterize people who don't write, and also probably those who don't write very well, as being simpleminded.

It's difficult not to find an element of elitism in this position, and some people may even see it as being ethnocentric, especially when writers like Leonard Scinto (1986) argue that written language is a "culturally heritable trait" (p. 171). Although there is no doubt that literacy provides increased opportunities for social mobility in the United States and in most Western nations, there must necessarily be some question in our minds as to the specific culture in which written language appears as a heritable trait.

In a pluralistic society like ours, we can speak of "American culture" in the abstract, but we must simultaneously recognize that the United States contains numerous subcultures—black, Hispanic, and American Indian, as well as the spectrum provided by socioeconomic status and recent, massive immigration—that simply do not place the same weight on writing that mainstream, upper-middle-class, Anglo-European culture does. Our task as teachers would most likely be far easier if indeed written language were a "culturally heritable trait." In truth, however, children from mainstream and nonmainstream backgrounds alike find much school-sponsored reading and writing to be complex and baffling puzzles.

The notion that writing exerts a cultural and psychological influence grew out of anthropological studies that attempted to explain why some cultures have reached a modern stage of development and why some haven't (see, for example, Finnegan, 1970; Goody, 1968, 1972; Goody & Watt, 1968; Greenfield, 1972; Lévi-Strauss, 1966; Levy-Bruhl, 1975; Luria, 1976).

In these studies, researchers gave a group of nonliterate, usually non-Western, subjects a task designed to measure cognitive abilities, then gave the same task to a group of literate, usually Western, subjects and compared the results. Colby and Cole (1976), for example, found that on tests of memory, nonliterate subjects from the Kpelle tribe in Africa performed far below the level of test subjects in the United States who were on average almost five years younger.

Similarly, Luria (1976) (who was a student of Vygotsky) found that the nonliterate subjects in his study had more difficulty categorizing and sorting objects than the literate subjects. The nonliterates' method of cognitive processing tended to be more concrete and situation-bound than the literates'. For example, Luria presented his subjects with pictures of a hammer, a saw, an ax, and a piece of lumber, then asked which object did not belong with the others. The literate subjects quickly identified the piece of lumber, since it, unlike the other objects, isn't a tool. The nonliterate subjects, on the other hand, seemed unable to clearly understand the question. They insisted that all the objects went together, since there was little use for a hammer, a saw, and an ax if there was no lumber to use in making something.

From Luria's point of view, that of a psychologist trained in the Western tradition, this functional response was wrong, and he concluded that the nonliterate subjects had difficulty formulating abstract categories. It may well be, however, that, as in the case of Piaget and Inhelder's (1969) mountains task, what was actually being tested had little to do with the ability to formulate abstract categories but had very much to do with understanding what the test was about.

We know, for example, that there are specific cultural characteristics related to accepting the attributes objects may have in common (see Rosch, 1978). Consider the often noted differences between English and Eskimo regarding the number of words used to describe snow. Even within a single culture there will be clusters of shared attributes that vary by gender and socioeconomic status. For many people in the United States, the term *car* embraces any vehicle that has four wheels and is used principally for personal transportation. Included are pickup trucks, station wagons, Jeeps, limousines, and Suzuki Samurais. For many other people, however, *car* refers only to sedans and coupes. Luria's findings could therefore simply be an instance of the nonliterate group's refusal to accept the designated category attributes, not a demonstration of an inability to establish abstract categories.

Moreover, we know that every recorded culture, whether literate or nonliterate, has (or had) some form of religious beliefs (see Campbell, 1959). Such beliefs tend to be highly abstract. We also know that collective terms are used in every recorded language to designate groups of people and things. For example, although not all languages have discrete terms for *brother* and *sister*, it appears to be a universal that they have a term for *sibling* (Ullmann, 1963). A culture where it is possible to own more than one cow will have some term equivalent to *cattle* or *herd*. On this basis, it would seem that the inability of nonliterate people to perform certain tasks, such as categorization, may not be related to their ability to reason abstractly.

These rather obvious difficulties beset most of the existing studies of literacy's effects on cognition. Another factor, however, is even more problematic. As Scribner and Cole (1981) point out in *The Psychology of Literacy*, to date the most detailed evaluation of the link between literacy and cognition, earlier researchers consistently conflated literacy and schooling. Given that it is in the nature of schooling to strip situations of their context and to emphasize nonfunctional intellectual experiences, conflating literacy and schooling may jeopardize the methodological integrity of the investigations. We can't readily determine any causal relationships involved, because we don't know whether the results were influenced by literacy or by schooling.

Furthermore, as a consequence of this conflation, the research generally fails to compare similar groups of subjects. In the case of Luria, for example, the groups he compared were not merely literates and nonliterates, but were literates with schooling and nonliterates without. These factors lead Scribner and Cole to state that such studies "fail to support the specific claims made for literacy's effects. . . . No comparisons were ever made between children with and children without a written language" (pp. 11–12).

In order to address such difficulties, Scribner and Cole were very careful to design a study that would distinguish between the cognitive effects of schooling and the cognitive effects of literacy. Their research was conducted among the Vai, a group of people in West Africa who developed an independent writing system early in the 19th century. The Vai script is used regularly for notes and letters, but there is no body of literature written in the script. Only about half the people who are literate in the Vai script have had some formal schooling, which means there was a large group of literate but unschooled subjects to draw on.

The researchers evaluated more than 1,000 subjects over a four-year period. First, the results showed that formal schooling has an effect on some cognitive abilities, but not on all. The schooled subjects were better at providing explanations, specifically explanations related to sorting, logic, grammatical rules, game instructions, and hypothetical questions. Outside the domain of verbal exposition, no other general patterns of cross-task superiority were found. Scribner and Cole suggest that schooling fosters abilities in expository talk in "contrived situations."

As for literacy itself, only four tasks showed any influence. Literates were better able: (1) to listen to uttered statements and repeat back their messages, (2) to use graphic symbols to represent language, (3) to use language as a means of instruction, and (4) to talk about correct Vai speech. Given the nature of literacy, we would expect such differences. They showed *no superiority* over nonliterate subjects in regard to classification, memory, deduction, and categorization. In other words, no evidence was found to suggest that literacy is linked to abstracting ability or cognitive growth. Summarizing their work, Scribner and Cole note: "Our results are in direct conflict with persistent claims that 'deep psychological differences' divide literate and nonliterate populations. . . . On no task—logic, abstraction, memory, communication—did we find all nonliterates performing at lower levels than all literates" (p. 251).

Further evidence against the language-influences-cognition view comes from studies of deaf children who have learned neither speech nor sign language. According to this view, we would expect such children either to have no thought at all or to have thought that is profoundly different from what we find in hearing children. Because it's difficult to evaluate cognitive processes without using language in some form, studies of deaf children's intellectual abilities are often less than definitive. Nevertheless, certain conclusions have been widely accepted. For example, after conducting a series of studies into cognitive development, Furth (1966) reports that "language does not influence development [among deaf children] in any direct, general way" (p. 160). Similarly, Rice and Kemper (1984) report that "deaf children's progress through the early Piagetian stages and structures is roughly parallel to that of hearing children" (p. 37).

Given the work with hearing-impaired children and the considerable weight of evidence Scribner and Cole bring to this issue, it seems reasonable to conclude that the major intellectual consequences of literacy are generally minimal, perhaps even nonexistent. Hence we may want to reevaluate the idea that students who come to us from cultures that do not stress reading and writing are suffering from some cognitive deficiency, as well as the idea that the written word is inherently superior to speech.

The Interactive View

So far we've seen that, at least in their strong versions, neither the cognition-influences-language view nor the language-influences-cognition view offers an acceptable account of the relationship between mind and language. Yet we've also seen that some aspects of cognitive development do appear to affect language, and some aspects of language development do appear to affect cognition.

The existence of simultaneous connections suggests that the mind–language relationship is probably best described by an interactive, reciprocal process. Support for this position is found in the discussions in the preceding two sections. Cognitive development *does* seem to influence language development in a general sense. Initial intellectual processes are object-related, and so are initial utterances. These initial processes are fundamentally performative, geared toward manipulating the environment, and so are initial utterances. And language *does* seem to influence some specific cognitive processes. Scribner and Cole found measurable cognitive differences between literate, nonschooled Vai and nonliterate, nonschooled Vai. Although these differences weren't profound and were in fact what we might predict intuitively given what we know about writing, they do indicate some influence of language on mental processes.

Additional support comes from a variety of sources (see Rice & Kemper, 1984), but one of the more elegant arises out of work with terms that indicate location. It is generally accepted that children's understanding of spatial relationships follows a set pattern. First to develop are notions of *on* and *in*, followed quickly by notions of *top* and *bottom*. Other spatial concepts, such as *between, behind,* and *across*, develop much later (E. Clark, 1980). The development of spatial concepts is reflected in children's acquisition of the terms to identify them. Dan Slobin, however, hypothesized that linguistic variables can influence the pattern of development: The pattern may not be uniform across cultures and languages, because some languages use complex grammatical features to indicate spatial relationships. This complexity might make it harder for children in those cultures to formulate notions of location.

To test his hypothesis, Slobin (1973) first studied a group of toddlers who were learning both Hungarian and Serbo-Croatian. He discovered that the children learned how to express location in Hungarian before they could do so in Serbo-Croatian. Of the two languages, location is easier to express in Hungarian. His follow-up study (Slobin, 1982) compared acquisition of location terms in four languages: English, Italian, Turkish, and Serbo-Croatian. Again, linguistic variables appeared to influence the development of spatial understanding. In this case, English and Serbo-Croatian proved more difficult than Turkish and Italian. Slobin points out, to cite one explanatory example, that Turkish and Italian use single words for the various spatial relations, whereas English and Serbo-Croatian have multiple terms, such as *on top of, next to, in front of,* and so forth.

From a teacher's perspective, the strength of the interactive model should be fairly clear. It seems to reflect a more accurate picture of the mind–language relationship, which emerges as a dynamic, with one faculty enhancing the other. It also is consistent with the large body of research we've already examined that indicates language use is best characterized as an individual acting on and being acted on by society. This view is inherently rhetorical, inherently pragmatic. Accordingly, we must seriously question the idea that writing is merely transcribed thought, as well as the idea that we can generate thought merely by engaging students in language tasks—reading and writing.

Pauses, Plans, Mental Models, and Social Actions

The superficiality of so much of what students write concerns many teachers. Complex topics and issues are dealt with simplistically, writers never venturing beyond the most obvious analyses. In classes from history to science, the badly written essay is the one produced by the student who not only hasn't mastered the material but hasn't thought about it deeply.

We know from the investigations into pausing and planning discussed in Chapter 2 that good writers spend more time thinking about what they write, perhaps developing and working from more elaborate mental models of the proposed text. You will recall that Flower and Hayes (1981) concluded from their research on pausing episodes that good writers and poor writers use pauses in different ways. Good writers engage in global planning that incorporates rhetorical concerns such as audience, purpose, and intention. Poor writers, on the other hand, engage in local planning that focuses on surface features.

Steve Witte (1985) suggests that when writers decide to compose, whether on their own or because of a teacher's assignment, they conceive an internal "pre-text" that has both global and local discourse features. Planning would therefore involve a complex process of formulation, monitoring, and revision of the pre-text. The physical act of writing would largely be the transcription of an already revised pre-text, which would account for the observation that experienced writers frequently do less revising on drafts but still produce writing superior in quality to that of their less-skilled counterparts. Quite simply, they have performed more revision during planning. If this is the case, it would seem our teaching should be directed toward getting students to focus more attention on planning at the global level and less at the sentence level. We would need to help them think more during writing activities.

Empirical support for these models and for the notion that good writing is linked to the amount of thinking students do during the composing process is difficult to obtain because of the very nature of the problem. How does one measure the mind at work?

The answer may lie in minute physical responses in certain muscles, such as those around the mouth and larynx, that appear to correspond with mental activity. These responses, usually called covert, or subvocal, linguistic behavior, can be measured only with the aid of special equipment, but they have been studied extensively over the last two decades. A large body of research now indicates that when people listen, read silently, solve math problems, remember, and write—that is, when they engage in almost any mental task—there is evidence of covert linguistic behavior. The more difficult the mental task, the greater the muscular response (see Conrad, 1972; Edfelt, 1960; Hardyck & Petrinovich, 1967; McGuigan, 1966, 1978; Sokolov, 1972; Williams,

1983, 1987). The link is so strong that many researchers are convinced covert linguistic behavior is a measurable manifestation of thought.

Williams (1987) found that the below-average writers in his investigation demonstrated much less covert linguistic behavior during pauses than the above-average writers. This finding suggests that the poor writers were doing less work on their internal pre-text than the good writers. Given the models proposed by Flower and Hayes (1981) and Witte (1985), we can even speculate that it was the global, rhetorical aspects of the pre-text that were being neglected.

Implications for Teaching

If poor writers are thinking about surface features rather than rhetorical ones, as seems indicated, we can understand why they so often produce essays that lack depth, essays deficient in identification of topic, articulation of intention, and specification of audience, even when these features are delineated by their teacher (see Bamberg, 1983; Williams, 1985; Witte & Faigley, 1981).

We don't know exactly why poor writers fail to spend much time planning their essays and thinking about their topics, but the problem is probably experiential and educational. That is, they haven't had much practice reflecting deeply on events and ideas, and they have been educated in an environment that doesn't consistently call for reflection. Much schooling, after all, relies on rote memorization. It seems clear that one of our goals as writing teachers should be not only to require reflection but to provide opportunities to practice it.

The model of the reciprocal relationship between mind and language is useful in guiding the direction we take in this regard. We can see that the mind-as-a-box metaphor (Trimbur, 1987) won't work if the box isn't very full, which will be the case with students who have generally been treated as empty vessels waiting to be filled. They haven't had much help in loading the box with ideas of their own. By the same token, we can see that reading and writing per se aren't likely to lead to more thought. Such activities have to be part of a social context that acts on each student—through questions, differences in perspective and opinion, demands for more detail—as the student attempts to act on the social context through writing and sharing that writing.

Implicit in the interactive model, given what we know about planning and mental models of discourse, is the idea of building new skills on old ones, which is what good teachers tend to do almost instinctively. But there is also the suggestion that writing assignments should be challenging if they are going to lead to cognitive growth. If by the time they come to us children are already very familiar with object-related cognition and language, we will want to be careful not to bore them with endless object-related tasks. Because narratives and descriptions are inherently object-related, students may not be challenged by such activities after one or two essays. Challenging tasks will be those that ask students to think, to formulate hypotheses concerning the way things are and to find support for their hypotheses.

In addition, the model suggests that writing assignments should be sufficiently related to the world of students as to be understandable. A teacher who asks students to examine why we do or do not have a comprehensive arms treaty with the Soviets is likely to be more disappointed with the resulting essays than one who asks students to examine why they attend a closed campus. This isn't to say that our students shouldn't know about arms treaties, political maneuvering, and diplomacy. These are important concerns. But they typically won't be of sufficient concern to children in elementary and high school for them to take such a writing task seriously, and our best efforts and intentions aren't likely to change this fact.

Indeed, we often find that "big topics" force student writers upon themselves, effectively isolating them from any recognizable social factors that could help make their writing meaningful. These topics are hard for most students because they don't yet see a connection between their world and the one reflected in the topic. They become like the children in Piaget and Inhelder's (1969) mountains task: They want to cooperate, they want to do well, but they just can't understand what they are being asked to do, or why they are being asked to do it.

To get a sense of the difficulty involved, you might consider how *you* would respond if you had to write about the arms treaty as opposed to, say, why you want to be a teacher. You are a part of the community of discourse for one topic, but probably not the other. You know quite a bit about teaching and working with young people, but you may know next to nothing about weapons, territoriality, and diplomacy.

Because you understand what is involved in discussing teaching, have in fact talked about it before with friends and teachers, you are connected to a community of many. On the other hand, unless you have significant expertise in international relations, you can't even know what the right questions are concerning an arms treaty, so you're forced to rely on your own ingenuity. That is, you are forced to withdraw into a community of one.

Conclusion

The interactive view of the mind–language relationship has two obvious advantages. First, it can help teachers avoid the error of assuming that good minds will always produce outstanding writing. Second, it helps teachers avoid the inevitable disappointment associated with the belief that having students write and read essays will produce good minds. It reflects the pragmatic notion that writers act on and are acted on by society.

This latter point has implications that may not be so immediately obvious, but that are nevertheless visible threads winding their way throughout this book. If one allows that texts and genres can be included in the term *society*, then when discussing mind and language we are once again coming to grips with reciprocal relationships. We have seen how these relationships influence style, reading, writing, and language/dialect acquisition. Classical rhetoric, particularly Aristotle's, provides a framework for understanding the inherent nature of reciprocal relationships, for in that tradition who one is (*ethos*) cannot be defined outside the society of which one is a part. In adopting a pragmatic view of writing, a chief task becomes discovering an effective means to help students learn how to define themselves through language.

A reasonable question at this point is how do we establish a classroom environment that reflects the pragmatic, psychosocial nature of writing. This is the focus of Part Two, where writing classes are viewed as workshops that enable students to interact as they develop compositions. The interaction forms a microcosm of the larger linguistic community, a place where dialogues about writing predominate.

PART TWO

Toward a Contemporary Methodology

CHAPTER 8

The Classroom as Workshop

Overview

Classroom workshops require a reevaluation of the writing teacher's traditional role, in which one lectures to the class about the characteristics of good writing or leads the class in a discussion of a professional model. They tend to shift the focus of the writing class from the teacher to students.

Peer work groups allow students to interact as they develop drafts of assignments. Students read each other's drafts in their groups, offering comments and suggestions for revision. Sometimes they may work on projects together, as a team. One result is a collaboration that resembles what takes place in natural writing situations. Students also take on more responsibility for their own learning and for their own achievement. Another result, one that teachers often overlook, is an opportunity to engage in cooperative problem solving that can enhance critical-thinking skills.

In addition to the rhetorical advantages workshops provide by giving students the opportunity to write and revise as part of a discourse community, they also allow teachers to move freely about the room to offer advice on papers that are still in draft form. Students can use this advice immediately to improve their revisions. In other words, workshops provide meaningful environments for teacher intervention and feedback during the composing process.

Structuring a Classroom Workshop

Having reviewed a significant portion of the research and theories relevant to writing instruction, we can begin a more specific discussion of practice. We saw in Part One that numerous investigations—ranging from classical rhetoric to language acquisition—emphasize the social and functional characteristics of discourse. In fact, a common feature of much recent work is the view that language is a psychosocial action used to interact with others. Repeatedly we saw that when children encounter writing in a functional way, they are more involved and learn better than when they aren't (see, for example, Chapters 2, 3, 4, and 6).

These investigations tell us something about how best to teach composition. They indicate that we should create a classroom environment that emphasizes the functional nature of language and writing. It should draw on what students already know about discourse, building new skills on old ones by connecting speech with writing, reading, and listening. And it should be highly social, providing students frequent opportunities to interact with each other through writing and talking about their writing. It should allow for collaborative learning in the richest sense. These investigations indicate that, in keeping with language acquisition, the key to improving one's writing skill won't lie in simply writing, but in receiving frequent feedback on work in progress and then using that feedback to revise effectively.

A *writing workshop*, mentioned briefly in Chapter 1, is fundamental to establishing such a classroom environment. If properly structured, it can greatly increase students' awareness of the rhetorical, functional nature of written discourse, and it can meet the other requirements for teaching success as well.

Workshops are relatively noisy places. Students are reading papers aloud, asking one another questions about their writing, and offering comments. If a workshop is quiet, it probably isn't working. Students are allowed to assume a great deal of responsibility for their own learning, which means not everyone will be doing the same thing. Some students may be working alone writing a draft, others may be discussing ways to improve a student's paper. Still others may be getting advice from the teacher in a short conference.

Writing workshops may seem chaotic to teachers who have been trained to think of composition pedagogy in a traditional way. Some teachers are initially threatened by the seeming lack of structure and control. But a successful workshop actually requires *more* structure and planning than a traditional classroom, because students must be kept busy as well as focused without being made to feel that the teacher is hovering over them.

What this means in practical terms is that you will need to devise lesson plans that move students through different activities during the class period. For example, you may spend 15 minutes analyzing a writing sample at the beginning of the hour, 25 minutes writing or rewriting, and then the final 10 minutes letting students talk about the work they just finished. Or you may use the first 15 minutes having students engage in role playing to enhance audience awareness, with the remainder of the hour devoted to writing and rewriting. The writing activity should be a part of every day's lesson. No matter what else you do, students should write for at least 20 minutes a day. Hour-long writing activities, however, usually aren't very productive, because students will lose their attentiveness. Nesting writing between two brief and related activities will help keep students focused on the task.

It should be noted at this point that legislated curricula and district-imposed programmed instruction often thwart our good intentions. Many districts, for example, limit writing instruction in English classes to one day a week. The other four days are reserved for literature and traditional grammar instruction. We shouldn't be surprised that Goodlad (1984) reports that high school students in the United States write only about 300 words a year. A more reasonable goal, even for elementary students, is 500 words a week, through drafting and revising. As a beginning teacher you may be reluctant to manipulate the curriculum in order to implement a more realistic approach to reading and writing in the classroom. But perhaps you should try.

Work Groups and Collaborative Learning

Before academics send an essay out for publication, they usually ask two or three friends to read over the manuscript and to offer some suggestions for improvement. Sometimes they use the suggestions in their revision, and sometimes they don't, but they always feel grateful to their friends for taking the time to offer constructive comments. Feedback of this sort, used to help revise a paper still in draft form, is often referred to as *formative evaluation* (see Huff & Kline, 1987). As the name suggests, it aims at helping the development of the writing and does not include any final appraisal of the draft's worth or value.

All public writing (that is, writing designed to be read by others) is a collaborative effort, in a sense. More often than not, it is a collaboration among friends, or at least coworkers. For reasons that will be discussed in the next section, we should make collaboration on writing projects a central part of our classrooms. It will allow students to read one another's drafts and then offer constructive comments that will guide revisions. An important first step toward developing a successful writing environment in the classroom, therefore, is to help students get to know one another as well as possible on the first day of class. Each student needs to come to think of the class as a group of friends who can be counted on for help, advice, and support. This kind of relationship takes more than a single session to develop, of course, but you can make a good beginning and set the tone of the class on that first day.

You can initiate a sense of community in the class several ways. An approach that works well for some teachers involves pairing students off and asking them to interview each other. They then use the interviews to introduce each other to the whole class. The problem with this approach is that it seems a bit too controlled and doesn't allow for the sort of bonding that's really needed to structure a successful workshop. With the idea of bonding in mind, many more teachers simply designate the beginning 20 minutes of the class as "get-acquainted time." Students are free to move about the room and free to talk with whomever they wish. It usually happens that small groups form that leave out two or three students, so you'll want to direct the interactions just enough to involve everyone.

Setting Up Work Groups

After students have had time to get acquainted, the next step is to make some evaluation of their writing abilities. Have students respond in class to a selected topic, after making it clear to them that the essays won't be graded, just used to help you become familiar with their skills.

In most classes, some students will have had richer experiences than others, and the wealth of background material they can draw on will put less fortunate students at a disadvantage when it comes to writing this initial essay. To ensure that you will be assessing students' writing skills equitably, you may want to consider making this initial writing task one that is text based: Students read a short passage you have selected and then use it as the basis for their writing. They are not necessarily writing about the reading selection, but the selection is relevant to their writing; it forms the background for the response.

Many teachers refer to this initial writing task as a "diagnostic" essay, but this seems to be a particularly inapt term, given its medical connotations. We aren't physicians working with diseased patients in need of healing. We're teachers working with normal students going through the normal process of mastering the language.

Use your evaluation of the initial essay to guide you in forming work groups. The skills displayed in this writing sample can help you ensure that membership is balanced in terms of ability. (It is perhaps worth mentioning that in the process view of writing instruction, work groups are sometimes referred to as "peer editing groups." This term can be misleading in the pragmatic environment we're trying to establish, because group members are responsible for so much more than mere editing.)

The educational benefits inherent in work groups are significant, as the next sections will show. At this point, we can summarize a few of those benefits. First, the cooperation required in group activities appears to lead students to work harder and to discover more than they do when they perform tasks on an individual, competitive basis (Crawford & Haaland, 1972). In addition, work in groups tends to improve motivation. Students who aren't strongly motivated to perform will be encouraged by those who are, and for all students the level of motivation seems to remain higher when participating in group work (see Garibaldi, 1979; Gunderson & Johnson, 1980; Johnson & Ahlgren, 1976). As noted in Chapter 6, cooperative work groups also provide an effective environment for interaction among mainstream and nonmainstream students (see D. Johnson, Johnson, & Maruyama, 1983).

The size of a group affects how well it functions. In groups of three, there is a tendency for two members to take sides against the third. In groups of four, there is a tendency for the group to split evenly whenever decisions are called for, so little gets accomplished. The ideal number is five, because it avoids these difficulties and allows for better interaction among members.

Before groups can function effectively, members must go through a bonding process that unites them in a common purpose. Once the bonding is complete, the group will work as a collaborative unit. For these reasons, groups should stay together the *entire term*. Moving students from group to group appears to offer greater variety in regard to feedback on drafts, but the advantage of variety is significantly offset by the lack of bonding that results from shifting students around. For the true cooperation that characterizes effective work groups, bonding is essential (see Huff & Kline, 1987). Without it, student feedback on drafts will rarely rise above a superficial level.

You may let students form their own groups, or you may assign membership, keeping in mind, of course, that it's important for students to feel happy about the groups they are in. Be alert in either case to the fact that best friends rarely work well together in a group. Not only are they reluctant to treat each other's writing objectively, they also have a pronounced tendency to discuss matters unrelated to the work at hand. In addition, you may find that if left to themselves, younger students may group themselves by gender. In some classes students may group themselves by race or language. None of these membership patterns is desirable, so if you allow students to form their own groups, you may have to reassign some members to achieve a more balanced distribution.

You will want to avoid situations where a group consists largely of very strong writers or largely of very weak writers. By using a mixture of both, the strong writers will be able to help the weak ones. Sometimes group balance may be a factor of the social network in the class rather than writing skills. As a result, many teachers find it desirable to have students respond to a questionnaire that helps identify the social network. Such a questionnaire will typically ask students who is the smartest person in the class, who is the best leader, who is easiest to get along with, and so forth. Even very young students will probably have some awareness of the existing network, and since the questionnaires are filled out anonymously, the responses are generally candid.

The very nature of work groups builds revision into the act of writing, so that young students are more inclined to see revision as a reformulation rather than an indication of failure. In this respect, work groups can be particularly important for very young children, who, as Scardamalia and Bereiter (1983) have shown, just don't *do* revision on their own. Yet revision is especially important to younger students, because they tend to operate on the surface level of written discourse, not the rhetorical level.

If you're lucky, the desks in your room won't be bolted to the floor, and students can arrange their seats into small circles that make working together easier. If they are bolted, the best procedure is to arrange students in small semicircles facing the front of the room. You accomplish this arrangement by seating group members in adjoining rows, with two students in one row and three in the next. This seating pattern will enable students to see each other as they interact, and it will also allow them to observe you if you need to address the whole class. Always try to have an empty desk or two separating the groups, if at all possible. Such separation not only leads to a greater sense of bonding within each group, but also creates a sense of privacy. Both are important.

Pedagogical Factors Related to Work Groups

Your use of work groups should be guided by several factors. As noted in Chapter 7, writing is a psychosocial action, which means in part that an individual writer influences and is influenced by his or her immediate discourse community. We've also seen that, in the pragmatic view, meaningful writing is related to problem solving and to critical thinking in the sense that successful writers will construct alternative mental models for a given experience. Work groups provide an opportunity for students to interact and to engage in cooperative problem solving that can enhance critical-thinking skills by asking them to adopt different perspectives.

It seems difficult to overestimate the importance of peer interaction in a positive learning environment. David Johnson (1980) tells us that such interaction contributes significantly to "internalization of values, acquisition of perspective-taking abilities, and achievement" (pp. 156–57). Working through problems in rough drafts together, discussing ways to make writing clearer and more meaningful lead group members to internalize values and to expand their role-taking ability. Expanded role-taking ability lies at the heart of cognitive growth (Flavell et al., 1968; Johnson-Laird, 1983), because it enables the formation of a repertoire of alternative mental models. Applying these models helps students become better, more critical readers of their own work, which in turn helps them become better writers (see Hawkins, 1980; Huff & Kline, 1987).

As mentioned earlier, collaboration on projects provides students an element of realism when they write, and there is evidence that they may actually learn more when collaborating than they do when working alone (Crawford & Haaland, 1972; Laughlin & McGlynn, 1967). In addition, some evidence shows that work groups have a positive effect on student motivation. Huff and Kline (1987) report that "students working together on assignments have more success in completing them, remain motivated longer, build a sense of group purpose that provides additional motiva- tion, tend to continue into other, higher tasks in the same subject area, and view the instructor more and more favorably as learning and success rates improve" (p. 136).

Students, of course, will need practice in collaborative learning. It will take them a while to feel comfortable helping one another with every aspect of the writing process, particularly revision. But because students will be sharing drafts of their papers *in progress*, they will be working in a largely risk-free environment, which means they will generally learn faster and more easily than they would otherwise.

Sharing Student Drafts

Sharing drafts in progress among work-group members can be accom- plished in several ways. Perhaps the easiest method for most teachers is to have students take turns passing drafts around in their groups. After every group member has read a particular draft, the group talks with the writer about the paper's strengths and weaknesses.

Teachers whose schools have large photocopying budgets and a relatively reliable copier can reduce the amount of time it takes group members to get through individual drafts. First, schedule revising sessions during which students spend class time writing and reading drafts aloud in their groups, commenting on one another's papers, and then revising. At the end of the period, students turn in their drafts, which you photocopy for the next day. Each group member receives a copy of the other members' papers. Unfortunately, few schools have the money or the equipment to handle the huge volume of copies this procedure generates.

Another approach asks each writer to read his or her draft to the work group. This method has the advantage of aiding both reading and listening skills, and writers are often surprised at how their writing actually *sounds*. They commonly will discover errors in logic, support, wording, and punctuation during a reading. The problem with this method is that it's difficult for group members to offer advice for improving a paper when their perception of it is limited to hearing it read aloud. At some point they will need to see the paper.

Social Bonding in Work Groups

To make the most of collaborative learning, you will have to help your students through the obstacles that naturally arise when people attempt any cooperative endeavor. Three distinct stages of development mark collaborative learning: the bonding stage, the solidarity stage, and the working stage. Your job is to help students through the first two and then to keep them on task throughout the third.

Before bonding can occur, two things have to happen more or less simultaneously. Students have to identify themselves with their particular group, and they have to feel that they aren't competing with fellow group members. Establishing this group dynamic requires a degree of skill and ingenuity, because in many cases students in writing classes are reluctant to work together in a constructive fashion. The myth of writing as a solitary act is pervasive, and students may also worry about individual grades. What we have to do is provide opportunities that will promote social bonding and a spirit of cooperation.

During the bonding stage, group members are adjusting to the idea that they will be working together closely for the entire term. They are trying to get to know one another, trying to establish a sense of community. During the solidarity stage, the group establishes a social network in response to the dominant and subordinate personalities of the members. Students recognize their strengths and weaknesses relative to their cohorts' and make the adjustments necessary for effective feedback during the composing process. For example, some students may have poor organizational skills but may be excellent editors. The result is usually a natural division of responsibility, with members sharing equal but different tasks. Also during this stage, students experience a growing sense of confidence in their abilities to evaluate one another's papers, which makes them feel more comfortable with their roles in the work groups. During the working stage, students come to see fellow members as a true support group that can be relied on for positive advice that will lead to a better essay. Students will often identify with their groups such that individual success on an assignment tends to be viewed as group success.

One technique we can use to enhance the bonding process during the first stage involves asking group members to complete projects that require the participation of all members. The members are essentially forced to work together. Such projects can take the form of reports, where students investigate a topic on their campus or community and write a group report, or they can take the form of panel presentations, where members research a topic and then share what they learn with the entire class. Periodic checks on student progress will ensure that each group member is taking part in the project and that no one is neglecting his or her responsibility to the other members.

Another technique involves competition. In all but a few esoteric cultures, competition serves as a healthy vehicle for bonding when it makes groups of people feel they are engaged in a mutual effort for a common cause. One effective way, therefore, to achieve group identity and bonding is to make it clear that the various work groups are competing with one another to produce the best possible writing. The prospect of competing with other classes tends to enhance the group dynamic even more.

The question, of course, is, *What* are groups competing *for?* In academics, unlike sports, the sheer joy of "winning" doesn't often work as a motivator, perhaps because of the higher level of abstraction involved. Grades are universal and strong motivators, but they generally fail to solidify the social bonds necessary to make collaboration succeed. In addition, there is evidence suggesting that competition between groups has little or no effect on achievement (see Johnson, Maruyama et al., 1981). Grades are generally individual rewards for achievement that can actually work against bonding. For the bonding stage, therefore, you will need to consider alternative rewards that will motivate students to compete seriously as groups. This is where your own ingenuity is invaluable, as the rewards will vary, depending on the personal inclinations of individual teachers and the degree of freedom allowed by districts and principals.

One potential motivator worth considering, devised many years ago by Staats and Butterfield (1965), is a "token economies" system, which has been used very successfully (often with modifications) in numerous classrooms. Students earn tokens of different values for their work; these can then be used like cash to "buy" items provided in the classroom. This system seems to lead to significant improvements in both motivation and performance. It is also readily adaptable to work groups. Rather than individuals earning tokens, groups earn them on the basis of the quality of their projects. In classrooms where students have access to computers but where computer time is generally short owing to the number of students who have to share terminals, I have observed that the most popular "item" for groups to spend their tokens on is computer time.

Addison and Homme (1965) developed a system similar to the one advocated by Staats and Butterfield, but tokens were used exclusively to purchase free time, during which students could engage in a "play activity." Computers and educational software, of course, now allow us more easily to turn play activities into learning activities.

Token economies seem to be extremely effective as motivators and thus would probably prove quite valuable in establishing a reward system to enhance group bonding. Yet we have to keep in mind that some parents and administrators frown on token economies. They feel uncomfortable with the idea of encouraging competition among students, and with the idea of linking education to what they view as classroom consumerism. Some teachers therefore avoid token economies while nevertheless using competition and rewards to solidify group identity. For example, several high school writing teachers in Los Angeles take work groups with the best records out for ice cream cones at the end of each semester. The biannual gatherings have become something of a ritual, and students work hard to stretch their limits, not so much for the ice cream but for the honor of being among a select few.

Computers and Work Groups

Over the next few years, advances in technology will profoundly alter the ways in which group members can interact and share their work. Some schools, for example, already have computer networks that allow students and teacher to view work in progress. In such a network, each group member has a computer linked to the teacher's terminal. Members can work on their individual essays, but at the press of a key or two they can see any one of the group's essays on all their screens. Not only can they then read the draft together, they can offer suggestions for revision through their own terminals, so that changes appear immediately in the draft, where they can be further evaluated to determine their effectiveness. Of course, work in one group doesn't interfere with work in any of the other groups.

In other schools, a similar network is connected to a beam projector that puts individual essays onto a large screen in the classroom. Although not quite as effective as the other system, because only one group (or the whole class) can use the screen at a time, it still offers a powerful means of sharing and commenting on drafts.

These systems exist now and are being used very successfully in schools that can afford them or that have faculty aggressive enough to write grant proposals for the equipment. If you find that your school doesn't even have a copier but still relies on a ditto machine, keep in mind that grant money is available for innovative projects.

Grading Group Participation

Some teachers believe that students need a rubric to work effectively in groups, so they provide "revision guides" for each assignment. Students respond to the guide questions after reading a draft and then return both the draft and the guide to the writer. Revision guides can take many forms, but the sample offered on p. 211 seems typical.

Revision guides can be very useful. Their structure, for example, helps accustom students to working in groups by giving them concrete tasks and clear-cut goals. Also, because work groups will be doing different things at different stages of a paper's development, revision guides can serve to direct appropriate feedback at each point, such as idea generation, initial draft, second draft, final revision, editing, and proofing. You can tailor a guide specifically to each stage of development, thereby ensuring that group members make the most of each workshop.

Revision guides also function to train students to become critical readers. You may therefore want to consider using guides initially as part of class discussions of writing samples, either from students or profession-

---

Revision Guide

YOUR NAME:

PERIOD:

DATE:

AUTHOR'S NAME:

Use the following guide to direct your reading of the rough drafts for this assignment. Answer each question fully so that the writer can use your comments to help his or her revising. Write on the back of this sheet if you need more space.

1. What point is the writer trying to make?
2. What specific details and/or support help the writer make a point?
3. Does the writer respond to all parts of the assignment? If not, what is left out?
4. Does the writer have an identifiable thesis? If so, what is it?
5. Is the paper interesting? Does it teach you anything? If so, what?
6. Is the paper well organized and easy to read?
7. Are the mechanics, like grammar and spelling, reasonably correct?
8. What do you like best about the paper?

---

als. Then, when they approach drafts in their work groups, they can model their behavior on what they have learned about critical reading.

You should be aware, however, that revision guides have certain disadvantages. For example, they tend to constrain discussions of papers. Students are inclined to respond in writing to the questions on the guides and to *say* very little more. Experience shows that even when directed to use the questions as a starting point for discussion, students fail to develop a true dialogue concerning drafts.

Also, should you decide to experiment with revision guides, be extremely careful about *how* you use them. You may observe teachers in your school who assign grades for students' participation in their work groups. For such teachers, the revision guide serves as a quick way to gauge some measure of involvement. One simply checks names off against the roll book. These cases reflect an unfortunate misunderstanding of the process approach to teaching writing. The reasoning is that if the instructional emphasis is to be on the process rather than the product, then the process ought to be graded in some way. Thus one gives a grade for each completed revision guide, for each rough draft, for each conference, and so on. In other words, formative evaluations become *summative evaluations* (see Huff & Kline, 1987), or final appraisals of worth and value.

Although group work is extremely important to improving student writing performance, the idea of grading group participation, or more abstractly, "process," can be counterproductive. We want writers to receive high-quality feedback from group members, but grading revision guides or rough drafts emphasizes quantity. The task focus shifts significantly from having a thoughtful draft to having a draft. Because grades are generally considered individual rewards for achievement, not effort, students are likely to treat work groups as meaningless busywork if they are graded on participation. As a result, the effectiveness of group work is seriously compromised.

We should keep in mind that when students are working well in their groups, when they are engaging in critical readings of each other's drafts and then following through with revision, their finished essays will show it. It therefore seems reasonable to suggest that the grades we give finished essays reflect group participation better than any separate or intermediate evaluation. They should serve as sufficient indicators of group involvement. In other words, students in effective work groups should be writing better papers than those in ineffective groups. Our motto in the classroom ought therefore to be: "Teach process, grade product."

The idea of student collaboration bothers some teachers who worry about authorship, but there is really no reason to be concerned that essays will no longer be the work of individual students. As noted in Part One, real writers simply do not produce in a vacuum; they receive assistance from a wide range of people whose contributions serve to make the finished piece better than it would have been otherwise. There is really little danger that the group will take over any given paper. In fact, teachers are far more likely to appropriate a student essay, giving so much guidance that the paper becomes something that a student can no longer claim as his or her own. Increasing the amount of group feedback and decreasing the amount of your feedback will help you avoid appropriating students' texts.

Teacher Intervention

The writing workshop is structured to allow students to work together on their compositions, but it is also structured to allow teachers to intervene frequently during the composing process. Such intervention gives guidance during the development of an essay, which is when it is most needed.

Intervention methods take two forms. The first involves circulating among the work groups as they write and revise initial drafts. You can regulate your level of intervention according to students' needs. With some students you may simply want to listen to the group discussion of individual papers. Where appropriate, you may add your own suggestions to complement those of the students. Groups may also call you over for advice or to listen to a passage that is giving them problems. With other students you may want to ask to look over a draft, do a quick reading, and then offer suggestions. Your aim in this method is to make fast evaluations and to provide concise, positive advice on how to improve the writing. If something is wrong with a sentence, a paragraph, or a whole paper, point it out, but then give the student concrete suggestions on how to fix it; don't just say, "This needs more work" or "This needs revision."

When circulating around the classroom and conferring with work groups, it's important to be aware at all times of your position relative to the entire class. You should make certain to situate yourself in a way that allows you to talk to one group while monitoring the others. There's no need to be obtrusive about this, of course, but merely keeping the class in your line of sight will discourage students who might be tempted by your turned back to become disruptive.

The second method involves conferences with students, probably the single most effective tool you can use as a writing teacher. Most conferences are with individual students, but occasionally you may want to confer with as many as three in a tutorial, if they happen to have similar problems. In conferences, the goal is to draw out of students what their intentions are, how they hope to realize them, and what techniques they are using to do so. Listen to students talk about their papers, then read through them to judge how successfully the draft matches what you've just heard. Chances are the match won't be perfect, and you begin focusing student attention on what the difficulties are and how to overcome them.

Two factors are crucial to successful conferences. First, students have to do most of the talking. If you find yourself saying more than your students, chances are you're beginning to appropriate the text. Remember, this is their writing, not yours, and the more they talk about what they are doing, the better they will understand it. Second, work on no more than two points at a time. If a student has a draft that lacks support for an argumentative claim, has no transitions between paragraphs, has numerous spelling errors, and lacks sentence variety, don't try to tackle everything at once. Select the most important points—in this case perhaps support and transitions—and work on those until the student shows marked improvement. In another draft or perhaps on another assignment, you can deal with, say, sentence variety and spelling. You should also keep in mind that writing takes many years to master fully. Don't frustrate yourself and your students by trying to achieve 20 or 30 years of work in a single conference.

Telling students about the rhetorical problems in their papers is one way to conduct a conference, but it may not be the most effective. What seems to work better is an approach that focuses on using questions to direct students' attention to features that need improvement. For example, if a paper lacks an easily identifiable thesis or purpose, you might ask the writer to tell you what he or she wants to do in the paper. More often than not, students will have an aim that just doesn't come through.

After listening to an oral statement of purpose, you can ask the student to indicate where the equivalent statement is in the text. If it isn't there, the student will recognize at that moment that an important part of the paper is missing. Because the writer has already formulated an oral statement of purpose, you can then offer advice on just where it might best appear.

You would use a similar approach if the problem were, for example, lack of details or lack of support. Suppose a student is working on a paper advocating that students be allowed to play portable radios on school buses. To support this claim, the writer states in the draft that: (1) she likes music; (2) she received a portable radio for Christmas; (3) the music makes the ride seem shorter; and (4) the bus driver said he wouldn't mind the music.

You might begin by asking the writer, What is the first question readers are likely to ask after they see the claim? The answer, of course, is *why*, and it provides the key to helping the writer understand that only reason (3) attempts to address the readers' question. The next step is to ask for more true reasons that will support the claim. If the topic is viable, the student will be able to think of more than enough reasons for the essay, and your task is to help sift through them to determine which are the strongest. If the writer *can't* think of more reasons, she may have discovered that radios on school buses isn't a viable topic for her.

Using an approach in conferences that emphasizes questions rather than statements has the advantage of prompting students to think for themselves about what they are doing. It engages them in the processes of critical inquiry and problem solving that are essential to continued improvement in writing performance, because they are discovering things about their writing for themselves. As a result, the revisions they make are their revisions, not the teacher's. In essence, this approach involves students in learning by doing, and that's the best kind of learning.

Admittedly, conducting a conference in this manner is not particularly easy, but we can better understand why it's important to strive for the inquiry approach if we put conferences in the framework of psychosocial actions. As has been mentioned several times throughout this text, student writers frequently tend to think of themselves as a community of one. The result is discourse that lacks a functional purpose; it doesn't exist as a social action. Questions during a conference serve to bring students' writing closer to the realm of oral discourse that they are familiar with. Questions provide the prompts and cues that are inherent in conversations but that must be explicitly developed in a text as part of the contextualization process. Questions, in other words, help students recognize unacceptable premises, gaps in rhetorical purpose, and the absence of the by-means-of relations associated with intentionality.

These social factors are balanced by psychological ones. A teacher's questions set up a dialectic context that can help students elaborate mental models of texts, and they can help students develop alternative points of view for a given experience, idea, or belief. Alternative points of view, or countermodels of experience, appear to be linked to reasoning ability

(Johnson-Laird, 1983), which suggests that the question approach to conferences may be a strong pedagogical tool in our goal to enhance students' critical-thinking skills.

Another factor you will want to consider as you prepare to conduct conferences is that they should be short. Some teachers try to limit them to five minutes, but that seems overly brief for most students. Ten to fifteen minutes is perhaps more realistic. Even at ten minutes per conference, you will need eight to ten class periods to meet with every student. Also, individual instruction can be quite draining, especially if you do it all day with 90–120 students. Given these realities, few elementary and high school teachers try to conduct more than three conferences per student per term, even though the benefits are so significant that they would like to conduct more. What you will need to do is hold one round of conferences and then evaluate how many rounds you can fit into your semester.

We can't leave the technique of conferences without saying something about classroom control. Students may be tempted to drift into socializing or horseplay if they sense that your attention is so consumed you aren't monitoring the class. For this reason, it's best to begin conferences several weeks into the term, after students have adjusted to their work groups and are used to the workshop environment. Also, you may want to plan some structured group activities during conference days. For example, you may ask each group to exchange drafts with another group, have students read the papers, and then have them write evaluation summaries of what they read. These would be returned with the drafts at the end of the hour. Equally effective is to schedule five-minute breaks between each conference that will allow you to leave your desk and to circulate around the room, monitoring group activities. You may see fewer students during the hour, but there is less chance of having one or two mischievous students disrupt the class.

Writing Across the Curriculum

The most significant pedagogical advantage of the workshop approach is that it brings a social component into the writing class. It allows students and teacher to interact on various levels to give individual writers a keener sense of how they and their discourse are part of a larger community. Other characteristics of the workshop approach, such as multiple drafts and revision, are simply part of this social component. Revision, for example, represents, in part, a writer's efforts to control the interplay of text and intentions so that he or she can bring about an effect in an audience.

Strange as it may initially seem, even though this approach can significantly improve classroom instruction, it is constrained by the very principles that make it effective. In a composition class, writing is essentially content-free. Teachers strive to provide content in their assignments, of course, but unless one asks students to write about literature or language, the content is external to the specific concerns of the class. Thus we see some teachers offering assignments that deal with political issues, national affairs, international events, and so forth. But most students don't know enough about such topics to write about them intelligently, so teachers are generally inclined to focus writing tasks on students' personal experiences, which more or less ensures that each student will have something to say.

The problems typically associated with these approaches are easy to identify and are related to students' understanding of discourse pragmatics. When students in an English class write about national politics, they may have difficulty recognizing any functional purpose for the task. They justifiably may want to know why they are writing, given that their audience—teacher and peers—is only marginally concerned with any issues that the essay may cover. You have already seen in *Preparing to Teach Writing* that a goal for teachers is to provide tasks that help students connect their compositions to real audiences, thereby making function and purpose implicit in the task, but quite candidly, there are limits to what one can do to make writing tasks functional. It demands unflaggingly resourceful ingenuity to devise meaningful assignments.

A more ideal environment, therefore, would be a classroom in which writing tasks are truly content based, where the audience exists primarily outside the class. Integrating such an environment with the workshop methodology, emphasizing as it does social interaction, would provide young people greater opportunities to learn more not only about themselves but about the world.

Until fairly recently, such an integrated environment was difficult to achieve, because teachers frequently gave little attention to writing tasks outside the narrow domain of English. The changes in writing instruction discussed in Chapter 1, however, have greatly altered educators' perceptions of what writing is about. Specifically, the idea that writing is a means of learning has had an important effect on the way composing is viewed in disciplines other than English.

Traditionally, students in science and history, for example, wrote primarily to demonstrate that they had mastered a given body of information. There was little concern for audience and intention. A composition reported certain facts that the teacher checked off much as though scoring a multiple-choice test. More and more, however, teachers in every field are becoming increasingly aware of the social nature of the learning process, increasingly aware of how thinking, reading, and writing are linked. It's understandable, then, that the traditional approach is being replaced by the pragmatic approach, which views writing as a vehicle for learning. Writing is now more than ever seen as a means of improving students' subject-matter mastery in math, science, history, and art, so teachers in these fields are not only adding more writing to their courses but, more important, are reevaluating the kind of writing they ask students to perform.

Writing across the curriculum is the name used to identify the effort teachers and administrators have been making over the last few years to give writing a more prominent role in classes other than English. We should note that writing across the curriculum isn't really a completely new approach to composition. Colgate College established such a program in the early 1930s, and UC Berkeley did the same in the 1950s (see Russell, 1987). The current approach is different, perhaps in that it seems to be more widespread; we find so-called WAC programs at the school level as well as at the college level.

How Writing Across the Curriculum Works

There are two popular models in junior and senior high schools for writing across the curriculum. The first consists of linked courses between writing classes and content-area, or base, classes. With this model, the school will designate selected classes as "writing intensive." The students in them will be simultaneously enrolled in composition classes in which the primary goal is to help them become better writers in the context defined by the content-area class.

Assignments in the composition course are drawn from readings and discussions in the base course. Whenever possible, the composition assignment should duplicate a writing assignment given in the base course. The evaluation students receive in their writing class is independent of their evaluation in the base course. Because the two instructors are often concentrating on different discourse features, it is possible for a given paper to receive a high evaluation from one teacher and a low one from another. An ongoing dialogue with the base-course instructor, however, tends to establish common standards for evaluation, so that grades rarely vary significantly. Such a dialogue allows teachers to discuss all assignments in advance and to share their evaluations of individual papers.

In the second model, writing teachers serve as resource persons for other faculty, providing suggestions on how to use writing in content areas. Their role is to give workshops on teaching writing, offering help on how to structure assignments, how to conduct conferences, and how to evaluate papers. The goal is to make teachers in fields outside English better writing instructors.

At the elementary level, writing across the curriculum comes closest to the second model. The difference, of course, is that one teacher is usually responsible for teaching all subjects. In this situation, writing across the curriculum focuses on developing ways to integrate writing as a way of learning and multiple subjects.

Some Practical Suggestions

It's important to keep in mind that the conventions that govern the typical English essay may not be totally applicable in other disciplines. Science reports, for example, often have a rigid structure of their own. If good writers are flexible writers, students stand to benefit from experience with a variety of composition requirements.

The range of writing activities that can be introduced as part of the work in a content area is as diverse as the disciplines themselves. For example, during art lessons, some elementary teachers may have children work in teams, as in the workshop approach. After finishing their artwork, the children can write stories for one another's pictures and then bind them into "books." Also at the elementary level, science lessons provide rich sources of writing opportunities. Jim Lee (1987) relates how several different writing tasks can be linked to a unit on garden snails. In an assignment that calls for description, students are asked to "Write an account of a day in the life of a snail." For narration, they are asked to "Write a story in which . . . [they] speculate or fantasize about how the snail got its shell." Then, for exposition, he offers the following:

> Suppose that the sun is moving closer to the earth each day. Using the theories of natural selection and survival of the fittest, project what physical changes might occur in the snail as it attempts to cope with its changing environment (p. 39).

In each of these tasks, students interact cooperatively in their work groups, but the latter assignment better utilizes the potential of collaborative learning. Illustrating the inquiry method in action, this hypothetical situation prompts students to brainstorm ideas as they examine the potential effects of the sun's shift. The writing assignment becomes a stimulus for learning, the social interaction of the work group becomes the vehicle for learning, and the resulting papers represent students' formulation of their learning.

Not long ago, several high school science teachers used the integrated approach—workshop plus content—when they brought writing into the chemistry lab and simultaneously took advantage of a nationwide essay contest sponsored by *Omni* magazine. Recent discoveries concerning superconductors—material that carries an electrical current with virtually no resistance—have made it incredibly easy to produce usable quantities of the superconductor 123, or $Y_1Ba_2Cu_3O_{7x}$. It is so simple to produce, in fact, that high school science teachers can have students make it in chemistry lab. Lab activities are nearly always collaborative endeavors, so these teachers were quick to recognize the advantages of the workshop method. A natural writing assignment would be an essay concerning the uses of superconductors, but during the fall of 1987 students in these Los Angeles classes had an added incentive. In November, *Omni* sponsored a contest for an essay describing the "most creative future superconducting invention" (Schechter, p. 76). First prize: $500.

As for mathematics, at first glance one might think that math class would be the last place to introduce a writing component, much less one that uses a workshop approach. After all, the students generally work with numbers rather than words. The possible exception, of course, is the dreaded "word problem." Over the last several years, math teachers have discovered that many of their students are adept at manipulating numbers, but when faced with a realistic situation that calls for a particular solution, such as a word problem, they are more often than not at a loss. Innovative teachers are finding that with a little assistance, students are able to write their own word problems, which they then exchange among group members and solve as part of their homework. Writing their own problems reinforces the fundamental mathematical concepts, giving students a better grasp of the principles involved, while simultaneously giving them the opportunity to practice their writing skills. The result is writing as a vehicle for learning at its best.

Promoting Writing Across the Curriculum

Over the last few years, writing-across-the-curriculum programs have proliferated throughout the country. Still, the majority of our schools have not yet committed themselves to formalized interdisciplinary writing. For beginning teachers, the lack of interdisciplinary writing programs is often particularly frustrating, because they clearly understand the inherent advantages and want to know how they may go about promoting writing across the curriculum in their schools.

Specific efforts must differ from campus to campus, but in general the most effective means of developing a program is to start very modestly with discussions among a few sympathetic faculty members inside and outside language arts. The aim is to listen to what they have to say about writing. Such talks usually reveal that most faculty members are concerned about students' writing skills and that they would like to do something about the low performance they observe. The problem is that they don't feel as though they have either the expertise or the time to do anything worthwhile.

Their self-doubts are certainly natural, but the truth of the matter is that one doesn't have to be trained in English to understand the principles involved in a pragmatic approach to writing instruction. Many teachers already use collaborative learning techniques, for example, which would make the workshop method seem less novel, less threatening. In addition, helping colleagues see new ways to take advantage of writing opportunities in their own classes is an important—and relatively painless—way to promote writing across the curriculum. Simply by asking students to write more frequently we are likely to improve their performance.

Ultimately, however, the real key to prompting writing across the curriculum among colleagues is to alleviate their fears that their work load will increase significantly if they ask students to write more often. All teachers work hard, but writing teachers work perhaps harder than others, owing to the number of compositions they have to read. Chapter 11 proposes ways to reduce the amount of paper-grading time commonly associated with writing instruction, and these methods can be used fairly easily by anyone interested in improving student writing performance. Generally, a small group's success with writing across the curriculum motivates other teachers to get involved, and that's when you can start planning a formal program.

Conclusion

One of the biggest obstacles we face in implementing writing workshops is our tendency to believe students incapable of handling the responsibility involved. Give us a class of basic writers, or one of nonmainstream students, and that tendency to believe is likely to become an outright conviction.

This obstacle, however, is based largely on a distorted view of students. Most are eager to please, eager to do well. Most are very responsible, whenever they are asked to be. What they often lack are chances to demonstrate their responsibility. This is just as true of under-achievers as it is of college-bound students. As we will see in Chapter 9, it is also true of LEP students. There is no doubt, of course, that if you turn your writing classes into workshops, over the years some students will prove themselves totally irresponsible, and the idea of collaborative learning just won't work. But for the majority, workshops and group activities are opportunities to experiment with adulthood.

When sometime in the near future you approach your first workshop session, keep in mind that the suggested methods discussed here represent simply an outline. The day-to-day mechanics of structuring your classes are likely to vary considerably. Moreover, you should keep in mind that it may take two or three years to begin mastering the many variables that contribute to a successful workshop environment. Be prepared to experiment along the way!

CHAPTER 9

Teaching the Nonmainstream Student

Overview

Nonmainstream students in this context are those whose first language is one other than English or whose first dialect is nonstandard English. Many times we find these two groups of students in the same class.

Traditional methods for teaching writing to nonmainstream students consist of providing drills and exercises to train them to use Standard grammar and usage. Students write very little under this methodology, and what writing they do is often limited to sentences and paragraphs. Only occasionally do they write whole essays.

At this point, it should be clear that the most effective way to improve students' writing skill is to give them opportunities to write and to provide them with frequent feedback on work in progress. In this view, the best method for mainstream and nonmainstream students alike is a workshop where students can interact, produce multiple drafts of papers, and receive direct feedback from the teacher. This chapter focuses the discussion of the workshop approach on the nonmainstream writing class, explaining why it will benefit students. It then offers some specific strategies for use with nonmainstream classes.

Nonmainstream Students

The term *nonmainstream* is often used to refer to a wide range of students whose linguistic and socioeconomic backgrounds place them outside the dominant Standard English culture. It is used here, however, as it was earlier in the text, to refer specifically to nonnative English speakers and to nonstandard-English speakers.

Initially, grouping these students together in a chapter about teaching methods may seem daring. After all, their backgrounds and experiences are often very different. Their difficulties with written discourse therefore have different causes and may in fact manifest themselves in different ways. For these reasons, among others, most discussions of teaching methods deal with nonnative and nonstandard speakers separately.

Nevertheless, these students do have many characteristics in common. Both groups are working to develop minimal proficiency in a language form that they have had few opportunities to practice. Their writing is equally prone to errors of structure and usage that initially seem to be the result of mere carelessness. And additional similarities can be found on another level: how teachers perceive these students. Both groups are usually deemed handicapped by first-language or first-dialect interference. Recent research notwithstanding, their attempts at Standard English composing are often viewed as being distorted by oral patterns from the primary language or dialect. Thus when teachers are confronted with the writing of nonnative English speakers and nonstandard-English speakers, their first impulse may be to give students sets of exercises aimed at implanting the written code through spelling drills, lists of verb forms, and copious examples of subject–verb agreement.

Although these common characteristics are important in their own right, for our purposes here they are secondary. Of primary importance in this chapter is that both nonnative and nonstandard speakers benefit from the methodology detailed in Chapter 8, a methodology that emphasizes the recursive, social nature of composing.

From Process to Product

We need to keep in mind that writing teachers are actually language teachers, that we deal with universals of competence, performance, learning, and acquisition that transcend individual language differences. The notion of universals suggests that the way we structure a class for nonmainstream students will be very similar to the way we structure a class for mainstream students. Both classes will be guided by a set of characteristics linked to what we know about the environment students need to become better writers.

Much of the rationale for this environment has already been put forward in previous chapters, but we can focus it a bit more here. Research over the last few years suggests that nonmainstream students work through writing tasks in about the same way that mainstream students do (Zamel, 1983). They develop a pre-text for the discourse that includes both rhetorical features and surface features. When they write, they engage in pausing episodes indicative of mental revisions of the pre-text, just as mainstream students do. They revise recursively, modifying their discourse plans as they go along. And with nonnative speakers, we find that planning and revising skills in L_1 transfer to L_2 (Jones and Tetroe, 1987).

Moreover, nonmainstream writers, like their mainstream counterparts, frequently use writing to clarify their thoughts on subjects. In other words, they use writing as a vehicle for learning. Their efforts require a high degree of interaction with the text, with their constructed audience, and with their intentions. To paraphrase Ann Raimes (1985, 1986), students "negotiate" with the text as they develop it; they engage in the sort of hypothesis testing described in Chapters 3 and 7.

If nonmainstream writers are to learn to negotiate with a text successfully, they need instruction that encourages risk taking. They need a methodology that promotes a high degree of interaction with the teacher and with peers, that allows them to write multiple drafts, to receive feedback as each draft is being developed, and to revise again and again and again. The only environment that currently incorporates all these features is the classroom workshop.

Turning a writing class with numerous nonmainstream students into a workshop may initially seem counterintuitive. Given the sorts of errors we find in their writing, there is always a strong temptation to resort to drills and exercises to reduce the level of primary-language or primary-dialect interference. In her much admired book *Errors and Expectations*, Mina Shaughnessy (1977) concludes that providing drills and exercises, along with a great deal of sensitivity to their difficulties, is about all one can do for nonmainstream students. The primary patterns they bring to school writing must be overcome, the common reasoning goes, and drill is the only way to accomplish the task.

But some recent research suggests that few of the errors nonmainstream writers make are the result of primary-language or primary-dialect interference.

As noted in Chapter 6, Farr and Janda (1985) performed a detailed discourse analysis on the speech and writing of Joseph, an 18-year-old BEV student enrolled in a remedial writing class. They concluded that dialect interference was not his major difficulty, even though the traditional view would suggest that the root of the student's writing problems lies in dialect interference. Farr and Janda state:

> Although features of Vernacular Black English are part of . . . [Joseph's] linguistic repertoire, VBE features occur relatively infrequently in his writing, eliminating nonstandard dialect influence as a major cause of his difficulty in writing. Furthermore, Joseph's writing evidenced many "literate" characteristics, i.e., devices which have been found to be typical of written English . . . . What, then, is the problem with Joseph's writing? Why was he placed in a remedial writing class . . . ? His writing does not appear to be language that was generated by a human being in an attempt to express or create meaning. The form is there; the functional attempt to communicate does not seem to be (pp. 80–81).

In a similar but more extensive study, Edelsky (1986) evaluated, during their first three years of elementary school, the oral and written discourse of a group of children whose first language was Spanish. Her results repudiate many of the notions commonly associated with bilinguals and literacy.

For example, she found very little code-switching between L_1 and L_2. She reports that most of the switching she found was "like slips of the pen" and that it decreased significantly by the time children were in the third grade (p. 152). This finding is important because L_2 writing is so widely believed to suffer from L_1 interference. Her data tend to confirm Krashen's (1980) view that second-language learners fall back on and use first-language rules, conventions, and strategies when they do not have the appropriate rule, convention, or strategy in their second-language repertoire (1980, pp. 73–74). In other words, they use skills they already have in L_1 until they acquire the rule in L_2. Thus rather than being prevented from acquiring a rule in the second language because they already have one in the first, they use first-language competence in a transitional way to master L$_2$. In this respect, Edelsky's findings echo those of other bilingual-education researchers (see Calkins, 1983; Dyson, 1982, 1983; Ferreiro & Teberosky, 1982).

Such research does not suggest, however, that we should completely ignore the problems students have with error. Improving the quality of the finished product is one of our long-range goals. But errors seem best addressed on the spot, as students are working on drafts in their work groups. They can be dealt with as part of the composing process through individual conferences, or through a presentation to the whole class, if several students are having similar difficulties. This approach keeps the emphasis on writing.

Studies like Farr and Janda's and Edelsky's, set in the context of contemporary writing research, have prompted numerous teachers to reexamine composition pedagogy for nonmainstream students. Quite simply, it now seems clear that the difficulties nonmainstream students have with writing stem less from linguistic features of the second language or the second dialect than from the complexities and constraints of the act of composing itself (see L. White, 1977). We are beginning to see that an emphasis on error correction is neither reliable nor effective in helping students eliminate errors in their writing.

Recognizing this fact, Edelsky (1986) explicitly calls for a new literacy methodology after having deconstructed what she terms the "myths" that guide literacy instruction for bilinguals. She calls for a new paradigm that will link reading and writing as top-down, pragmatic activities. This new paradigm will not treat reading and writing as separate skills, nor will it treat writing as a set of separate subskills. Instead, it will view writing as a social action, as a means of interacting with others.

This entire text, of course, is an attempt to establish just such a paradigm, and the methodology associated with writing workshops explicitly deals with the issues Edelsky raises. As has been stressed repeatedly, our final goal is to improve the writing our students produce, but that improvement will more effectively come about by changing the way students approach writing tasks. By enabling them to better control the process of writing, we give them the means to improve the product.

The Nonmainstream Workshop

We've already seen how the workshop method focuses on giving students new strategies for composing. In many ways it is designed to break down old and persistent myths concerning what writing is about. Most students believe, for example, that writing should be easy, or that it's some sort of innate talent that one is either born with or not. Although this may be true in some cases, it certainly isn't in most. And in any event, the notion that writing skill is predicated on talent denies the fact that good writing is just plain hard work. Yet the myth persists, and students commonly think their first draft of an assignment should be their final draft.

Writing workshops are structured so that students produce multiple drafts, engage in collaborative activities, and so forth, gaining a clearer understanding of what writing entails. For nonmainstream students, who may feel inferior to their mainstream counterparts, this understanding is important; they begin to see that their problems with written discourse are similar to those that all writers have.

In fact, what we know about language acquisition suggests that the classroom workshop provides a social dimension to school language use that is often crucial to the developing literacy of nonmainstream students. Acquisition of communicative competence in literacy requires meaningfully interacting with others who encourage reading and writing. Yet it's common to find that nonmainstream students come from family backgrounds where literacy isn't stressed: Parents will seldom read to their children, and they may never do any writing, which means the children lack effective models for literate behavior.

The writing workshop allows nonmainstream students to talk, of course, but it also asks them to talk in the language of the school—Standard English—as they discuss one another's work. When they collaborate on drafts, trying to make them better, they engage in problem-solving activities that enhance their critical-thinking skills. Thus the benefits of group interaction are far-reaching: Students not only exercise their cognitive abilities but exchange ideas that can enhance vocabulary, clarity, and meaning.

The process of working through multiple drafts and revisions has additional advantages for nonmainstream students. It provides the opportunity to experiment with language in a largely risk-free environment. Mistakes during the drafting process are allowed, perhaps even encouraged, because they are an important part of learning.

We already know some of the consequences of the fear of failure. S. Harter (1981) notes that students who are overly concerned with task failure will simply withdraw, refusing even to make an attempt at a given activity. Rose (1984) suggests that fear of making mistakes is an underlying factor in writer's block. Dulay, Burt, and Krashen (1982) suggest that fear of failure and subsequent rejection will prevent second-language learners from interacting with native speakers of that second language. It therefore appears that students who avoid errors are avoiding risks, are playing it safe, working with what they already know, and therefore aren't learning. The workshop provides an environment that minimizes the possibility of rejection and its accompanying fear and anxiety.

The personal and pedagogical benefits of such an environment are unmistakable. As nonmainstream students take more risks, they expand their repertoire of skills, which in turn leads to greater success with Standard English and to a growing sense of confidence in their writing ability (see Kantor, 1985). Confidence and success are two of the more significant pillars of academic achievement, which has led Diaz (1986) to argue, in regard to nonnative English speakers, that "the development of confidence in writing that can accompany the use of process techniques brings . . . a powerful and important by-product for ESL students in learning to write in English" (p. 173).

Structuring Activities

The ideal classroom would have a balanced mixture of mainstream and nonmainstream students. Where such a balance exists, the Standard English speakers can work with the nonmainstream students in a "buddy system" that enhances the skills of both. Frequent reading of drafts written by Standard speakers will work to familiarize the other speakers with the rhythms and construction patterns of English. Standard speakers benefit from attempting to explain the nuances of their own language or dialect, often articulating linguistic principles they had never thought of before. For example, prepositions commonly cause nonnative speakers serious problems. In Spanish the preposition *en* means both *in* and *on*, so a native Spanish-speaking student is likely to write something along the lines of "I got in the bus, and after we arrived I got in the car." Native English speakers' linguistic competence provides them the knowledge that we get *on* buses but get *in* cars. Yet it takes some thought to figure out the underlying principle, which is related to the size of the vehicle, that dictates the preposition we use.

Most multicultural classrooms in metropolitan areas, however, rarely have a balance of mainstream and nonmainstream students. Usually the student body will be predominantly Hispanic, Asian (Korean, Cambodian, Laotian, Chinese, Vietnamese), and black. But a "buddy system" can still work in this environment, because the nonmainstream students more often than not will be at various levels of English proficiency; the more fluent students can help the others.

When it comes to structuring learning activities, elementary teachers in nonmainstream classes frequently have to deal with tutorial programs that, although put together with the best of intentions, can seriously handicap instruction. In larger districts, particularly, schools will provide learning specialists for many nonmainstream students. These specialists no doubt provide a valuable service, but they also complicate the teacher's job, because individuals and small groups leave the class at various times throughout the day for tutoring. Teachers in this situation have to maintain the utmost flexibility in order to fit whole-class activities into those hours when all the students are present, doing group work and conferences when some students are missing.

Middle school and high school teachers face a different problem, one that has already been raised. Curriculum guidelines may dictate drills and exercises, and implementing a workshop may stir administrative displeasure. In addition, nonmainstream writing classes at these levels are commonly the dumping ground for students with discipline problems. This is not to suggest in any way that nonmainstream students are troublemakers or that they can be stereotyped as such. The difficulty isn't in the students but in the nature of the classes—traditionally places where students simply sit and fill in the blanks in workbooks. Administrative thinking in this case follows a circuitous route: The idea is that the drills and exercises will at least keep difficult students in their seats. Of course, some educators believe that large numbers of such students would cease to be discipline problems if school were more meaningful and allowed young people a greater voice in their own education (see Freire & Macedo, 1987).

We should note in this case that workshops actually enhance one's ability to deal with discipline problems. With students in work groups, the troublemakers are isolated from the whole class, more visible, and easier to control.

Speech and Writing

Generally, nonmainstream students' oral skills in Standard English will develop in advance of their writing skills. For this reason, teachers should introduce specific writing activities that involve speaking and listening. This methodology enables students to build writing skills on oral skills. The activities described in this section are designed to work with mainstream and nonmainstream students alike, because the two groups are occasionally mixed in a single classroom.

Videotape machines are very useful tools when introducing writing activities that include speaking and listening tasks. Just to offer one example, you can bring in tapes of television shows and movies and let students watch the first 5 minutes of the program. Then turn off the sound and let students watch for another 10 to 15 minutes. The first writing task is to produce dialogue for the characters. The assignment should be written collaboratively by groups, because students can read their work aloud and stage a competition for the most inventive dialogue, the most dramatic, the most humorous, the most realistic, and so forth.

The next step is to play the tape back with the sound on so that students can compare their work with the original. Practicing dictation can improve students' grasp of sound-to-symbol correspondences, so you may want to replay the tape in short segments to allow students to write down the dialogue they hear. You can circulate among groups to monitor the degree of accuracy between the tape and students' taking down of the dictation.

The differences between the students' dialogue and the original are likely to be interesting. These differences form the foundation for another writing assignment: an analysis that compares and contrasts student versions with the original. A final and related assignment will ask students to summarize the story elements of the portion of the tape they viewed, then to speculate on how the story or episode actually ends. When their speculative essays are completed, they can view the entire video and compare their versions with the actual story.

A stimulating variation on these activities involves videotaping students as they act out or read the dialogues they have produced for shows. You can then play the recording back so that the entire class can comment on the reading, offering suggestions for improvement and providing feedback on language use. Seeing oneself on camera has a powerful effect on most people, and students will be motivated to give complete attention to their performances. The language context in this case is so meaningful that language use tends to improve significantly on the basis of the feedback offered by the class and you.

Stories, essays, and newspapers provide similar sources of writing activities. You can read a portion of a newspaper article, for example, then develop a wide range of writing tasks, from letters to the editor to follow-up stories on local events. After an initial experience, students may want to bring in their own materials to use as the basis for their next assignment. Such an activity can be especially meaningful if the class has many nonnative English speakers. Students can bring in community newspapers written in their primary language to share with the class. Often these papers present local news that students outside that community will not know about. Thus the experience can be doubly educational.

Learning the Mainstream Culture

In addition to language, mainstream cultural assumptions present perhaps the biggest obstacle nonmainstream students have to hurdle on the road to writing proficiency and academic success. Very often, teachers take their frame of reference for granted and fail to see that their students don't share it, which makes communication impossible.

A former student of mine, for example, learned that she couldn't get her fifth-grade class of inner-city students to write acceptable essays about California Indians until she taught them about oak trees and acorns. Oak trees, of course, are common throughout much of the United States. In California they dot the hillsides, and they figure significantly in the early history of the state. California Indians used acorns as a dietary staple, grinding and bleaching them into a meal they ate like porridge.

When presenting the lesson on the Indians, this teacher assumed that her students knew what oak trees and acorns were. When she collected and read their papers, however, she realized her mistake. The next day, she brought to class acorns, oak leaves, and some bark to help make the lesson concrete. She now has files of objects and artifacts to help provide comprehensible input for the numerous mainstream cultural assumptions that are part of her curriculum.

We should note, however, that acculturation works two ways. Students should be encouraged to write about and explore their own cultural heritage. Writing tasks that ask students to examine some aspect of their own culture and compare it to a mainstream equivalent, in fact, offer students socially meaningful ways to use composition.

Conclusion

The idea that we should use similar methods for mainstream and nonmainstream students alike may take some getting used to. The traditional notion of having nonstandard and nonnative speakers working on grammar and vocabulary lessons is deeply ingrained in the American educational system. What we currently know about language acquisition and writing performance, however, suggests that the process of writing development is the same for both groups. The product differs, obviously. The writing of nonmainstream students will have significantly more errors than that of their mainstream counterparts. But these errors will not be remedied through traditional methods. They can, however, be dealt with developmentally if we treat them as a normal part of language/dialect acquisition.

Students will benefit most from a classroom environment that reduces the amount of error correction and that increases the level of social interaction and constructive feedback on work in progress. In other words, they will benefit most from a workshop approach to writing instruction. The chief characteristics of this approach are summarized below:

1. Frequent opportunities to practice writing, with equally

frequent opportunities to receive significant feedback from peers and teacher.

2. Regular opportunities to confer individually with the teacher to discuss work in progress.

3. A meaningful context for writing; assignments that are related to students' daily experiences and lives.

4. Opportunities to practice a variety of rhetorical strategies aimed at different audiences.

5. An emphasis on multiple revisions of drafts before a paper is submitted for evaluation.

6. An emphasis on collaborative learning.

7. Frequent opportunities to combine reading and writing as reciprocal activities.

8. Major reduction in the amount of direct instruction in gram mar and mechanics, with a corresponding reduction in the attention given to error correction.

CHAPTER 10

Writing Assignments

Overview

Numerous factors contribute to successful writing assignments, but developing a *sequence* that allows students to incorporate skills they have practiced in previous work with new skills they are trying to master is absolutely crucial. In addition, a well written assignment will make clear to students what they are supposed to do, how they are supposed to do it, who the students are writing for, and what constitutes a successful response.

The traditional view, the process view, and the pragmatic view of teaching writing all take the importance of sequencing into account, but the pragmatic view has a different understanding of what constitutes an effective sequence. In both the traditional and the process views, sequencing is usually linked to a taxonomy of behavioral objectives and cognitive development through the various rhetorical modes. Students begin with narration and description, producing personal-experience narratives or simple firsthand descriptions. They then go on to definition, comparison/contrast, and process, until at some point they reach argumentation (see Lindemann, 1987).

Underlying this sequence is the notion that rhetorical complexity and cognitive complexity are essentially the same thing. In the traditional view particularly, students are often considered incapable of coping with abstract cognitive tasks, so classroom instruction focuses on writing assignments that are deemed rhetorically concrete. The discussion of language and cognition in Chapter 7 should make the difficulty inherent in this line of reasoning relatively clear. Cognitive processes and language develop interactively, each influencing the other, and they are not the same thing.

The distinct nature of rhetorical complexity and cognitive complexity should affect the way we sequence assignments, because the rhetorical demands of a task may be far different from the cognitive demands. For example, close analysis shows that true narration is perhaps the most rhetorically demanding of all the modes, even though it may be less demanding cognitively than argumentation. Beginning a sequence with narration therefore appears to be at odds with what we know about learning. It is the equivalent of asking a child to walk before he or she can crawl.

The pragmatic view of teaching composition offers a sequencing alternative that focuses on the functional nature of writing and on the social and intellectual demands placed on students at any given moment rather than on modes. It suggests that an effective sequence should build on students' communicative competence and should ask them to use essays to perform specifiable social actions. We frequently find the pragmatic view influencing assignments in writing-across-the-curriculum classes. Many teachers in these classes have discussed writing with colleagues outside language arts and have determined that most of the writing students do in classes other than composition and most of what they are likely to do outside of school calls for three general skills: analysis, exposition, and argumentation.

In the pragmatic view, argumentation is particularly important because it links writing to problem solving, which as Chapter 7 noted enhances critical-thinking skills. In the pragmatic, psychosocial view developed in *Preparing to Teach Writing*, almost all writing is inherently argumentative owing to its rhetorical nature. Poetry and narrative fiction, for example, can be seen as representations of reality that a writer wants an audience to accept. The intentional component makes the writer's representation argumentative.

The pragmatic sequence for assignments would focus primarily on argumentation—although it may include narration—because in the broad application argument can incorporate all the other discourse modes. Moving students from less difficult to more difficult tasks could be accomplished by varying the kinds and sources of information students may use to support claims and/or representations of reality.

One of the numerous advantages in adopting the pragmatic view is that it allows teachers to apply a viable theoretical framework to a curriculum often highly constrained by textbooks and district guidelines. Teachers are commonly asked to address seemingly quite disparate writing tasks, such as essay exams, analyses of literature, and research papers. Seeing all these tasks as inherently argumentative allows for greater instructional continuity, because the rhetorical skills students are trying to master are very similar across tasks.

Making Good Writing Assignments

When students turn in essays that have little to say and that are boring to read, teachers will often blame the students for not trying. Actually, the problem may be in the assignment. There is no such thing as "the perfect assignment," but some are definitely better than others and lead to more thoughtful responses from students. What factors do we need to consider to make our assignments as good as they can be?

Planning

First, good assignments take time and planning. Teachers who put together a writing assignment the night before class are neglecting their students. You should develop assignments in advance to ensure that they are as thoughtful as possible. You will need to sequence assignments so that they are a careful blend of the old and the new. It's generally best to start with something students already know how to do fairly well, adding just enough novelty to make the task interesting and challenging. In addition, you will want to be aware of district guidelines that specify the particular skills students are expected to master from grade to grade. This awareness will help you avoid tediously repeating skill-building tasks that students have already practiced.

As you plan your assignments, focus on asking students to perform new tasks that incorporate and build on skills that were practiced in previous work. Remember, the goal of sequencing is to guarantee successful learning. For example, you could begin teaching analysis by asking students to write about something concrete, like a sporting event, and then go on to ask them to analyze something more complex, like a film or a story. We can find an analogy for this methodology in swimming. Beginning swimmers are pretty good at sinking, so some swimming coaches start lessons by having children go underwater. By adding strokes and kicks, the children turn their sinking into swimming underwater. From that point, it is a short step to swimming above water.

It's difficult to keep a sequence in view if you develop each assignment separately during the course of the term, so most effective teachers put together all the assignments before classes start. They simply outline the work for each quarter or semester, with due dates for all papers, then hand out copies to students on the first day of class. Two additional advantages of this approach are obvious: Students will be prompted to begin planning their writing early, and there will be less room for argument in regard to late papers.

If, during the term, you need to add an assignment to the outline for some reason, let students know as far in advance as possible that a change is required, and tell them why. Be certain to type up the additional assignment and hand it out to the class. Avoid giving any writing assignment orally, and avoid writing any on the board; at least half a class will not hear an oral assignment, and the majority of the other half will misunderstand it or forget it an hour later.

About the only time you should consider putting an assignment on the chalkboard is when an opportunity for using writing as a learning activity arises spontaneously out of the classroom dynamic. In this case the assignment will be written in class, and you shouldn't grade it. For example, one of my student teachers during the fall 1987 semester was preparing her ninth-grade class to write an editorial about a presidential candidate of their choice. As the students were discussing the ongoing campaign, it became clear that the majority of them had only a fuzzy notion of what characteristics an American president should have. She stopped the discussion at that point and had the class write for 15 minutes on desirable presidential characteristics. She wrote the task on the board, and the writing activity effectively engaged students in prewriting that helped them develop ideas.

Good writing assignments are also relatively brief, although they generally provide enough information to put the task in a context and to help students discover a purpose for the writing. Some teachers mistakenly assume that the more detailed they make the assignment, the better students will respond, but this just isn't the case, as was discussed in Chapter 2. Overly detailed assignments lead to "cognitive overload" that inhibits writing performance. An assignment that consists of a single directive, however, is probably too brief because it fails to offer a context.

Features Every Assignment Should Have

At this point you should be starting to see that writing good assignments is far from easy. Next to evaluating students' papers, it is perhaps the most difficult aspect of teaching composition. To write a good assignment, you have to consider the rhetorical nature of the task you are setting. As Erika Lindemann (1987) notes, teachers must decide *what* they want students to do in an assignment, *how* they want them to do it, *who* the students are writing for, and what constitutes a *successful response* to the assignment.

Generally speaking, assignments that lack the rhetorical aspects previously outlined are problematic because students find it extremely difficult to develop a meaningful purpose for their responses. Many teachers rely on class discussions to specify these rhetorical aspects, but this approach seems unsatisfactory for most writing tasks, especially those that students will complete out of class. Some students won't be listening, and others won't take notes, relying on their memory to complete a task that they won't begin until hours or even days later.

Class discussions of assignments are important, of course, but they shouldn't be used to convey information crucial to the satisfactory completion of the task. They are excellent opportunities to start students talking about their writing, articulating not only their understanding of the assignment but their initial conceptualization of how they plan to proceed. Such discussions are best begun in work groups, where the give-and-take of ideas can be more rapid owing to the relatively small size of the group. Group discussions can serve as a form of brainstorming, stimulating both ideas and questions that can then be shared with the class as a whole.

Let's summarize the characteristics we have just examined. Good assignments generally will:

1. Be part of a sequence designed to develop specific discourse skills.

2. Tell students exactly what they are expected to do. The mode of the response should be clear.

3. Tell students exactly how they are expected to write the assignment. If students are expected to use a formal tone, this expectation should be stated; if students are expected to use outside sources to support a claim, this expectation should be stated, and so on. You may include here practical specifics such as whether the paper should be typed, due date, length, and so on (see Tarvers, 1988).

4. Tell students something about the purpose and the audience for the paper. What is the paper supposed to do? Who other than the teacher should the writer be addressing?

5. Tell students what constitutes success, including some statement regarding the criteria you will use to assess the quality of the response.

Sample Assignments

To begin making these characteristics more concrete, we can examine some sample assignments collected from teachers at various grade levels. These particular samples are presented out of the sequences they belong to, simply to make our analysis a bit easier at this point. Some sequenced samples are presented later in the chapter.

(1) (For a group of third-grade students studying poems; the teacher was linking reading with writing.) We have been studying poems for two weeks. Last week we wrote our own version of *Over in the Meadow*. We took Olive Wadsworth's poem and put in our own words to tell a story. Now I want you to write another poem. I want this poem to be all your own. Tell your own story in

rhyme. The story can be about yor dog or cat. It can be about your favorite toy, or even your best friend. Just make it your own special poem. When all the poems are finished, we will put them together in a book. Then we will make copies so everyone will be able to read your poem. We will even make enough copies so you can give one to a friend.

(2) (For a group of ninth-grade students studying poetry; the teacher was linking reading with writing, focusing on analytical skills.) On your last assignment, you analyzed three of Charles Webb's prose poems to get ready for his visit to class. For this next assignment, I want you to begin with your earlier analysis and then to add to it an evaluation that explains which poem you like best and *why*. Successful analyses will support the explanation with good reasons and illustrations from the text. We will then mail our essays to Mr. Webb, who has promised to respond to several of them.

(3) (For a group of twelfth-grade students studying analysis; the teacher was focusing on relating writing tasks to situations students might encounter outside school.) Last week we studied the brochures we received from the travel agency to decide where we would like to spend our ideal vacation. Suppose that the agency were to sponsor a contest that would send the winner wherever he or she wanted to go, all expenses paid. All you have to do to win is write an essay explaining why you want to vacation in the spot you selected; and write the *best* essay. That is your task for this assignment. Each peer group will choose its best essay to enter into the finals, and then the whole class will choose from the final four which one is the winner. Our judging criteria should include knowledge about the vacation spot and the reasons the writer wants to vacation there.

Observe how in each case the teacher provides a background for the task, tells students what they are supposed to do, how they are supposed to do it, and what she will be looking for as she evaluates responses. In (2), for example, students can see that the reasons they supply to support their analyses will be a significant factor in the teacher's evaluation. Notice also that the assignments are not overspecified; the teachers did not overwhelm students by providing too much detail in regard to audience, purpose, assessment criteria, and so forth.

It may be useful to contrast the preceding assignments with some that are not particularly successful and to examine why the latter don't work very well. The following samples were collected from various public school teachers, and they were not part of any identifiable sequence:

(4) (For a group of twelfth-grade students studying exposition; students had previously discussed film plots and had spent some time analyzing the movie *E.T.*) Pretend you are E.T. How would you describe your school to the folks back home? Keep in mind that you would know nothing about Earth and its customs.

(5) (For a group of seventh-grade students studying exposition; students had recently read an essay about how to build a kite.) Describe the process of making a peanut butter and jelly sandwich to someone who doesn't know how to make one.

(6) (For a group of tenth-grade students studying exposition; students had just finished a unit on poetry.) Everyone has done something they felt ashamed about later. Describe an event in which you did something that made you feel ashamed.

(7) (For a group of tenth-grade students studying exposition; students had previously read a short story in which the main character enjoyed reading.) For this assignment you will write a comparison and contrast paper. Be certain to describe each of your topics in detail. Select one from the following choices: (a) compare and contrast two types of music such that readers will understand why you prefer one to the other; (b) compare and contrast the sort of books you enjoy reading today with the sort of books you enjoyed reading five years ago, and describe how your taste has changed; (c) compare and contrast a place, such as a neighborhood, you knew as a child with how it is today.

These last four assignments are problematic for several reasons. In (6), narration and description are confused; the narrative is stated in terms of describing an event. The list illustrates a further confusion in that the teachers who wrote the assignments seem to mistake what students find interesting with what is personal. Outside the warm intimacy of close friendship or the anonymity of religious confession, not many people are prepared to voice their personal shame. I would suggest that we teachers just don't have the authority to insist that our students reveal their private lives to us or to anyone else.

In addition, there is a serious question as to the significance of some of the assignments. Under what circumstances would anyone ever be expected to explain rather than show how to make a peanut butter and jelly sandwich? The E.T. assignment is cute, if one likes E.T., and there is something to be said for role playing. But why *that* role? Aren't there many others that ultimately are more immediate, more challenging, and more educational?

Assignment (7) is especially interesting because it gives students choices regarding the exact nature of their responses. Initially, this technique may seem very appealing, but closer consideration shows that the teacher isn't doing students a favor here. As is often the case when students have several choices for their responses, the question of validity arises because students will be performing quite different tasks on this assignment, depending on the topic they select.

Although there are several different kinds of "validity," in this case the term refers to the idea that assessment criteria must match what is being measured. In most instances, and clearly in assignment (7), what is being measured isn't simply a broad construct like "writing ability" but is much more specific. For example, topics (a) and (b) call for analyses that substantiate conclusions—a weak form of argumentation—whereas topic (c) calls for simple analysis. Any subsequent assessment of responses will be invalid if even one student makes a selection different from the rest of the class, because the assessment criteria must be different. And if this problem isn't serious enough, we also have the fact that students may be confused when they perceive that they are told they can perform significantly different tasks and still meet the requirements of the assignment.

Developing Sequenced Assignments

In writing classes, the idea of sequencing and building on skills students already have is often linked to Bloom's (1956) taxonomy of educational objectives, which of course owes much to the work of Piaget (1956, 1962). You will remember that Piaget describes children's cognitive development as a movement from the concrete to the abstract, and that he argues that children younger than about 11 are incapable of abstract reasoning. The pedagogical implication of these developmental claims is fairly straightforward: Teachers should give students concrete tasks until they are old enough to work with abstract ones.

This notion has had a major effect on composition pedagogy. In a large number of elementary and middle schools, we simply don't find students working on analysis or exposition, because they are deemed incapable of the level of abstract thought required to carry out the tasks. Instead, they are asked to engage, year after year, in self-expressive discourse of the narrative, descriptive, what-I-did-on-my-summer-vacation variety. For students in high school, we see a sequence that almost always starts students out with narration and description. They then work through the various rhetorical modes of definition, comparison and contrast, analysis, and so forth, until they finally reach argumentation, if there is time left in the semester.

Both the sequence and its rationale are problematic, however. Notice that they reflect very strongly the cognition-influences-language view discussed in Chapter 7. In other words, once students reach a sufficient level of cognitive development, they will be able to practice more demanding discourse modes, such as argumentation. We've already seen that there are numerous reasons for rejecting this view, but here I would add another related specifically to sequencing assignments. As we usually find it embodied in assignment sequences, the cognition-influences-language view seems to suggest that cognitive complexity is the same as rhetorical complexity, that the ability to engage in abstract cognitive tasks is the same as the ability to engage in abstract rhetorical tasks.

Cognition and language, however, are most certainly separate faculties (see Fodor, 1983; Glass, Holyoak, & Santa, 1979; G. Lakoff, 1987). There does appear to be evidence to support the position that, generally speaking, argumentative discourse is cognitively more demanding than, for example, a simple description or narrative report (Williams, 1983). Quite the opposite appears to be true, however, concerning rhetorical complexity: Description and narration are likely to be more rhetorically demanding than argumentation. It would therefore seem a mistake to equate cognitive complexity with rhetorical complexity. In other words, an abstract cognitive task is simply not the same as an abstract rhetorical task.

A Problem with Narratives

If we distinguish cognitive demands from rhetorical ones, the practice of beginning a writing sequence with narration becomes highly questionable. A close analysis shows that *narration* is quite different from what we may think of as "narrative report." We can differentiate them on the basis of *meaning* (what is said) and *message* (what is meant). Narration usually has a message that demands a high level of rhetorical sophistication to convey. Even narratives noted for their entertainment value, such as *Raiders of the Lost Ark* and *Star Wars*, tend to edify as well as entertain, and in this regard their rhetorical demands are great. Narrative reports, on the other hand, are almost entirely meaning. They remind us of Sergeant Friday in the old *Dragnet* TV series: "Give me the facts, Ma'am, just the facts."

We begin to better understand just how great these demands are if we consider narratives in the rhetorical context discussed in Chapter 2. Narratives, like assertions, are claims for a particular representation of reality. (A narrative report simply records reality.) The goal of writers is to get readers to accept the representation. In fact, one measure of a writer's narrative success is the believability or acceptability of his or her representation of reality.

But argumentation is also involved with representations of this sort, although we distinguish argumentative success on the basis of how well writers make their claims acceptable via proofs and support. In other words, when writers make claims, they are simply asserting a representation of reality that they want readers to accept, and the presentation of evidence and the manipulation of warrants (premises) are designed to accomplish this goal. Given this similarity, it seems reasonable to suggest that narration is a special form of argumentation, special because it uses plot and characters to make and support claims in an implicit rather than an explicit manner. Other genres, such as poetry, also appear to fall into this category.

It is extremely difficult to write on the implicit level, and unless you've attempted to convey a message solely through the narrative interaction of people and events, you may not fully appreciate just how hard it is. It's so much easier to write: "The purpose of this paper is . . . ." Yet good narratives don't do that, although good arguments frequently do. What this analysis suggests is that narration may actually be more rhetorically demanding than argumentation, which may help to explain why student writers tend to produce simple narrative reports when asked to produce a personal-experience narration. If narration is rhetorically more demanding than argumentation, then any sequence that includes narratives should place these assignments at the end of the sequence rather than at the beginning. Students would thereby work on tasks that truly allow them to build on skills, moving from less-demanding to more-demanding activities.

A Pragmatic Alternative

So far our discussion suggests that the most common approach to sequencing assignments—starting with narratives and working through to arguments—may be fundamentally flawed. Personal narratives, for example, seem to require a high level of rhetorical sophistication to convey a message implicitly, and our students are unlikely to possess such sophistication, particularly at the beginning of the term. We have already examined the factors that should influence our search for an alternative sequence. Effective writing assignments will be those that require critical thinking, formulation of hypotheses, and syllogistic reasoning, giving students the critical tools necessary to engage in what Paulo Freire and Donald Macedo (1987) refer to as valid "interrogation and analysis."

If, as the first two chapters of this text suggest, our principal task is to help students better understand themselves and the world around them, if, as Giroux (1987, pp. 10–11) suggests, our goal in making students literate is to enable them to "locate themselves in their own histories and in doing so make themselves present as agents in the struggle to expand the possibilities of human life and freedom," we will want to develop a sequence of assignments that, above all, challenges students to think.

Currently, there is no evidence that the traditional approach to sequencing accomplishes this goal. In fact, it often seems that the repetitive nature of the modes approach and the unavoidably arhetorical practice of presenting modes in isolation actually have a negative effect on student perceptions of writing. The endless round of personal narratives, definitions, and comparison/contrasts, for example, fails to offer intellectual challenges to students who understand that there are few demands for autobiography outside the walls of the English class and perhaps even fewer demands for definition essays.

Our discussion of pragmatics has noted that young people use language as a means of social definition. In school and out, they are frequently called upon to analyze and to reach conclusions on the basis of their analysis. Just as frequently, they are called upon to defend their positions. It would therefore seem that a viable sequencing alternative would be related to analyzing and arguing in whole essays. Support for this position comes from writing-across-the-curriculum programs. Numerous program administrators have conducted surveys of teachers in their schools to identify the most common types of writing across subject areas. The consensus is that analysis and argumentation are the two modes students practice most outside composition classes (also see Britton et al., 1975).

It is entirely possible, of course, to argue that the frequency of analysis and argumentation in subjects other than English offers a rationale for focusing on narration and description in composition classes. Britton et al. (1975), for example, suggest that language learning takes place in the intimate environment of the family and that "expressive" discourse, which includes personal narratives, should be encouraged as a means of continuing language development. The problem with this argument, however, is that it assumes that students receive active writing instruction in classes other than English. Yet we have far to go before we see widespread writing instruction in other disciplines. So for the time being, we have a situation where students are asked to engage regularly, at least outside their composition classes, in the two modes of writing in which they receive the least instruction.

Given that the rhetorical aspects of argumentation are relatively straightforward, dealing primarily with matching proofs to audience, a sequence that focuses on it would allow students to practice relatively concrete rhetorical skills. For middle and high school students, you might begin by asking them to use personal experience to support a claim. The next step would be to ask them to develop their own data, perhaps through interviews, direct observation, or simple questionnaires, to support a claim. The final step would be to ask them to use secondary sources (books, magazines, newspapers, and so on) to support a claim. In this kind of sequence, analysis is implicit, as students will analyze support to determine whether it is suitable to the task.

An immediate advantage to focusing on argumentation is that it allows teachers to deal with a range of writing tasks that otherwise would seem unrelated. In the traditional modes sequence, creative writing, essay exams, and research papers don't really have a place because they are not "modes," per se. Yet these are common writing tasks that teachers must face. The pragmatic framework allows us to view each of these tasks as a form of argumentative discourse in which the writer's goal is to establish an acceptable representation of reality or claim. What varies is the type of support available to support the representation or the claim: In the research paper it will be documented sources; in the essay exam it will be information from the class textbook and from the teacher's lectures. Seeing these tasks as inherently argumentative allows for greater pedagogical continuity, because the rhetorical skills students are trying to master are very similar across tasks.

More Sample Assignments

The three assignments that follow, taken from a series of six, reflect how one teacher actually organized an argumentative sequence. They were written for a class of tenth graders:

(8) Last summer the school board met to discuss potential health hazards to students resulting from the growing number of reported AIDS cases. The question before the board was whether or not school nurses in the district should be allowed to distribute condoms to sexually active students who ask for them. Before making a decision this fall, the board wants to hear from the community to weigh the arguments for and against this proposed policy. As a student at this school, you will be directly affected by the board's decision. Based on what you know about the needs of students on this campus, write an essay that will influence the board members to support your position on the proposed policy. Successful papers will be free of surface errors, will provide detailed reasons for your position, and will recognize an alternative point of view. (After we evaluate the final drafts, we will mail the essays to the board.)

(9) In the last assignment, you drew on your own knowledge to support your claim. This assignment asks you to draw on the knowledge of others. Last year three students at this school were suspended for drunkenness on campus. Our principal is very concerned that many students may be doing poorly in their classes because they are often "under the influence." In the superintendent's office there has been talk of random locker searches to cut down on the amount of drinking on campus.

Many parents believe the superintendent is overreacting and are reluctant to support searches. Our principal must consider both sides of the issue before making a decision. Your task on this assignment is to advise the principal. Your advice, however, may not be very influential if you speak solely for yourself. You will therefore want to interview at least ten other students (and perhaps some teachers) to find out their views on the matter. Use their reasons for or against the searches to make your advice more informed and more significant. Successful papers will present findings clearly and objectively; they will include some background information for the reader. (After we evaluate final drafts, we will forward them to the principal for consideration.)

(10) Your last assignment helped you distance yourself from the point you wanted to make by asking you to use other people's views, rather than just your own, to support your position. This assignment will take you one step further in that direction by asking you to go to the library to find books, magazines, or newspaper articles that have information you can use to support a position. Once you complete this assignment, you will be well on your way to mastering the sort of formal, argumentative writing that you may have to use in the future. Keep in mind that written arguments, unlike oral ones, are not so much concerned with "winning" as they are with getting readers to accept your view. Term papers, for example, are opportunities for you to express your views on a particular subject in a reasonable and well supported way. If your reasons are good ones, then a reasonable reader may agree with what you have to say. We all have multiple views because we are connected to many people and many ideas. We have views about history, science, literature, society, government, and romance. Give some thought to the range of views you have and select one that is of particular value to you, then write an argument, supported with information you find in the library, that will get readers to accept your view. Successful papers will be clearly documented; they will use library sources to support your view such that the tone is objective.

You will note that the first two assignments are specific to this teacher's school; they aren't generic. Such specificity will be characteristic of assignments designed to evoke functional responses. They engage students in the world around them as much as possible so as writers they can consider immediate experiences. Also, such assignments take advantage of the fact that much argumentation reflects a need to make a decision about some course of action. The third assignment is far less functional, being essentially the sort of task students are often asked to do in a research paper. It's important to understand, however, how this assignment follows naturally from the other two. The distance between writer and content increases progressively from the first assignment to the last. In addition, the third assignment makes it clear that students are supporting a personal belief, just as they were in the first assignment. This idea is usually absent in most research tasks, even though a majority of the research that people do when writing is conducted with the aim of supporting a personal view or representation of reality.

Collaborative Assignments

An important advantage to setting up work groups is that they increase the opportunities for meaningful collaboration among students. In the pragmatic view of writing, collaboration is a natural part of the writing process because writing is a social action. Thus collaborative assignments move students closer to realistic contexts for composing and are likely to motivate students to do well.

A goal of such assignments is to get students to work together on a group project, and often groups will be in competition because they may be working with the same material. Consider, for example, the following two assignments. The first was written for a class of fifth graders, the second for a class of twelfth graders:

(11) Surveys of young people show that just about everyone would like to be on television reading the evening news. Few will ever get the chance, but it is fun to dream of gathering the news and reporting it. For this paper, you will have the chance to be a reporter. Each group will find a topic about the school or our neighborhood and report on it. Each group member will work on one part of the report, and then the whole group will put the parts together to make a complete paper. After the reports are finished, groups will read them to the class so we can have our own "evening news"! Remember to supply details for every story and to avoid making your report sound like a conversation.

(12) In the minds of most people, an expert is someone who knows all the answers in a given field. This is a common and somewhat misconceived view. But there is another way of looking at things.

> In this alternative view, a knowledgeable person, an expert, isn't one who knows what the answers are, but one who knows what the *questions* are in a given field. On this assignment, each group will be responsible for explaining what the significant questions are in a given field, whether it be criminal law, local government, American history, film, computer technology, or whatever. Divide the work among group members such that everyone has a task and everyone writes part of the report. Give your papers a professional tone. Keep them free of spelling and punctuation mistakes. Be sure to explain the questions in detail, and discuss why they are relevant to all of us.

These assignments illustrate how collaborative assignments can be structured, although we should note that (12) is not as strong as it could be because it fails to inform students what function the task will serve. Generally, the only conceptual problem you may have with collaborative assignments is finding tasks that lend themselves to group work.

Monitoring collaborations is a bit more difficult, because you will have to guard against any effort in each work group to make one or two members responsible for the whole project. Although it is often a good idea to have one member act as a "chief editor" to delegate the work and to oversee combining the several parts into a coherent essay, we want each member to be productive. Perhaps the most effective way to monitor collaborative assignments is to pay careful attention to workshop activities. If you see students who seem idle or who aren't writing, ask them to show you the draft they are working on. If they have little or no work to show, you'll know that some students are trying to shirk their responsibility.

Experience shows that students not only enjoy group projects enormously but also learn a great deal about the writing process from them. They gain a new appreciation of audience, for example, when their ideas, style, and tone have to be compatible with those of the rest of the group.

Relating Writing to the Real World

The pragmatic view of composition instruction suggests that we teachers have to start recognizing the rhetorical nature of written discourse, in part through our assignments, before we can expect students to produce meaningful essays. In other words, meaningful assignments are likely to lead to meaningful writing.

If students were performing a "real" writing task, one arising in the natural context outside school, their writing would be directed by the social conventions of the stimulus. Writing a love letter or making a diary entry, they would automatically take into account such factors as audience, purpose, intention, and tone.

Most school-sponsored writing assignments, however, provide little in the way of context, so student responses often seem pointless, vague, and rambling. Thus we will want to take care to develop into each assignment a context for the response. This doesn't involve simply describing a supposed audience or asking students to role-play. Rather, it involves setting tasks that allow students to do something with their writing other than simply turning it in for a grade. We've already seen in Chapter 1 a useful method of providing a real-world context: arranging for pen pals.

Other methods to help you relate assignments to the world outside the classroom abound. A personal computer and the appropriate software now make it possible to produce, quickly and easily, high-quality copy in either a newspaper or magazine format. Teachers with access to such equipment can organize a publishing program for their writing classes, where student writing is printed for everyone to read. Such programs seem to be particularly successful with elementary students, who are eager to enhance their writing with artwork (some of which can be done on the computer).

Students in junior and senior high can benefit greatly from contact with local businesses, either through field trips or classroom visits by businesspeople, which introduces them to the demands of writing in the workplace. This introduction can be followed by a unit on business writing, where students establish their own company, with the work groups taking on the roles of its various divisions. Assignments can simulate the wide range of written discourse we find in business. In addition, assignments dealing with reports and proposals lend themselves nicely to oral presentations, so teachers can draw on the advantages inherent in a whole-language approach to activities.

Students of all ages can benefit from visits by working writers in the community. Some communities are fortunate to have published poets, essayists, or even novelists as residents, and many times these writers are pleased by invitations to visit schools. Most communities are served by newspapers and radio stations, and it's possible to have journalists, copywriters, or disc jockeys come to talk about their work. Radio disc jockeys are often especially popular, because their music and on-air chatter make them local celebrities. Yet few students are aware of the fact that DJs are often reading a script when broadcasting. This discovery can make a lasting impact on their perception of writing.

Conclusion

For too many years we have mistakenly assumed that all an assignment required was a task that got students writing. Even with the renewed vigor of composition studies over the last dozen or so years, we still often talk about students' writing deficiencies as though the essays they produce are not connected to what we ask them to write, and it seems reasonable that we can do much to improve students' writing by giving them better assignments.

But what is meant by "better assignments"? Many teachers assume it means simply that we search harder to find topics students will be interested in or that we rack our brains thinking up activities that are somehow the ultimate in fun. This view is probably off track. We do want students to be interested in their work, and we should like to think that they may even enjoy it from time to time, but we shouldn't confuse interest and fun with learning. They aren't the same things.

In the account offered in this chapter, better assignments are ones that allow students to do something with their writing. They are assignments that tell students in a direct and straightforward way what they are supposed to write and how they are supposed to write it. They are assignments that exist in a context, or what James Moffett (1968) calls a "universe of discourse." That is, assignments and the responses they generate are linked to the worlds we and our students inhabit—worlds because we teachers are connected to the realms of intellect and reason and history, whereas students are connected to the realms of action and emotion and the moment and iconoclasm. Good assignments will serve as a bridge between those worlds. In them we will ask students to be a little more intellectual and perhaps a little more traditional, and perhaps we will be forced to ask ourselves to be a little *less* traditional.

Functional assignments that evoke functional responses, particularly as reflected in writing-across-the-disciplines programs, suggest that the traditional notions of what it means to "learn how to write" may be generally misconceived. In other words, mastering writing may involve not a generic ability but many specific ones. Exploring this issue, Patricia Bizzell (1987) states that "one learns how to write particular kinds of texts, for particular audiences, in particular languages that may be greatly removed from one's native tongue" (p. 581). If we accept this position, we must not only reevaluate thoroughly the rhetorical nature of our classrooms and our assignments, we must also alter our understanding of what good writers are: people who know how to write many different kinds of texts.

Evaluating this ability will involve something more than writing comments on a paper and then putting a grade on it. As we've already seen, the comments themselves are unlikely to help students improve their skills, and now we are at a point where we have to ask ourselves what our grades mean. What is the relationship between what students do when writing and the grades we give their papers? This is the question explored in the next chapter.

CHAPTER 11

Assessing Writing

Overview

Writing teachers probably devote more time to evaluating students than anyone else in education, yet as Ed White (1986) notes in *Teaching and Assessing Writing*, they generally know little or nothing about assessment. This paradox is made even more problematic, White tells us, by the fact that most writing teachers are arrogant about their ignorance. The net result is that, with some important exceptions, such as the training provided by the National Writing Project, writing assessment in the United States may be characterized as chaotic and unprincipled.

Assessing student papers is one of the most important things we do, because the decisions we make about how we give grades affect students' lives, sometimes significantly. For this reason alone we need to know more about assessment. And certainly if we want to be the best teachers we can be, we will want to understand more clearly what is involved in evaluating writing. An in-depth analysis of writing assessment would fill an entire book; this chapter is intended simply to help you avoid some of the pitfalls associated with grading student papers.

To accomplish this aim, we can examine three factors of the utmost importance to writing teachers: assessment *validity*, assessment *reliability*, and the amount of time grading papers usually involves. Validity is related to matching what we are measuring to what we are teaching and to what our assignments ask students to do. For example, an instructor who devotes much of her class time to teaching grammatical terminology but who grades students on their skill at writing descriptions is involved in invalid assessment. Reliability is related to the consistency of evaluation. If an assessment procedure is reliable, then neither the administrator nor the time of administration will significantly affect evaluation.

Validity in writing assessment is a difficult issue to address, because writing is such a complex behavior. Reliability, however, is strongly influenced by assessment methodology, which is in turn related to the time involved in evaluating student writing. Over the last several years, the field of composition studies has generally adopted *holistic scoring* as a means of increasing reliability and decreasing the time required for evaluation. The chapter addresses the question of reducing the paper load associated with grading writing and then provides a detailed discussion of two popular, time-saving evaluation procedures.

The first, holistic scoring, is a procedure in which compositions are read very rapidly by at least two people who aim at getting an overall impression of the quality of the writing. Reliability is ensured by "socializing" readers, that is, by cooperatively reaching a consensus regarding the characteristics of good writing, as defined in a preestablished *rubric*, or scoring guide. Analyzing writing samples that reflect the characteristics described in the rubric is part of the socialization process, and it ensures a high degree of reliability during assessment. This chapter presents holistic scoring as a method students can use to evaluate their own writing.

The second procedure, portfolio grading, is a variation of holistic scoring and is also highly reliable. Students periodically select the best compositions they have written up to that point and submit them to a group of teachers for evaluation. The teachers then score one another's papers and calculate an average score for the entire portfolio.

Both holistic scoring and portfolio grading can significantly reduce the amount of time it takes to evaluate student writing. Both are also completely compatible with the pragmatic as well as the process approaches to writing instruction.

Validity: What Are We Measuring?

Most researchers who study evaluation have found widespread confusion over what writing teachers are assessing when they give students grades on their papers. Are they measuring "writing ability," or are they measuring students' performance on a given task at a particular time? Many people, both in and out of education, assume that the grade is a measure of writing ability. In fact, you may share this assumption and may never have questioned it. But careful consideration suggests that this assumption may be wrong, or at least simplistic.

We begin to see the difficulties in this assumption when we note the patterns of students' writing growth. Any given class will have good, average, and poor writers. At the end of the term, all the students will show growth, all will have improved their language skills to some degree. But generally the patterns remain the same: Those who were good writers at the beginning of the term may at the end be excellent writers, those who were average writers may now be good writers, and those who were poor writers may now be average writers. In terms of overall writing ability, it's unusual when students skip ability levels. We just don't often find students who start a term as poor writers and end it as excellent writers, perhaps because growth in writing is such a slow, incremental process.

Nevertheless, we often find students of all ability levels whose performance may differ from assignment to assignment or from task to task. Students who have been writing C– papers for weeks will get excited about an idea or a project, will work away at it for days, and will produce B work or better. But then the next assignment finds them really struggling to put together something meaningful. By the same token, students who generally are very good writers will occasionally stumble, producing a paper that is barely passing. In both cases, it is hard to say that the grades on these uncommon papers truly reflect overall writing ability. But they do appear to reflect a degree of success on a particular task.

It may be, of course, that when we add up all of a student's grades at the end of the term we have some indication of overall writing ability, so perhaps we're measuring ability after all. We should note, however, that ability is a comparative concept, which means that in each case we have to match it against something else. University writing teachers experience the reality of ability's comparative nature every fall, when tens of thousands of freshmen enter college having received nothing but A's on all their high school essays. These students are also crushed by the tens of thousands when they can't earn anything higher than a C in freshman composition.

This experience suggests that the terms "good," "average," and "poor" writers are constrained by context. We can apply them with a degree of accuracy only when the group we base our comparisons on is fairly limited and well defined. But if this is the case, then even cumulative or averaged grades may not be true indications of writing ability, at least not in any absolute sense.

What we're left with is the idea that the grades we put on papers are related to performance on a specific task at a given time, not to the broader concept of ability. Indeed, it looks more and more as though writing ability itself is coming to be viewed as the application of quite specific rhetorical skills to equally specific rhetorical situations. In other words, one doesn't simply learn how to write, but rather learns how to write very particular texts for particular audiences (Bizzell, 1987; Faigley et al., 1985).

This isn't to suggest, however, that we *cannot* measure writing ability. But any straightforward effort to do so in a composition class is likely to have undesirable pedagogical consequences.

We know that we can usually determine what a teacher is evaluating by looking at the way he or she teaches, because what one intends to measure will affect methodology (see Faigley et al., 1985; Greenberg, Wiener, & Donovan, 1986). For example, teachers who want to evaluate how successfully students use writing in a social context, how they respond to specific writing situations, and how they revise are likely to use a method that stresses making students feel good about themselves as writers, providing realistic writing situations, and offering ample opportunities for revision. They will probably search for relevant, interesting topics, and they will probably make much use of workshops and conferences, where instruction is as individualized as possible. Grades in this case will reflect a complex array of abilities, such as cooperation with others during group activities, not just writing ability.

Evaluation can also serve a pedagogical function, as when poor writers occasionally receive an average grade on a paper that is barely passing in order for the teacher to build their self-confidence and sense of accomplishment. Evaluation in this case is not a measure of writing ability at all but is, if anything, a pedagogical tool used to manipulate student behavior and attitudes.

If one were concerned strictly with measuring writing ability, there would be no need to consider the relevance of writing assignments, and certainly one wouldn't use grades to manipulate behavior. The chief interest would be in making certain that the assignments were *valid tests* of writing ability. Each assignment would be structured so that the good writers would consistently receive high grades on their responses and the poor writers would consistently receive low grades. The issue would be how accurately the task and the subsequent assessment measure students' abilities.

In trying to determine what we teachers are measuring when we assess writing, we're really dealing with a question of *validity*, or the match between what's being taught and what's being evaluated. It's our responsibility as instructors to give more attention to validity in writing assessment, because it is crucial to just about everything that takes place in a writing class. Quite simply, we need to be certain that we are truly measuring what we believe we are teaching (E. White, 1986).

If, for example, revision is an important part of our instruction on every project, we need some way to account for this skill when we evaluate students' work. Some teachers therefore assign grades or scores to rough drafts, as well as to participation in work groups. This approach has at least two drawbacks, however. First, it reflects an attempt to grade process, even though composing processes appear to differ from person to person and from task to task. There really is no such thing as *the* composing process, and evaluation is only valid when we measure similar student behavior against a preestablished standard. Second, this approach defeats the purpose of formative evaluations by adding a summative component that too easily results in a shift in focus from, for example, having a rough draft to having a good rough draft. Such a shift is significant and counterproductive because it reinforces the erroneous perception students have that the only difference between a first draft and a final draft is neatness.

It seems that a more effective means of evaluating something like revision skill would involve having students submit their rough drafts along with final drafts to allow for comparisons between the revisions and the finished product. By comparing the initial drafts and then matching them against the final draft, one can more clearly evaluate how successfully any given student is grasping the skill being taught. The grade on the final draft, the summative evaluation, would therefore reflect the quality of the finished paper as well as revision skill, because realistically the two are inseparable. In other words, one grade would indicate an overall assessment.

We saw in Chapter 10 how assessment validity can be affected by the way one structures assignments. If teachers give students poorly planned tasks that allow them to choose from a list of topics that call for different kinds of writing, teachers have no principled way to evaluate responses. If one student writes a narrative report and another an argument in response to the same assignment, which may ask for description, our criteria for what constitutes a successful response will vary from essay to essay, seriously compromising evaluation validity. Often students who attempt the more difficult task, the argument, will receive a lower grade on the assignment than they would have received had they performed the easier task and written a narrative report. Under these circumstances, teachers have almost no way of knowing *what* they are measuring.

Reliability

The second problem we face in evaluation is uniformity of assessment, or what is called *reliability*. Suppose, for example, you wrote a paper in one of your English classes that your professor thought was very good. In fact, suppose she thought it was so good she passed it around among her colleagues and asked them to tell her how they liked it—in other words, she asked them to assess it. If her colleagues' assessments are *reliable*, they should all see it as a very good paper. Thus we see that reliability simply describes the degree of consistency from one evaluation to another. But it need not be limited to different evaluators of the same paper: If your professor came across the paper a year or two later, she would still think it was well written, if she is a reliable evaluator.

In our own classrooms, we will want our evaluation of students' writing to be as reliable as possible for several reasons. Students need to know that assessment is consistent and objective, not capricious and subjective. Just as important, we will want reliable evaluations throughout our schools to avoid situations in which a student receives D's on written tasks in one class and A's in another. Unfortunately, reliability doesn't usually occur spontaneously. Unless teachers in a school work together to make their assessments reliable, some students will indeed get high grades on papers in one class and low grades in another, even though their writing remains pretty much the same from teacher to teacher. The problem is that different teachers will look for different things in a well written assignment—hence the inconsistency in evaluation. In such circumstances, students are forced to conclude, quite correctly, that writing assessment is largely subjective, which has the effect of motivating them to write to please the teacher.

Writing for that audience of one, of course, is just another arhetorical exercise that fails to improve discourse skills. A key, then, to better writing performance may well lie in making our assessment more reliable. The only way to accomplish this task, however, is to reach an agreement on what constitutes good writing and what doesn't. As difficult as such agreement may initially appear, it isn't very hard at all. Later in the chapter we'll explore how it's done.

Evaluating Under Curriculum Constraints

We've noted that formative evaluations are crucial to writing improvement because students need immediate feedback when they are engaged in writing tasks, not when the tasks are completed and the opportunity for revision has passed. We've also seen that writing-related tasks, such as revision and group participation, are best evaluated as part of the overall grade for each writing assignment.

Nevertheless, in many districts curriculum constraints may mandate that some writing-related tasks be assessed separately. For example, you may be expected to give grades on spelling, usage, and vocabulary. But teaching spelling and vocabulary without a meaningful context gives students no immediate means of integrating the arhetorical activity (say, memorizing a vocabulary list) with the social action of writing. As a result, they are likely to forget the words on the list shortly after being tested.

You will therefore want to discover ways to relate such tasks directly to writing, while maintaining a separate evaluation. We can outline this procedure using vocabulary words as an example. If your students were writing about the nation's space program as part of a writing-across-the-curriculum effort, you could introduce as part of their background reading a set of new vocabulary words related to space. You could assess students' mastery of the vocabulary items, perhaps through summaries of the reading, and assign grades. You could then ask students to use these words when they wrote essays. Once their compositions were finished, you would assign a separate grade for writing performance that does not include an evaluation of vocabulary items.

This particular approach has the effect not only of expanding students' vocabularies but improving their writing (Duin & Graves, 1987). Your evaluation of the writing-related tasks may in this way be separate from your evaluation of compositions, but the tasks themselves will be well integrated into the context of writing.

When you are expected to directly evaluate usage and so forth, the amount of paper you have to keep track of grows very rapidly. To facilitate collecting, storing, and recording these various components, it's wise to set up a filing system where students may keep their work in folders for each assignment. You may want to use a hanging file for each class member to hold student folders. Each folder will contain all the materials, such as usage handouts, vocabulary items, and rough drafts, that are part of every writing assignment. You should attach a checklist to the inside of the folder for all the materials; as students submit them, you merely check each item off. You can include grade columns for each activity, thereby streamlining the recording process.

Reducing the Paper Load

As important as validity and reliability are, there is a third problem in writing assessment that sometimes gets overlooked. It is the *time* it takes to evaluate student papers. The problem is especially acute at the junior and senior high school levels, where teachers often have as many as three or four writing classes each term. Four classes with an assignment a week creates a crushing paper load. If teachers spend 15 minutes evaluating and commenting on each paper, they will need 30 hours a week to assess them all. Faced with such a paper load, most instructors do not give an assignment each week. But reducing students' writing assignments is not really an acceptable way to reduce the paper load, because students have to write frequently if they are going to improve.

The crux of the problem is the way teachers assess student writing. Most teachers, even those who have adopted a process approach to instruction, use a very traditional grading method. They read each finished paper, writing comments in the margins as they go along, concluding with a summary comment at the end of the essay, then affixing a grade. This process is extremely time consuming, taking anywhere from 15 to 40 minutes a paper. In addition, research over the last 15 years or so suggests that it is a largely ineffectual method, offering little that acts to improve students' writing performance. How, then, should you approach written comments on your students' papers?

Teacher Comments on Papers

Given the labor-intensive nature of writing comments, teachers have only two choices when deciding on a method. They can assign little writing but try to provide very effective written comments, or they can assign much writing but make few, if any, written comments. My classroom observations over the last dozen years have consistently found teachers opting for the first choice.

The rationale for this choice is that comments are an effective pedagogical tool. In theory, the teacher uses them to engage in a kind of discussion with writers, pointing to those things done well, those things done not so well, then offering suggestions and advice not only on how to fix the weak parts of the current paper but on how to improve the next one. Students are expected to study the comments, learn from them, and transfer this learning to other assignments.

When this theory is put into practice, however, several problems arise. Many teachers use abbreviations, such as AWK (for "awkward"), AMB (for "ambiguous"), and MM (for "misplaced modifier"), that students usually find cryptic. Even if a teacher takes the time to teach the various abbreviations and symbols to students, some question remains as to how effective they are pedagogically. Telling students they have misplaced a modifier doesn't really help them understand its proper placement.

Furthermore, it doesn't do students much good to know what's wrong with a paper after the essay is completed and graded. Unless comments are made on a draft that students will revise, they have no chance to incorporate comments into their texts, and they have no chance to practice the immediate skills they are supposed to learn. Of course, once you start marking rough drafts, your work load can increase exponentially, because good papers commonly require three or more drafts.

Moreover, research indicates that students do not use written comments to improve their performance from one paper to the next (Gee, 1972; Hausner, 1976; Schroeder, 1973; Ziv, 1981). In an unpublished study conducted a few years ago, Faye Pitzman at UCLA reported that the only comments students paid attention to were personal ones that reflected an interested reader interacting with the text. Students were likely to remember comments like, "This is an interesting point; it reminds me of . . . ." But they were unlikely to remember comments about organization, rhetorical devices, or surface features.

Part of the problem is that when teachers make comments on final drafts, they almost always use them in an evaluative way to justify their grades, especially low ones. In fact, an informal survey I conducted two years ago showed a definite correlation between the grade a paper received and the amount of red ink applied in comments. The lower the grade, the more red ink. Students quickly learn how this works, so they tend to look at the grade and ignore the comments (see Sommers, 1982; Ziv, 1981).

Regardless of research and theory, however, the pressures to apply comments must be acknowledged. Written comments on student essays are so thoroughly institutionalized that parents, administrators, fellow teachers, and certainly students expect them as a matter of course. To forgo them completely takes a bit of daring, even though everyone concerned may be better for it. If after reading the next sections on alternative grading procedures you still feel compelled to put written comments on papers, the following suggestions may prove helpful.

First, read papers twice, rather than once. The first time you read them, do it very quickly, almost skimming, but not quite—*and make certain that you don't have a pen or pencil in hand.* The goal is to get a sense of the strengths and weaknesses of the papers, to mentally grade them, actually, but without making any marks. When you finish the first paper, compare it with what you think an excellent response should be. Set it aside. Then, as you start on the rest of the essays, compare them not only to your mental model of an excellent response but to one another. As you finish each paper, put it with other papers of similar strength, setting up three stacks, one for excellent, one for adequate, and one for unsatisfactory. (If you feel more comfortable with four stacks, make four, but don't go beyond this number.) When you're finished reading, you will already have graded the papers mentally, and you will have made no marks on them.

The next step is to read the papers a second time, more slowly, making comments in the margins as you read. If you have been successful in your workshops you will already have seen each paper at least once, and you will already have established a dialogue concerning the content and form. Your comments should be continuations of each dialogue. They should be just the sort of things you would tell the writers if they were beside you.

Typical comments will focus on changes students made or failed to make during revisions, what you like about the paper and why, and what impact the content has on you as a reader. They may also take the form of questions similar to those you used when conferring with the writer during the rough-draft stage of the assignment. In any event, it is extremely important that you indeed respond as a real, interested reader during such evaluations, not as a teacher. Remember, the grade is already fixed in your mind, and as a professional you shouldn't allow yourself to be drawn into justifying an evaluation. Also remember that when a final draft is in your hands, instruction is over for that assignment. Any weaknesses you see are better addressed on the first draft of the next task.

Keep comments brief, and avoid entirely any temptation to rewrite any sentences and to engage in any editing by circling spelling, usage, or punctuation errors; these problems should have been corrected during writing workshops. Severe mechanical problems in final drafts indicate that you need to monitor groups more closely. If you include a final comment at the end of the paper, don't put it next to the grade. To emphasize the separation of grade and comments, you may want to put the grade on the back of the paper, where it will be as far away from your writing as possible. Try to limit final comments to three sentences that, like what you put in the margins, focus on either your response to the content of the paper or elements of change that you identify as being linked to workshop revision. As a reasonable goal, try to limit yourself to about five minutes per paper. Spending more time may lead to your overmarking the essay, or to your attempting to justify the grade you are giving it.

Holistic Scoring

Until about 20 years ago, few people gave much thought to methods of evaluating writing. If teachers wanted to determine how well students wrote, they gave an assignment, read the responses, and put grades on them. Occasionally, writing needed to be assessed outside the classroom for large groups of people, as in college entrance examinations. A multiple-choice test was used more often than not, something along the lines of the *Test of Standard Written English*.

Some teachers and researchers, however, were concerned that these traditional methods weren't very effective. Lack of reliability was deemed the biggest problem with classroom assessment, and lack of validity was deemed the biggest problem with large-group assessment. In the latter case, people argued that the only way to measure writing was to ask students to write and that multiple-choice tests were invalid.

In the 1960s, Educational Testing Service (ETS), the group that sponsors the *National Teachers Examination,* the *California Basic Educational Skills Test,* and the *Advanced Placement* tests, decided to explore the possibility of developing a valid and reliable way to evaluate writing. After several years of effort, ETS came up with the method known as *holistic scoring* (see E. White, 1986). It quickly became popular as an effective means of testing large numbers of students, especially at the university level. Since 1977, for example, the

University of Southern California has used holistic scoring to evaluate the final exam—an essay written in response to a text-based stimulus—in freshman composition. About 3,000 students take the exam every semester. Even though each response is read and scored three times, the grading is completed in a single weekend.

Only recently, however, have individual teachers started using holistic scoring in their own classrooms as a means of reducing their paper load while simultaneously increasing the reliability of assessment. This procedure requires training students to accurately evaluate each other's writing and being willing to give students more responsibility for their own success or failure on tasks. Although holistic scoring is used more frequently in junior and senior high schools, growing numbers of elementary-school teachers are using it with their students.

The rewards are significant for everyone involved. An entire batch of essays can be scored in a 50-minute class session, freeing your evenings and weekends that otherwise would be devoted to marking papers. Because they are assessing their own writing, students gain an increased sense of control over their learning, especially if, as recommended, holistic scoring is used in conjunction with writing workshops. And the teacher–student relationship changes. Because the teacher is no longer assigning grades to papers, he or she can be accepted more readily as a resource person, or coach, who can help improve skills.

As the name suggests, holistic scoring involves looking at the whole essay, not just parts of it. It is based on the notion that evaluating writing skill does not consist of measuring a set of subskills, such as knowledge of punctuation conventions, but rather of measuring what Ed White (1986) calls "a unit of expression" (p. 18). Some things are more important than others. For example, quality is more important than quantity, and content and organization are more important than spelling and punctuation.

The goal, then, is to make an overall assessment of the quality of the writing as a whole. Strange as it may initially seem, readers make this assessment more reliably if they read a paper very quickly. Skilled holistic readers will therefore take only about a minute or two to go through a two-page paper. The more time readers take to get through a paper, the more inclined they are to begin mentally editing, focusing on the surface errors. A typical two-to-three-page paper should take student readers no more than four minutes to complete.

The previous discussion of reliability noted that even good writers may receive different assessments from different people, because each evaluator is likely to look for different qualities in a given paper. Thus unless evaluators agree in advance to look for the same qualities during an assessment, there is little chance that their reliability will be high. Holistic scoring solves this problem through a process of "socialization" during which evaluators agree to reach a consensus on a specific set of criteria, called a rubric. (Note that when you provide the rubric with each assignment, there is no need to include assessment criteria in the assignment itself.)

Rubrics for older students usually use a six-point descending scale to gauge the quality of each response. A paper that scores a 6 is very good; one that scores a 2 is not very good at all. But no direct correspondence exists between numeric scores and letter grades. Translating scores into grades is a separate procedure and should not even be discussed as part of a round of holistic scoring.

Organizing Holistic Scoring in the Classroom

A workshop approach to writing instruction will make incorporating holistic scoring into your activities easier, because students will already have been working together in teams before your first scoring session. Note, however, that holistic scoring does not *require* a workshop approach to be successful.

Keep in mind that your student evaluators have to agree on the characteristics of good writing before any scoring can begin, so the first task is to analyze some writing samples that show a range of skill, from good to bad. The object is to begin training students to be more critical readers. As a new teacher, you may need to borrow samples from colleagues if you don't already have some on file. For the first socialization, the most critical to the success of the entire procedure, you will need at least a dozen sample papers, which you will want to evaluate carefully in advance and assign a score on the basis of a rubric you have developed for them. *Remember, the samples must all be on the same topic for valid assessment.*

On a practical note, if you are teaching four writing classes of 25 students each, you will have to photocopy a huge number of pages in order to give each class member a copy of your 12 (minimum) samples. The cost can be daunting, even in a school with a liberal photocopying budget. Making transparencies of the samples for use on an overhead projector is perhaps the easiest way to solve the problem, although it has its difficulties. Handwriting doesn't transfer very well, which means you may have to type the samples. Not only does typing involve additional work, but it may affect students' evaluations of their own papers, unless you insist that students write the majority of their papers out of class and then insist that they be typed. But unless your school is unusually wealthy, the transparency method is probably the best alternative.

Students' existing rhetorical competence will enable them to make accurate assessments of the samples in most instances. At this point, as you are evaluating samples together, you will want to introduce older students to the concept of upper-half and lower-half essays: Upper-half essays are those that can be considered a competent response to the task, lower-half essays can't.

Your role is that of "chief reader." You will use your greater experience with written discourse to help students see why one piece of writing is better than another. This role is vital to the socialization process, because it's common to have students disagree over the merits of a particular paper. They will need you to resolve the disagreements. Also, you will often need to guide students to ensure that their assessments agree with yours, because your assessments will be more informed and therefore more refined. Thus as chief reader you are essentially providing a role model for critical reading. But your guidance in all cases must be persuasive rather than coercive. A rubric is invaluable in this regard, because it objectifies evaluations: A paper is poorly written because it has lower-half characteristics.

As the class is discussing the characteristics of the writing samples, ranking them informally as upper-half and lower-half, you will want to list distinguishing features on the board until a pattern emerges that enables the class to make further distinctions within each category. Some upper-half essays, for example, will be better than others, just as some lower-half essays will be worse than others. The goal is to produce a general outline of the six-point scale that students will use on their rubrics.

This first stage may take four class sessions, and you will probably use all twelve samples. With some classes, socializing may take even longer. It's important that students reach agreement, so try not to rush them. The time certainly isn't wasted, because students are practicing critical-reading skills every time they evaluate samples.

Once students have recognized and practiced their ability to assess writing, they are ready for the next step, which is the introduction of a general rubric you will have written in advance for your course. This general rubric will serve as the basis for the specific rubrics you and the class will develop for each writing assignment. You will probably want to construct your own general rubric, but the examples that follow seem typical for their respective grade levels, and you may want to use one or the other as a model, depending on what age group you teach. The first rubric was developed for an elementary class, the second for a high school class focusing on argumentation:

General Rubric 1

A Very Good Composition:

has a beginning that lets readers know clearly what the composition is about;

gives readers much information;

is interesting;

has fewer than three errors in capitalization and spelling.

A Good Composition:

has a beginning that lets readers know what the composition is about;

gives readers some information;

has at least one interesting point;

has fewer than five errors in capitalization and spelling.

A Composition That Needs More Work:

does not let readers know what the composition is about;

does not give readers much information;

has no interesting points;

has more than five errors in capitalization and spelling.

General Rubric 2

In general, thoughtful, critical responses to the assignment will be placed in the upper half; in addition, those that demonstrate global organizational and argumentative skills will usually be rewarded over those that merely demonstrate sentence-level competence.

UPPER HALF

6-point essays will:

> have a clear aim, a strong introduction that clearly states the thesis to be defended, and a thoughtful conclusion;
>
> effectively recognize the complexities of the topic, thoughtfully addressing more than one of them;
>
> contain strong supporting details and a judicious sense of evidence;
>
> be logically developed and very well organized;
>
> use a tone appropriate to the aim of the response;
>
> show stylistic maturity through sentence variety and paragraph development;
>
> be virtually free of surface and usage errors.

5-point essays will:

> have a clear aim and a strong introduction and conclusion;
>
> effectively recognize the complexities of the topic, addressing more than one of them;
>
> contain supporting details and a good sense of evidence;
>
> be logically developed and well organized;
>
> use a tone appropriate to the aim of the response;
>
> have adequate sentence variety and paragraph development;
>
> lack the verbal felicity or organizational strength of a 6-point essay;
>
> be largely free of surface and usage errors.

4-point essays will:

> have a clear aim and a strong introduction and conclusion;
>
> recognize the complexities of the topic;
>
> contain supporting details and a sense of evidence;
>
> display competence in logical development and organization, although it may exhibit occasional organizational and argumentative weaknesses;

use a tone appropriate to the aim of the response;

display basic competence in sentence variety, paragraph development, and usage.

LOWER HALF

3-point essays will:

acknowledge the complexities of the topic and will attempt to address it, but the response will be weakened by one or more of the following:

lack of a clear aim, thesis, or conclusion;

lack of sufficient support or evidence;

supporting details may be trivial, inappropriate, logically flawed;

flaws in organization/development;

inappropriate tone;

stylistic flaws characterized by lack of sentence variety and/or paragraph development;

frequent usage and/or surface errors.

2-point essays will:

address the topic, but will be weakened by one or more of the following:

thesis may be too general or too specific;

makes a vacuous or trivial argument;

lack of support or evidence;

lack of organization;

inappropriate tone;

serious stylistic flaws;

serious usage and/or surface errors.

1-point essays will:

be seriously flawed in terms of argument, organization, style, or usage/surface errors.

Allow students to review the general rubric for several minutes, then go through it point by point with them to clarify terminology and meaning. If students are working in groups, allow them to discuss the rubric among themselves before proceeding. Next, have them reexamine the sample essays already discussed and, in the case of older students, assign scores to each. If students are in work groups, have each group discuss the assigned scores to resolve disagreements. In cases of disagreement, students should use the rubric as a guide. Finally, use the board to tabulate scores for each paper and compare them with the scores you gave, keeping in mind that your scores serve as anchors to help students adjust their evaluations.

Split Scores

Perfect agreement on any one paper scored by 25 to 30 people is very difficult to achieve, so you should expect some variation in the scores assigned to the samples. For example, suppose you originally gave a paper a score of 4. In class, twelve students give the paper a 5, ten give it a 4, three give it a 6, and two give it a 3. The high and the low scores would be dropped because they are off the norm established by the rubric. The paper would probably receive a final score of 5/4, unless you had compelling reasons for arguing that the paper isn't good enough to rate a 5. This latter situation does occur, because students will often raise scores a point above yours to avoid being critical. A 5/4 score simply indicates that a paper is a weak 5 or a strong 4, depending on one's interpretation.

Such a one-point difference in scores is acceptable in holistic evaluation, and a 5/4 is usually viewed as a single score. A two-point difference, however, is not acceptable. For example, suppose you give a sample a score of 4 and twelve students give it a 6, ten give it a 2, and five give it a 4. In this case, the students who assigned the 6 and the 2 must be directed to pay closer attention to the rubric, for they are off in their assessments, one group assessing the paper too generously, the other assessing it too harshly. In an actual reading, there is a strong chance that this paper will receive one score of 6 and one of 2. Papers with scores that vary by more than a point are called "splits." During actual scoring, splits go to you, the chief reader, for another assessment. You are the final arbiter in such instances. The scores are not simply averaged; you must carefully evaluate the paper and assign a score.

Scoring Student Papers

To reduce subjective factors during scoring, students' names should not appear on their papers. Assign each student a code number at the beginning of the term, recording the number in your record book next to each name. If you are using work groups, you should number them as well. If you have five students in Group 1, their code numbers would be 1-1, 1-2, 1-3, 1-4, and 1-5. Instruct students to use the code number rather than their names whenever they turn in a composition.

You will need to work out a new rubric for each writing assignment you issue, because usually every task will be different and will make different demands on students. Give students copies of the rubric before they begin writing their papers, so that it functions as a concrete guide as they are working on drafts. With the exception of the general rubric, you should involve pupils as much as possible in setting these rubrics, for their participation will give them a greater sense of control over their achievement.

Setting a rubric consists of carefully examining the assignment and reaching a consensus regarding the characteristics of *good, average*, and *weak* responses. The best way to structure the activity is to have on hand at least *three* sample papers written in response to the assignment, although more is preferable. Students can then analyze the papers and work through the rubric on the basis of their analysis of how other students responded to the assignment.

Again, as a new teacher you may find this approach difficult unless you have already established a file of writing samples. Colleagues should once more serve as a valuable resource for papers, as long as you are also willing to use their assignments. If you aren't, or if you are not able to obtain enough samples for both the initial socialization and the first round of assignments, you may want to analyze a professional model that approximates the type of task you plan to assign. This approach has some drawbacks, however. Students are likely to have some difficulty relating the model, and therefore the rubric, to their own writing. In addition, they will have only one sample essay rather than several, which will limit their understanding of the range of possible responses.

Yet the only other alternative is to focus intensely on the assignment and to use your experience with varieties of discourse to help students identify the characteristics they should strive for in their papers. In effect, you help them discover what will characterize an upper-half response and what will characterize a lower-half response.

Setting Anchor Scores

After you have collected students' papers on a given assignment, you will have to resocialize the class. This means you will again need a set of sample papers for students to evaluate. In this instance, however, the set need not be as large as the one you used for the initial socialization because much of what constitutes good writing will already be partially internalized. Three or four samples are usually sufficient. Your aim is to provide samples that illustrate a range of responses, so you will want at least one very good composition, an average one, and a weak one. If you haven't collected samples in advance, you may use student samples pulled from the compositions you are preparing to score.

Selecting samples from the compositions students submit means you have to read all the papers in advance of the scoring. Reading them holistically generally doesn't take very long. Simply read the first paper and mentally evaluate it according to the rubric. Then read another paper and compare it to the previous one. If the papers are of about the same quality, put them together in a pile, but if they differ, put them in separate piles. As you complete each one, put it in a stack of similar papers, so that when you finish you have three, or in some cases four, stacks indicative of quality. Finally, pull a sample paper from each stack, reading it holistically a second time and assigning a score. You won't want to use the work of the same students over and over again, so note in your record book the names of the students whose compositions you chose as samples.

Conducting the Reading

After you have analyzed the anchors and reached a consensus on scores, the class is ready for the actual reading. If you are using work groups, separate the papers by group, giving Group 1 the papers of Group 2, and so forth. With each assignment, alternate the arrangement to avoid any regularity of grouping.

Reliability and validity will be seriously compromised if readers are able to see one another's scores, so you will need some self-adhesive patches—round labels—to cover each score. These are available in stationery stores. When a reader finishes a paper, he or she must affix a patch over the score before passing the composition on for another reading.

Normally, papers are read two times by different students, although some teachers recommend three readings. Huff and Kline (1987) suggest that in a workshop each paper should be read by all the members of each group, but going beyond three readings makes converting scores to letter grades more difficult, because one has to decide in advance what range of scores is acceptable. For example, the one-point difference in scorers' assessments would have to be altered to prevent a paper from receiving scores that range from 1 to 5 in a group of five readers. With three readings, the easiest procedure is simply to add scores. Thus a paper scored 4, 4, 5 would receive a score of 13, a paper scored 2, 3, 4 would receive a score of 9, and so forth. Two readings, however, allow for the easiest conversion of numeric scores to letter grades, without a significant loss in reliability. In fact, several years ago ETS dropped third readings and now uses two on both the *National Teachers Examination* and the *California Basic Educational Skills Test*.

After all the compositions have been scored, direct students to remove the patches covering scores. They should then hand the papers over to you so that you can return them to their owners. Once students have had a minute or two to look at their scores, they should pass them back to you.

Your task at this point is twofold. First, you will need to check scores for any splits (scores that vary by more than one point). These you will have to reassess. Second, it is usually a good idea to read through all the papers one last time to compare the scores the students gave with those you would give. In some cases you may find that a paper has been evaluated incorrectly, and you may want to change the score. Letting students know in advance that you will check their evaluations has a way of making their reading more accurate, and it also tends to make most students feel more comfortable with holistic scoring. They understand that you are there helping guide their judgments.

Converting Numeric Scores to Letter Grades

There are no definite guidelines for converting numeric scores to letter grades, because teachers differ in how they perceive grades. Some teachers, for example, may want a simple assignment: 6 = A, 5 = B, 4–3 = C, 2 = D, and 1 = F. This sort of distribution seems entirely appropriate for most grading situations, but it may make students unhappy, considering that the average grade in most schools seems to hover between a B and a B+.

Generally, it is a good idea to put the score distribution on the board for students. This gives everyone a chance to see how he or she did in comparison with everybody else. If no papers score a 6, students will often be inclined to argue that A grades should begin with the highest score, even if it is a 3. Your task is to explain that it isn't unusual for a class to have no A's on a given assignment and to resist grade inflation as best you can. More often than not, establishing letter grades is a matter of compromise, with you trying to reduce inflation and students trying to increase it.

After going through the process of compromise many times with many different groups of students, it seems that the following grade equivalencies arise again and again. I offer it just to give some idea of the direction the compromise is likely to take:

6 = A	4/5 = B	3 = C-
5/6 = A-	4 = C+	2 = D
5 = B+	4/3 = C	1 = F

Portfolio Grading

Some teachers object to holistic scoring on several grounds. Many believe, with some justification, that putting grading in the hands of students will only aggravate the already bad state of grade inflation. Others believe, again with some justification, that no matter how carefully one socializes students they will never be as accurate in their assessments as teachers, owing to the disparity in maturity and reading experience. Still others are convinced that it's a mistake to grade every composition students produce, because students will be inclined to focus on grades rather than process. And finally, some believe that student writing performance can be assessed accurately only by an outsider, not by the students' teacher or by the students themselves.

Portfolio grading has, in a sense, developed in response to these objections. It is based on holistic scoring procedures in that it involves a rubric, socialization of readers to the rubric, and rapid reading of compositions. It differs, however, in several important respects.

First, portfolio grading requires the participation of several other faculty members. In a typical grading situation, for example, three instructors—*A, B, C*—will evaluate student papers for each other. Teacher *A* grades the papers of teacher *C*; teacher *B* grades the papers of teacher *A*; and teacher *C* grades the papers of teacher *B*. Papers are then exchanged in the opposite direction to obtain the second reading. Ideally, however, the grading group should consist of six members; this enables teachers to avoid a mutual exchange of papers.

Second, to reduce the paper load, students' compositions are not assessed as each one is completed, nor is every paper evaluated. Instead, students keep their work in individual files that are stored in the classroom. After several papers are finished, students select the best three or four, depending on the teacher's directions, for assessment.

Let's assume, for example, that you have students write a paper each week, for a total of 15 compositions each semester. Five weeks into the term, you announce your first grading session and ask students to select the best 3 of their first 5 compositions. (Additional grading sessions would occur during the tenth week and at the end of the term.) These 3 compositions go into a folder along with each assignment and the rubrics you have worked out with students for each task. You then meet with your colleagues, each of you carrying a stack of folders and sample papers. Together you discuss the various rubrics and the sample papers until you reach a consensus on scoring standards. You then exchange stacks of folders and begin scoring, using the six-point scale (or three-point for elementary students) previously described.

After each portfolio has been read twice, the scores on the individual papers are averaged into a single score for the entire portfolio. Thus if a student received 5's on one composition, a 5/4 on the second, and two 4's on the third, his average score would be 4.5. This score would then be converted to a letter grade following the procedure outlined previously.

Portfolio grading has some clear advantages. It forces students to consider readers other than their teacher and their peers as part of their audience. It may make the paper load slightly smaller than holistic scoring, because there's no need to read papers to check student scoring. And it creates a sense of collegiality often missing among faculty members. On the other hand, it presents one obstacle that is frequently difficult to overcome: persuading several other teachers with busy schedules to participate. What should be clear, however, is that either holistic scoring or portfolio grading is a significant improvement over traditional methods of assessment.

Sample Rubrics and Sample Papers

The following sample rubrics and papers are offered to help you better understand how rubrics are used to assess writing. The score—or in the case of the elementary samples, the evaluation—each paper received in holistic assessment is shown at the end of the response:

Assignment 1 (grade 6)

Two years ago, the school board of Ocean View School District voted to ban gum chewing in all schools. At next month's meeting, the board members will evaluate the ban and decide whether or not to make it permanent. Write a composition either for or against gum chewing. Take a position and then support it with good reasons and examples. We will send the finished compositions to the district office so the school board will know how students feel about the ban.

Rubric: Assignment 1

A Very Good Composition:

has a beginning that lets readers know clearly what the composition is about and what the writer's position is;

gives several good reasons for that position;

is interesting;

has fewer than three errors in capitalization and spelling.

A Good Composition:

> has a beginning that lets readers know what the composition is about
>   and what the writer's position is;
>
> gives some good reasons for that position;
>
> has at least one interesting point;
>
> has fewer than five errors in capitalization and spelling.

A Composition That Needs More Work:

> does not let readers know what the composition is about;
>
> does not state the writer's position clearly;
>
> does not give good reasons for why the writer takes that position;
>
> has no interesting points;
>
> has more than five errors in capitalization and spelling.

Sample 1
The Right to Chew Gum

The school board banned gum at school two years ago, probably because gum can be pretty messy if kids spit it on the ground or put it under desks. It banned gum because it believed that students can't be responsible enough to handle gum chewing. I not only disagree with the ban but I disagree with the idea that we aren't responsible.

Lets readers know what the essay is about.

States position.

We know the board has the power to ban gum, but it isn't so clear that it has the right. As long as students act responsible and don't spit their gum on the ground or pop it in class, gum chewing doesn't hurt anyone. It is a private act. We may be kids, but that doesn't mean that we don't have the right to eat what we want or say what we want or chew what we want, as long as it doesn't bother others.

Reasons that support the position.

The problem is that the board never gave us the chance to act responsible. If there was a problem with kids abusing the right to chew gum, the board should have explained the situation to us. It should have told us what would happen if we didn't stop abusing the right. But it didn't do that. Instead it just banned gum chewing without ever talking to us. That isn't fair.

(*A very good composition*)

Sample 2
No gum On Campus!

I agree with the school board's decision to ban gum chewing in Ocean View School District. Chewing gum is real messy. If you spit it on the ground it gets stuck to your feet and you can't get it off your shoes. If you chew it in class it can be real loud so that you can't hear what the teacher is saying. And maybe if you blow bubbles the other kids won't be able to hear either, especially if the bubble pops and makes a loud noise.

States a position, but unlike the previous response there is no introduction to let readers know what the essay is about. We have to infer the purpose of the response from the first sentence.

If teachers step in the gum that you've spit on the ground they can get mad. That means that everybody gets into trouble because one person spit his gum on the ground. That isn't right. Only the one who spit the gum should get into trouble. But if you don't know who spit it in the first place, then I guess it's right that everybody gets punished.

Reasons that support the position.

We're here to learn things and I think that chewing gum in class can keep us from learning. We can get so involved with chewing that gum that we don't pay attention to what the teacher is saying. The next thing you know we end up dumb and we can't find jobs when we grow up and we have to go on welfare.

Chewing gum is just a bad idea. I support the ban.

(*A good composition*)

Sample 3
Chewing Gum

I think the ban on chewing gum is stupid. I have friends in Sunnyside school district and they can chew gum. If they can chew gum, we should be able to chew gum to. It doesn't hurt anything and it's relaxing. Also it keep us from talking in class. It's hard to talk and chew at the same time. So I think the school board should forget about the ban and let us chew gum like my friends in the sunnyside district.

(A composition that needs more work)

The writer assumes that the reader shares the context and therefore knows what the paper is about. This assumption is characteristic of weak responses. Note that there is no background information; from the first sentence we know only that gum has been banned. The reasons offered to support the position are irrelevant and/or trivial.

Assignment 2 (grade 8)

The United States is a country of immigrants. Essentially we all have roots extending somewhere else. Over the last few years, more and more people have become interested in tracing their roots, turning into amateur genealogists. Using all the resources available to you, including interviews with family members, trace your family history as far back as you can and write a report of your investigation, telling readers what you discovered.

Rubric: Assignment 2

6 — A six-point essay will be characterized by all of the following features:

establishes a context for the essay by providing background and
> purpose;

purpose will be easily identifiable, although not stated directly;

addresses the complexities of human behavior;

operates on a very high level of significance;

is rich in detail;

is well organized, easy to follow, easy to read;

tone is entirely appropriate to the task and the audience;

has variation in sentence and paragraph structure;

is virtually free of spelling, punctuation, sentence/paragraph errors.

5 — A five-point essay will be characterized by all of the following features:

　establishes a context for the essay by providing background and
　　purpose;

　purpose will be identifiable, although not stated directly;

　addresses most of the complexities of human behavior;

　addresses significant points;

　has many details;

　is generally well organized, easy to follow, easy to read;

　tone is generally appropriate to the task and the audience;

　is generally free of spelling, punctuation, sentence/paragraph errors.

4 — A four-point essay will be characterized by the following features:

　establishes a context for the essay by providing background and
　　purpose, but the context will not be as detailed as the five-point
　　response;

　purpose may not be easily identifiable;

　addresses some of the complexities of human behavior;

　addresses a few significant points;

　has some details;

　is organized, although may not be as easy to follow as the five-point
　　response;

　tone may occasionally be inappropriate;

　may have occasional spelling, punctuation, or sentence/paragraph
　　errors.

*3 — A three-point essay may be characterized as having some combination
　of the following features:*

　attempts to establish a context for the essay by providing a background;

　attempts to provide an identifiable purpose;

　addresses few of the complexities of human behavior;

　attempts to address at least one significant point, but overall the
　　composition tends to be trivial;

　is not very detailed;

　is not well organized;

　frequent errors in punctuation, spelling, and paragraph structure.

2 — *A two-point essay will significantly compound the problems of the three-point essay.*

1 — *A one-point essay may be characterized by as having some combination of the following features:*

    lacks background;

    the purpose may be unidentifiable or may be stated explicitly;

    lacks details;

    may be off topic;

    fails to address the complexities of human behavior;

    composition is trivial;

    is unorganized and hard to follow;

    uses inappropriate or inconsistent tone;

    serious surface errors in spelling, punctuation, or sentence/paragraph structure.

Sample 4
Realizing the American Dream

I feel very unfortunate not to have known my great-grandfather on my father's side of the family. He passed away in 1972, the year I was born.

His name was Anton, but my mother says everyone called him Poppi. Poppi was born in 1880 in Norway, where he learned to be a tailor by apprenticing himself when he was only 13. At nineteen he was so well trained that he decided to open his own small shop, and during his first year of business he was successful enough to take on two apprentices. But at the end of that year he was ordered to fulfill his military service. Being against war and weapons, he preferred to leave his country rather than serve in the army. In the summer of 1900, he set sail for America.

When he arrived on Ellis Island, he immediately arranged to travel to Minnesota, which at that time had several large Norwegian communities. Knowing almost no English, Poppi felt he would have an easier time surviving among people from

The writer doesn't establish a context for the essay, but the purpose becomes clear as the paper develops: tracing family heritage.

a similar background, people who spoke his
language. With the small sum of money he had
brought with him, he opened another tailor shop.
He owned the shop until 1940, making a modest
living for himself and his wife and children. In
1940 he had to sell the shop because more and
more people were buying ready-made clothes
rather than having them tailored. Without a shop
of his own, he had to find work where he could,
so he and his family moved to St. Paul, where he
worked in several department stores, altering the
ready-made suits and pants customers bought off
the rack.

Note the richness of detail.

Poppi's only daughter married Paul Alphaus,
who was my grandfather and who I always called
Grandpa Alphi. He was born on a farm in Iowa.
Even when he was a young boy he was determined not to become a farmer like his father,
because there was no way to make a good living
on the farm. So while many of the other farm boys
quit school to go to work in the fields, Grandpa
Alphi studied hard and finished high school. After
he finished, he enrolled in a small Lutheran
college not far from his home. He got good grades
and enjoyed the work, but he had to drop out at
the end of his first semester because he ran
out of money—his family couldn't help him,
either.

The writer addresses the complexities of human behavior as called for in the rubric.

Grandpa Alphi was good with numbers,
which may be a reason why he was offered a job
as bookkeeper at a local insurance company. He
worked hard in those early years. He took classes
evenings and on weekends that were offered
through the insurance company, and he studied
banking and investments. Five years latter, after
his studies were finished, he was given an award
for his high grades. He worked at the insurance
company for forty-six years, until the company
went out of business. He then went to work at the
local bank as a senior trust officer, a job he kept
until 1986, when he finally retired at age 79. Living

in a small town made job opportunities scarce, but Grandpa Alphi managed to succeed through determination.

My grandfather on my mother's side was John Walter, who I knew as Pop Pop. He was born in 1915 in Pennsylvania. Pop Pop had to drop out of school after the ninth grade because of the Depression—his family needed him to work and to bring in extra money. Jobs were scarce, but he found work in a lumberyard, where he worked stacking lumber until the war started. Then he began working at a local arsenal making bullets. After a year, he went on to the shipyards in Philadelphia, where he worked as a welder.

After the war, Pop Pop sold jewelry, while in his spare time he made lawn furniture out of scraps of metal, using the welding skill he had picked up during the war. He liked the furniture work so much that he borrowed money to open his own shop, where he made wrought iron railings, furniture, and interior rails. He never seemed to make much money, but somehow he managed to put his two daughters through college. After thirty years of welding, Pop Pop retired, only to die a year later of cancer. On his deathbed he told us not to feel sad, because he had lived a good life and had done just about everything a man could hope for.

The significance of the account becomes clear in this final sentence.

(*Holistic score* = 5)

Sample 5
Mother's Love

During World War II, with all its abandonment and loneliness, Harrison Richards met Mary Rogers. Harrison was from Port Orchard Washington, where, at age 18, he was drafted and sent to Southern California, where he was stationed. Mary was living in San Diego.

They began seeing each other and before long Mary became pregnant at the age of 16. Har-

The writer attempts to establish a context for the essay, but doesn't succeed. We could just as easily be reading the introduction to a short story as to an essay about family history.

rison and Mary got married before the baby was
born because the war was still going on and they
wanted to be married in case Harrison had to leave
for combat. Mary's parents accepted her pregnancy
and the marriage because she was one of their
favorite children. In the hot, dry month of July,
1942, Mary gave birth to a little baby girl she named
Hilda LaVerne and she became a mother for the
first time. Needless to say, at the age of 16 she was
still a child herself and not responsible enough to
handle a child. After the baby was born Harrison
left for the war and was never heard from again. It
had just been a wartime romance for him and he
knew that it was too great a responsibility for him
to handle. Mary didn't even acknowledge that she
had a child, she didn't even want to give the child
Harrison's last name.

 Mary would leave the baby with her brother
and his wife to take while she went out on dates
and late night parties. Mary's sister-in-law showed
more love and attention to the baby than Mary did.
In 1947 Mary decided to give the baby up for
adoption, and her brother and sister-in-law decided
to adopt the baby because they were unable to
have children because she had Scarlet fever as a
child which caused her to get a hysterectomy. They
changed the baby's name to Tonya LaVerne, and
after that Mary never made any attempt to see her.
Mary got remarried in 1955 to Bud Hevert who
owned his own floor covering business. Mary
owned her own beauty shop and was doing good
for herself now that she had given up Hilda. When
Bud and her would come to family get togethers
she wouldn't even act like Hilda, who was now
Tonya, was her real daughter. Even Mary's grandmother, Myrtle Lola Chrissy Moore, treated her like
she wasn't part of the family.

 Mary met a construction worker and began to
see him behind Bud's back. Bud became suspicious
of her because she would work late hours to see
this man and she was always acting tired. One

Note the surface errors.

The writer attempts to address the complexities of human behavior, but the account lacks details.

Note the problematic paragraph development; we should reasonably expect new paragraphs at sentences 3 and 5.

night, in 1966, Bud followed her and waited in the parking lot to see what was going on. He saw the man enter the shop with a six pack so he decided to go in. He found them together in the back room and shot them both dead, then he turned the gun on himself. Tonya was 13 when she found out about being adopted and she has never acknowledged Mary as her mother. She is not ashamed of her and she doesn't hate her for giving her up because she got a mother who would show her the love she needed. Tonya married Wayne my father in 1966 and they had a daughter that they named Trisha in 1972. Tonya gives her daughter the love and attention that a natural mother should give a child but that she received from an adopted mother.

Again, we find poor paragraph development and numerous sentence errors.

(*Holistic score* = 3)

Sample 6
Brothers

The year was 1865 and it was the beginning of the Civil War. Samuel Lloyd was 17 years old. He had never fought in a war before. Now here he was assigned to General Rosser's troop and he was expected to fight and to kill. He had been called in for duty from his West Virginia home and had expected to be in battle within days. However, he and the other troops found themselves marching South for weeks only to see the abandoned burned down plantations and homes of Southern Virginia farmers. They continued this monotony until they reached the border. He found there the action that he had anticipated in the previous weeks.

The writer seems unaware of the audience and what readers may know: We can reasonably assume that most 17-year-olds haven't fought in a war before.

The North fought a long and hard battle. The casualties number almost 600 for the South. As they set out the next morning to head North and take their prisoners to a camp, Sammy Lloyd was called to the back of the line to help a dying

The shift in focus here defeats reader expectations. Given this sentence as the first in this paragraph, readers expect the next sentence

prisoner. While he was approaching the man, he could hear him coughing with all his might in his body. Sammy reached over to roll the man on his back to ease the coughing. As he did so he saw that it was the face of his only brother staring up at him. Sam Lloyd never forgave himself for having been a part of the killing of his own flesh and blood. The war that he so anxiously awaited had brought him nothing but hardship and sorrow and it left him cold and bitter.

to say something about the North, but instead it refers to Southern casualties.

The writer provides nothing to connect the narrative to the assignment.

(*Holistic score* = 2)

Assignment 3 (grade 12)

In the minds of most people, an expert is someone who knows all the answers in a given field. This is a common and somewhat misconceived view. But there is another way of looking at things. In this alternative view, an expert isn't one who knows what the answers are, but one who knows what the *questions* are in a given field. Your task for this assignment is to find out what the questions are in a given field, whether it be math, chemistry, history, or business. Begin by interviewing one of your teachers, asking him or her about the significant questions in the field. Then use the library to get additional information. Your paper should be 3–5 pages. It should not only identify the questions but explain why they are significant, how they are being investigated, and why they are relevant to readers.

Rubric: Assignment 3

6 — A six-point essay will be characterized by all *of the following features:*

It will be well organized: (a) it will clearly introduce the topic and provide an interesting and detailed background for the essay; (b) it will then move to the body of the paper, where it will identify the significant questions, explain in *depth* why they are significant, how the questions affect the field, how the questions are being investigated, and why the questions are relevant to readers; in each case the author will provide abundant details and examples to illustrate his or her points; (c) it will have a conclusion or summation that offers a more explicit statement of relevance;

it will be factual and *highly* informative, providing readers with new information;

it will be coherent; each of the several parts will flow together
smoothly;

the tone will be objective and appropriate to the task;

stylistically, the essay will demonstrate variety in sentence structure and
paragraph development;

the essay will be virtually free of surface errors.

5 — A five-point essay will be characterized by all *of the following features:*

It will be well organized: (a) it will introduce the topic and provide an
interesting background for the essay; (b) it will then move to the
body of the paper, where it will identify the significant questions,
explain why they are significant, how the questions affect the field,
how the questions are being investigated, and why the questions
are relevant to readers; in each case, the author will offer details
and examples to illustrate his or her points; (c) it will have a
conclusion or summation that offers a more explicit statement of
relevance;

it will be factual and informative, providing readers with new
information;

it will be coherent, although the various parts will not flow together as
smoothly as in the six-point essay;

the tone will be objective and appropriate to the task;

stylistically, the essay will demonstrate variety in sentence structure and
paragraph development;

the essay will be largely free of surface errors.

4 — A four-point essay will be characterized by all *of the following features:*

It will be organized: (a) it will introduce the topic and provide a background for the essay; (b) it will then move to the body of the paper,
where it will identify the significant questions, explain why they are
significant, how the questions affect the field, how the questions are
being investigated, and why the questions are relevant to readers;
the author will offer some details and examples to illustrate his or
her points, but they may not always be effective or appropriate; (c)
it will have a conclusion or summation that offers a more explicit
statement of relevance;

it will be factual;

there may be occasional transitional flaws that prevent the various parts from flowing together as smoothly as they should; the tone will be objective;

stylistically, the essay will demonstrate some variety in sentence structure and paragraph development;

the essay may have occasional surface errors.

3 — A three-point essay may be characterized as having one or more *of the following features:*

It will not be well organized, as characterized by *one or more* of the following: (a) it will introduce the topic but will not provide an adequate background for the essay; (b) it will move to the body of the paper, where it will identify the significant questions, but it will fail to explain in much detail why they are significant, how the questions affect the field, how the questions are being investigated, and why the questions are relevant to readers; the author may attempt to offer some examples to illustrate his or her points, but they will generally be ineffective; (c) it will have a conclusion or summation that attempts to offer a more explicit statement of relevance, but the conclusion may be confused or may be merely a repetition of what has already been said;

it will be factual but uninformative, telling readers things they already know;

it will have significant transitional flaws that prevent the various parts from flowing together smoothly;

the tone will be inconsistently objective or inappropriate to the task;

stylistically, the essay will lack variety in sentence structure and paragraph development;

the essay may have frequent surface errors.

2 — A two-point essay may be characterized by as having one or more *of the following features:*

organization will be seriously flawed in that the writer fails to offer adequate background information;

there will be insufficient details in the body of the paper, and the summation may not be relevant to the topic;

the tone may be inconsistent;

the frequency of mechanical errors increases.

1 — A one-point essay may be characterized by as having one or more *of the following features:*

will be unorganized, lacking background and context, details of fact, and a summation;

the tone will be subjective and inappropriate;

the essay will have serious mechanical errors.

Sample 7
Math

When most of us think of mathematics, we think of practical applications, such as using math to balance a checkbook. Such applications of math are used everyday by many different types of people. For example, economists use differential calculus to determine the maximum and minimum points on supply and demand curves. Civil engineers use principles of trigonometry to calculate the tensions on certain beams on truss bridges. Even school teachers use algebra to set bell curves for exams.

The first paragraph supplies a background for the response; it relates math to readers.

But the field of mathematics is actually much more complex. Another aspect of math is theory, which deals with explanations of why mathematical equations and theorums, such as the quadratic equation, work. This side of math is also called pure mathematics. If this pure math cannot be applied, it is virtually useless. Therefore, a very significant question in the field is brought forth: How can pure math be related to applied math?

A good use of a rhetorical device here: thesis, anthesis.

The writer identifies the significant question in the field.

This important question has had a great effect on the field of math. The field has been split into two parts: pure math and applied math. Researchers in pure math deal with theoretical principles and come up with abstract theorums. Although pure math by itself is not practically used, research is very important because it broadens the field of math. A broader field in turn gives applied mathematicians more to work with. Greater importance is being given to applied mathematicians, because they make math useful, by applying it to practical matters. They include research-

Note the effective use of the transition here

ers in many fields, some of which are in the natural sciences, engineering, and business. They in turn broaden many other fields, such as chemistry, economics, and electrical engineering.

The writer explains how the question has affected the field.

Many different approaches have been tried to find a sure method to apply pure math to answer all the questions in a given field. In one technique, trial and error is used to try to apply mathematical principles to a certain case. If a mathematical principle works, it is attempted with many other similar situations. If this approach can be repeated over and over in every case, a formula or equation is derived, which can be applied in practical situations. Unfortunately, this technique does not always work, because the same repetitive steps can rarely be used for all cases. Also, numerous complexities frequently come up, which in turn bring up more questions to be answered.

Here the writer discusses how the question is being addressed in the field.

In another technique, abstract mathematical principles are converted into physical models. These models link the pure math to certain applications. A good example of this method is the differential analyzer. Most problems in physics and engineering involve differential equations. The problem was that in theory the solutions of this type of equation are rarely expressed in term of a finite number and therefore cannot be practically used. But in 1928, an engineer named Vannevan Bush, along with his staff at MIT discovered that when differential equations are applied to physical situations, a finite answer is not necessary if a graphic solution is obtainable. Using this fact, they designed and constructed the first differential analyzer. Today these analyzers are used throughout industry.

In conclusion, how we can relate pure math to applied math is a very significant question, not only in the field of mathematics itself, but also in many other fields. A universal answer to this important question would make many aspects of mathematics more useful. For normal people like you and me, the answer would greatly speed up technology. Many more practical applications would lead to many new inventions and break-throughs that would have a great impact on the way we live.

The writer ends the essay by again relating the topic to readers.

(*Holistic score* = 5/6)

Sample 8
The World of Economics

Most people do not notice that the movies shown during the summer are either comedies, adventures, or teen related, while those played in the winter are dramas and adult comedies. We might wonder why this is. During the summer months, what type of audience can a film bring it? Young people. Also for us, the summer means good times and lots of adventure. Most of us want to keep those good times rolling and do not wish to take on a serious film. This interesting observa-tion has to do with economics, because econom-ics has to do with each and very one of us.

The writer attempts to provide a context for the response, but the connection isn't clear.

The shift in tone here is inappropriate.

Note that the topic is not adequately linked to the introduction; as a result, readers have to make connections for the writer.

The people who create and produce films we watch need to answer three questions before they can get the film rolling. In fact these are the same questions that every nation, economist, business-man, and individual needs to be able to answer, because without them products would not be cre-ated and an economy would not exist. We need to know what to produce, how much to produce, and whom to produce it for.

The question what to produce is significant because if we do not know what to produce, then we won't have certain goods or services. An economy cannot exist without production, and the more products available the stronger the economy and the cheaper the product. The cheaper the product the greater the demand for the product. The more demand means more product sold,

This paragraph marks the beginning of a simple outline organization, in which the writer dis-cusses each of the three questions in turn, without attempting to interconnect them.

which creates a healthier economy. Therefore if we can answer what to produce, more of our wants will be satisfied, the goods and services will be cheaper, and the economy will be growing. This makes us happier and our nation stronger.

However before the good or service can be produced, it must be known for whom you are producing it for. We need to know if there is a market for the product. If there is not a market for the product, there is no reason to produce it. Music groups are a good example. Music groups provide a service however if there is not a demand for their type of music they will not be able to sell albums. If they do not produce a product that is desired, it does not help economy. In fact groups in demand could increase the cost of their material, because they now hold a monopoly on the music that is in demand. This means higher prices for you and me. This question is investigated through market research. These individuals study the market system and predict what is and what will be in demand. This helps companies create future products, which help satisfy our wants and desires.

Although what and for whom to produce it for is known, how much to supply or produce is still unanswered. The less product that is produce the cheaper it is to produce it. For example, it is cheaper to buy the materials to wall paper one room then it is for a whole apartment complex. More materials, supplies, and hired help need to be bought and it takes more time. However, items with little demand are not heavily produced and cost more. For example, there is little demand for dialysis machines, so few are produced. There is a monopoly on these machines because they are needed. So manufacturers can charge as much as they see fit because, although it is small, there is always a demand for it. Therefore, how much product is produce affects the price that you and I

The writer's attempt to relate the topic to readers is not very effective here.

An obvious question at this point: Are readers primarily producers, as the writer suggests, or consumers?
The surface errors are beginning to accumulate.

The writer doesn't make any distinction between marketing and economics.
Again, the attempt to relate the topic to readers isn't very effective.

have to pay. However, we decide how much
demand there is for the product by deciding
whether to purchase it or not.

As it can be determined, these questions are
always being asked and answered. They affect everyone because the products are produce for us
and bought by us. They are investigated through
market systems and market research. These
questions affect the field of economics, because
they are economics. Without these questions,
there would be no products and therefore no
economy. Economics is the study of how goods
and services get produced and how they are
distributed. Consequently the study of what, for
whom, and how much to produce, is economics.
The attempt to answer them gives us the field of
economics.

*Has the writer really
demonstrated this
assertion? No.*

*By the time readers reach
the end of the essay, they
have received essentially
no new information.*

(*Holistic score* = 3)

Sample 9
Questions in french

At one time, people concentrated on learning
as much as possible about their native language.
This was sufficient until society became more
complex and knowing more than one language
was almost essential. As one strolls the isles of a
local grocery store, one notices products with
names derived from the french language. Some
examples are Lean Cuisine, Au Gratin and Le
Jardin, all three of this parents have french words
in their title. The television companies even
broadcast a Perma Soft commercial spoken in
french. These are just two subtle examples used to
show the need to have a knowledge of the french
language is increasing. This has caused many
people to seriously consider or go forth with the
learning of french. One can not simply learn a
language overnight. It requires determination

*Lower-half essays
usually have obvious
surface problems.*

*Readers must ask when
society became so
complex that knowing
more than one language
was essential.*

*Note the suggestion that
readers need to know
French in order to buy
frozen dinners and
perfume. The writer is
clearly struggling.*

*Actually, commercials
are far from being
"subtle."*

along with an effective method. This has raised a very significant question in learning the french language. Despite research, the question still remains of what is the most effective method to adopt in learning the french language.

The writer offers these truisms, but most readers will have a hard time understanding why.

One of the methods of teaching concentrates on grammar translation. This method involves translating from french to english as well as from english to french. Students translate sentences, paragraphs, and even complete sentences. The translations are checked for accuracy in grammar usage, proper word placement in sentences, accent marks, and consistency of the choice of words. This method has advantages but is not free of disadvantages. Since there is little oral work, the students are not familiar with correct pronunciation, the ability to perform well on dictation and communicate with other french speakers. Researchers have found this is an effective method in learning how to read and write the language but feel more oral activities. They also have found through grammar translation, students appear to be able to retain their knowledge of french over a long period of time.

Severe structural errors force readers to guess at exact meaning.

A second method of teaching french involves audio-linguism. This method is based on listening to cassettes of french conversation and students will learn by repetition. There is some written work involved since students are asked to write what is heard on the cassette. The information heard ranges form daily conversation to sentences with specific exceptions in french. Researchers have found this method to be less practical since one is confined to listening to the french spoken and many are bored with this. Since many people learn through repetition, it quite effective.

The final method is communative competence. Their is a great amount of concentration on the ability to understand french in day today situation and the culture. The majority of this would

There is little here to distinguish this "method" from the audio-lingual approach.

include oral work. Students learn greetings, answering and asking questions, interests and information concerning the french culture. There is more emphasis on the ability to be able to say a sentence correctly than the ability to write one. Researchers have found students in this type of class were able to cummnicate but their writing and grammar skills were not quite strong. They felt a student had a liberal education in french but more precision was needed to help the student have a better grasp of the language.

Deciding on which method to adopt in teaching french is an unanswerable task. Choosing one method would satisfy all french students. Researchers have found a certain amount of certains performed will in each method of teaching. Experts in the field of foreign language study feel they are not at liberty to pick a single method because, as mentioned earlier, who is to say which is the best method. Research on the french language continues. There have been many cons found for the communative competence found since many feel the purpose of learning a foreign language is the ability to communicate. Researchers have stated there should always be a purpose behind taking the foreign language. The question remains unanswered concerning the most effective method to adopt in teaching a foreign language.

Readers must ask "why" at this point, considering that the essay set out to provide an answer but obviously failed.

(*Holistic score* = 1/2)

Conclusion

It isn't unusual for writing teachers to ignore assessment issues. Perhaps the problem is that assessment seems too closely associated with the social sciences to be of much interest to those in the humanities. There appears to be little doubt, however, that traditional lack of concern for assessment is destined to change during the next few years.

First, increasing numbers of writing teachers are coming to recognize that almost everything we do in the composition class is linked to evaluation (see E. White, 1986). Indeed, as I stated in the early part of this chapter, what we measure in a writing class will significantly influence how we teach. Second, concern about assessment seems to be growing nationwide. The Reagan administration's report on public education, *A Nation at Risk*, published in 1983, focused attention on the plight of our schools and cited low teacher salaries as a major contributor to the low level of education that has become a national disgrace. As a result, teacher salaries are going up. But the increase in salaries is linked to increased demands for accountability. The only practical means we currently have to effect greater accountability is through greater emphasis on assessment.

Both holistic scoring and portfolio grading already occupy important roles in this new emphasis on assessment, because they have been tested and used for a number of years now. They are far from being perfect measurement devices, of course. Neither effectively addresses questions of validity, for example. Nevertheless, they are extremely useful tools in any writing class, and your job will be easier if you utilize one of them.

APPENDIX 1

Writing Myths

All writers are concerned with form to one degree or another. At the elementary and secondary levels, the focus of writing instruction is often on simply—or perhaps not so simply—producing complete sentences, correct spelling, and correct punctuation.

Generally, as teachers give more and more attention to matters of form, they rely more and more on rules to explain to students what writing is about. These rules can come to regulate every aspect of writing, such as the spelling, number of paragraphs that make an essay, sentence length, and so on. In some classes, the consequences for violating these rules are dire. A misplaced comma or a misspelled word has been enough to earn more than a few students an F on a given assignment.

Accuracy and correctness in form are clearly important. Also, classroom experiences can be trying, as when Suzie or Freddy asks for the twentieth time why commas and periods go inside quotation marks rather than outside. It's just easier to tell them, "Because that's the rule!" Nevertheless, we need to keep in mind that a large part of what we do with writing is governed by conventions—conventions of spelling, genre, and punctuation. Rules too commonly are understood as laws, which they are not. Conventions are quite arbitrary and therefore changeable. At any point it would be possible to hold a punctuation conference of teachers, writers, and publishers to adopt some alternative to what we currently use.

Several rules come not under the heading of *convention* but rather the heading of *myth*. They seem to get passed on from teacher to student year after year. The complete list is longer than I will discuss here; for example, I once worked with a teacher who would not allow his students to begin a sentence with the word *there*. (When students asked one afternoon what the rule *was,* he told them that he couldn't explain the rule, but it was enough that *there* just sounded bad.) I've included those myths that appear to be the most common and widespread.

Sentence Openers

Every year thousands of students are told never to begin a sentence with a coordinating conjunction, such as *and, but,* and *for,* or with the subordinating conjunctions *because* and *since*. The origin of this prohibition probably lies in the fact that many students transfer some speech patterns to writing.

Information supplied by the context of a conversation allows us to use sentences in speech that are shorter than those we characteristically use in writing. Moreover, we often express utterances that aren't sentences at all, in the strict sense, but are simply parts of sentences, which in composition we usually term *fragments*.

If, for example, you were to tell your roommate that you're going to the market this afternoon, and he or she were to ask you why, most likely you would respond with: "Because we're out of milk." This response is not a sentence; it is a *subordinate clause*. It has a subject and a predicate, making it a clause, but the subordinating conjunction *because* makes it a modifier, in this case supplying information related to your reason for going to the market. Since modifiers must modify something, they are dependent, and by definition dependent clauses are not sentences. If you had not taken advantage of context in this exchange, your response to your roommate's question would have been: "I am going to the store because we're out of milk." Here the dependent clause is attached to its independent clause, "I am going to the store." But having already declared your intention to go to the store, you could limit your response to the subordinate clause.

This rather long explanation is designed merely to suggest how prohibitions against certain sentence openers may have originated. The goal may have been to reduce the number of fragments that potentially could be produced when students transfer a pattern very common in speech, like "Because we're out of milk," to writing. Yet the answer to sentence fragments lies in students understanding the nature of sentences, not in arbitrary prohibitions that have no basis in fact. There simply are no rules, conventions, or laws that decree sentences cannot begin with conjunctions.

Actually, sentences in English can begin just about any way one chooses, and this becomes apparent to anyone who looks closely at published writing. Authors will open sentences with *and* or *for* or *because* quite regularly. In an unpublished study of sentence openers that I conducted some years ago on 100 well known authors of fiction and nonfiction, using 500-word excerpted passages, 9 percent of the sentences began with a coordinating conjunction.

Sentence Closers

Even stranger than the prohibition against opening a sentence with a conjunction is the prohibition against ending a sentence with a preposition. There is evidence that this myth has circulated for many years; Winston Churchill is commonly reported to have mockingly responded to the injunction against prepositions by saying: "This is the sort of English up with which I will not put."

Students are often told it is ungrammatical to end a sentence with a preposition, but this is simply not the case. In certain types of constructions, such as questions, English grammar allows for *movement* of prepositions. The two sentences below, for example, mean the same thing and are both grammatical:

(1) In what did you put the flowers?

(2) What did you put the flowers in?

One might argue that (1) is more formal than (2), but one can't argue that it is more "correct." Issues of formality have nothing at all to do with correctness; they are related to "appropriateness," much like questions of dress. Sentence (1) probably sounds a bit awkward to most readers, and it would sound awkward, and probably incorrect, to elementary and high school students.

We shouldn't dismiss the issue of formality, of course. A characteristic of good writers is their ability to move easily from one kind of writing task, and one level of formality, to another. Our students therefore need to be able to adjust to the demands of formal writing. It seems reasonable to suggest, however, that very few writing conditions these days are so formal that (2) would not be just as appropriate as (1).

For inexplicable reasons, people with an overconcern for matters of structure actually spend time thinking up truly ungrammatical constructions that occur when a sentence ends with a preposition. Two I encountered some years back are:

(3) It was really funny, the way which Fred ate in.

(4) We gave money for fame and fame for love up.

We understand these to be versions of:

(3a) It was really funny, the way in which Fred ate.

(4a) We gave up money for fame and fame for love.

The problem here is not particularly complex. The writer of (3) and (4) actually violated English grammar to produce examples of ungrammatical sentences ending with prepositions. English grammar doesn't allow movement of a preposition attached to a pronoun like *which*, except in questions. Furthermore, in (4) the problematic *up* isn't even a preposition. As a particle, it is part of the verb *gave*. Although English grammar does allow particles to move, they can do so only under certain conditions, as in the sentences below:

(5) Fred looked up the number.

(6) Fred looked the number up.

That is, particles can *only* move to the right of the noun that immediately follows the verb + particle phrase.

Students *do* have problems with prepositions, especially nonnative speakers. Producing ungrammatical constructions by putting prepositions at the end of sentences, however, is not one of these problems. Because so many English sentences can and do end with a preposition, passing on the myth that they cannot will only confuse students.

To Be or Not to Be:
Weak Verbs/Strong Verbs

This myth maintains that writers should avoid using forms of *to be*. Very often forms of *to be* are classified as "weak verbs," and all other verb forms are classified as "strong verbs."

The idea that some words are better than others lies at the heart of the weak verb/strong verb myth. A kernel of truth exists here, but it is a truth that must be qualified. Words themselves have no value. They only assume value when they are put together with identifiable intentions in specifiable contexts, thereby achieving specifiable effects. The words that make up our codes of laws are very valuable, as is our Declaration of Independence and our Constitution. The words that make up our literature are valuable not only because they move and inspire the individual human spirit but because they are part of our heritage. The words that we utter in friendship and in love are valuable because they weave the fabric of our lives. But words, in and of themselves, have no value, which makes it highly questionable to propose that some words are better than others. Our first reaction to such a proposal must be, "In what context?"

The origin of this myth lies, perhaps, in the tendency of many young writers to focus on two aspects of their individual realities: first, the existence of things, and, second, the classification of things. The short essay that follows, written by a sixth grader and presented unedited except for name changes, illustrates this focus in a typical manner. The assignment asked students to describe an important experience in their lives:

> The Olympics at my school **were** on June 6, 7, 1986. There **was** a lot of different events and I **was** in a 400 meter relay with three other people. We **were** from South America.
>
> We had very fast runers. They **were** Erica, Peter, Jack, and myself and my name **is** Jason. Peter **was** first to run 100 meters then Erica then Jack, and I **was** anchor. I came in 1st place.
>
> It changed the way people felt about me in a positive way. Now I have races against more people.

The bold type highlights the various uses of *to be;* we see how this verb form establishes existential relations ("The Olympics at my school were on June 6, 7, 1986") and classifications ("We were from South America").

The difficulty the student faces in focusing on existence and class is that he captures none of the excitement that he assuredly felt when he won his race. His tone is that of a police report or an insurance policy (typical narrative reporting). It is inappropriate for this particular assignment. In this case, the various forms of *to be* simply reflect a much larger problem, one related to the purpose of the writing task. The writer doesn't appear to have a solid grasp of what exactly a description of a memorable event is supposed to do.

It's important to note, however, that if the student were asked to write a report or to describe a procedure, then it might be inappropriate for him to use verb forms *other* than *to be*. Blanket injunctions against *to be* forms and characterizations of them as "weak verbs" are therefore not only incorrect but seem to miss the point entirely, which is that good writers are flexible and know how to adapt their prose to fit a given task.

The Poor Passive

Passive constructions are interesting for several reasons. They allow us, for example, to reverse the most common order of subject/object positions in sentences, as in:

(7) Betty kicked the ball.
(7a) The ball was kicked by Betty.

In (7) we have a simple active sentence, where *Betty* is the subject, *kicked* is the verb, and *the ball* is the object or the recipient of the action conveyed by the verb. We might also say that *Betty* is the topic of the sentence. In (7a), however, the situation is different. The terms *subject, verb,* and *object* still apply, but now there are additional words and *Betty* is no longer the topic of the sentence—*the ball* is. Also, there is some question as to whether the meaning of an active sentence changes if one switches it to the passive. In most cases the meaning doesn't appear to change, but in others a strange ambiguity arises:

(8) Everyone at the party spoke a foreign language.
(8a) A foreign language was spoken by everyone at the party.

This section is headed "The Poor Passive" because many students are told they should never use passive constructions, that all sentences should be active, yet as *this* sentence demonstrates, passives are very useful constructions. They allow for a distancing among writer, object, and agent that is essentially mandatory in some forms of writing, and that is tactful and polite in others. They also allow for greater sentence variety.

This isn't to suggest, of course, that students should be told to use nothing but passive constructions, and it's unlikely that they *would* even if encouraged. Most English sentences begin with the subject, and they generally follow a subject/predicate—that is, subject/verb/object—word order. This places a natural constraint on the use of passives. Students who are native speakers have a tacit awareness of this word order by about age eight or nine, so overuse of passives is rarely a problem. In fact, in many cases students don't begin using passives with much regularity in writing until they are told *not* to use them. The irony here is obvious.

Short and Sweet: Misconceptions About Sentence Length

The myth that sentences need to be short and simple to be readable involves a paradox. On the one hand, with the exception of sentence-combining exercises, students are told from sixth grade through college that they should make their sentences as short as possible. On the other hand, all the research related to writing development in children indicates that growing maturity as a writer is reflected in longer constructions (see Hunt, 1965; O'Donnell, Griffin, & Norris, 1967; Dixon, 1970).

We may come closer to understanding this paradox if we consider that one characteristic of immature writing is a compounding of clauses. Fourth graders in Hunt's (1965) study, for example, wrote very long sentences, averaging about 70 words each, because they compounded clauses, generally using the conjunction *and*. The following passage illustrates this sort of compounding. It comes from a sixth grader who was asked to write a response to a recent ban on gum chewing at his school:

> I think children at this school should be able to chew gum and I think it should be for fourth and up because those grades are the more mature grades and they would not spit it on the floor. If you were chewing gum you would not be able to talk but you must throw away your wrappers, and spit out your gum in the trash before recess, lunch, and Physical Education. This morning Rita Brown was chewing gum, the teacher caught her and she didn't get in trouble. You could only chew it, not throw it, or play with it and if it started getting out of hand you could abolish the priviledge.

The sentences in this passage aren't especially long, but they tend to be "run-on"; that is, the student has joined independent clauses with conjunctions, but without the usual comma at each joining. It's easy to see why one might be tempted to tell the student: "Write short sentences!" The student understands where to put a period, if not a comma, so dotting the essay with periods will take care of some of the run-on sentences. However, breaking each of these long sentences into shorter sentences would simply trade one problem for another. If the change were made on the basis of independent clauses, the result would be choppy, at best, as we see in the altered version below of the "Rita Brown" sentence:

> This morning Rita Brown was chewing gum. The teacher caught her. She didn't get in trouble.

The effect is a Dick-and-Jane style that becomes virtually unreadable after a paragraph or two.

Francis Christensen (1967) observed that really good writers, professionals who make a living at writing, don't write short sentences. They write long ones, short ones, and some in between. Students, he noted, usually have little trouble with the last two categories, but they have serious difficulty with long sentences, because the tendency is to engage in compounding with *and* and subordinating with *because* until the sentence approaches gibberish. An important task of the writing teacher, in his view, is to help students master long sentences that truly reflect maturity in writing. The key, according to Christensen, lies in short independent clauses that have modifying constructions attached to them, usually following the clause. Sentence (9) illustrates this principle:

(9) The misconceptions have existed for decades, being passed from teachers to students, year after year.

The independent clause in (9) is *The misconceptions have existed for decades*, and it is followed by two modifying constructions: *being passed from teachers to students* and *year after year*.

Several studies have found a relation between overall writing quality in student essays and sentences that fit the pattern of short independent clause followed by modifiers (see, for example, Nold & Freedman, 1977; Faigley, 1979). These findings suggest that when working with students at the sentence level, teachers should not ask for shorter sentences, but for longer ones with short independent clauses.

Conclusion

The attitudes we bring to teaching and the things we tell our students can have long-lasting effects on their lives. Students seem particularly susceptible to our attitudes and assumptions about writing and writing ability. Our attitudes and assumptions become their attitudes and assumptions. Given the importance of writing, not only to students' education but to their work and place in society, we do them a terrible disservice if we perpetuate the misconceptions that prevent a clear understanding of what writing is about. One of the more difficult problems a teacher can face is the student who has come to believe that he or she can't write and, moreover, can't learn to write. Too often this false assumption is accompanied by a set of "rules" related to sentence structure that can lead to so much attention to form that ideas never have a chance to be developed. Nothing of worth gets written, and the student reinforces his or her own sense of defeat.

As stated at the outset, this appendix discusses only some of the myths that surround writing. The purpose here was not to be comprehensive but to provide a starting point for discussion and learning, to stimulate readers to examine critically their own understanding of what writing is about. It's often said that teachers teach just the way they themselves were taught, and this observation may explain in part why the misconceptions in this appendix have been handed down from generation to generation. In trying to dispel these misconceptions, this appendix dares readers to become risk takers, to challenge their preconceptions about writing.

APPENDIX 2

Sample Essays

The following essays are offered for the purpose of practice evaluations. They were written in class by a group of high school seniors in Southern California who had studied argumentative strategies in English class. They had 45 minutes to complete the task.

For several weeks before the assignment, the community and the campus had been talking about establishing a smoking area for students who smoke. The proposal was controversial, because it is illegal in California for anyone under 18 to buy, possess, or use tobacco. Thus the school would be condoning an illegal activity were it to establish the smoking area.

The writing assignment follows. You are encouraged to use the sample rubrics in Chapter 11 as the basis for a rubric for this task.

> The school principal is proposing to establish a smoking area on campus for students who smoke. In an argumentative essay, take a stand either for or against this proposal. Completed essays will be forwarded to the principal for his consideration. Be certain to state your position clearly after providing appropriate background information. Provide good reasons or support for your position, using convincing details. Finally, include a conclusion that states the significance of the topic for the whole campus.

Essay 1
On Campus Smoking

The fact that more students than ever before are smoking on campus has caused a lot of discussion among students and teachers. Our school newspaper, *The Scroll*, even ran a series of articles about it. On the one hand, smoking is illegal for anyone under 18, so students who smoke, and teachers who let them, are breaking the law. On the other hand, by the time a person reaches high school he/she is old enough to make some decisions on his own, so restricting smoking may be a limitation on his/her rights.

Now the district is toying with the idea of setting up a special area for smokers. The aim is to clear out the restrooms, which would reduce the fire hazard that comes from students lighting up around wastepaper bins that are often overflowing, and to put an end to the silly game of "hide and seek" played out between students and teachers. The students hide to have their cigarettes, and the teachers try to find them.

There's no doubt that the idea seems initially to make sense. Students could be open about their habit. They wouldn't have to sneak around behind the gym or in the restrooms to have a smoke. Nonsmokers would really appreciate being able to walk into the restrooms without choking on the smoke-filled air. Smokers wouldn't have to dodge cars as they rush across the street to Paris Liqour to grab a quick one between classes, which means they would have fewer tardies. They could simply step over to the smoking area, have their cigarette, then go on about their business. Everyone would be happier: students, teachers, and administrators.

What all these good arguments ignore, however, is that existing California law prohibits minors from buying, possessing, or smoking cigarettes. That law isn't likely to change in the near future, considering the clear health problems tobacco causes. Until the law does change, the school district is really in no position to even propose a smoking area, unless administrators want to put themselves in the awkward position of aiding and encouraging criminal behavior among students. That's a bad position to be in, and it comes from their considering a bad idea.

Essay 2

Our school newspaper recently reported that the school district is thinking about setting aside a special area for smokers. I think this is good idea because so many students at W.H.S. smoke. They smoke out in the parking lot or in the restrooms. They smoke out behind the gym or across the street at the liqour store. There are probably more smokers at this school than there are nonsmokers.

The simple truth is that if a teenager wants to smoke there's no way to stop him/her. I know that a lot of parents don't want their kids to smoke, but the kids do it anyway. They are always willing to take a chance of getting caught whenever they want to smoke, because they are as addicted to their cigarettes as a junky is to heroine. Talking to them isn't going to help, neither is having teachers chase them out of the restrooms. All that does is make them resent their teachers more than they already do and make them dispise school more than they already do.

In some ways it's like so many other things that adults do but don't want teenagers to do. Sex is a good example. Grown-ups are all the time telling teenagers they shouldn't have sex, but we do anyway because it feels good and we figure we're old enough to make our own decision about it. And there sure aren't many adults who would give up sex. Sex isn't bad for us if we're in the Pill, so it's our decision regarding what we want to do with our bodies. Alcohol is another example. Adults are always telling us not to drink, that it's bad for us, but those same adults will have a drink before dinner, wine with their meal, and then a nightcap before going to bed.

Smoking is a little more complex because it is bad for our health. But its our lungs and our health problems. In fact, the smoking area would let us smoke away from nonsmokers, so that our cigarettes don't pollute the air for them. All in all, it's a good idea. We are old enough to decide what to do with our bodies. We're going to do it anyway because we're addicted. And it would be good for nonsmokers.

Essay 3
I Don't Think There Should Be a Smoking Area

It seems that everyday we hear another report on the news about how bad smoking is for smokers and nonsmokers around them. Now the principal's office is thinking about putting in a smoking area at Westminster High School. In my opinion, this would be a mistake, and in this essay I'll point out some of the reasons why.

First, the school would in effect be encouraging students to smoke if it set aside this special area. Given the fact that smoking is illegal as well as the fact that it causes lung cancer, heart disease, and emfazima, smokers should be given help to kick their habit. They shouldn't be told by their school that it's o.k. to ruin their health and comit a crime.

Second, we know that cigarette smoke is not only bad for smokers—it's bad for people who don't smoke but who just happen to be standing around. If there was a spot on campus for smokers, what would their nonsmoking friends do? The smokers would probably smoke more freely and more often, which means that they would spend all their free time in the "smoking zone." Their nonsmoking friends sure wouldn't want to be around all that smoke, so they would stay away. The result would be that the smokers and the nonsmokers would rarely talk to each other. Friendships might end, and that wouldn't be good for anyone. As it is now, smokers have to sneek a quick smoke between classes or at lunch, so their nonsmoking friends still have time to be with them.

Finally, a lot of students probably wouldn't use the smoking zone because they would just go back to smoking where they usually do. A lot of students smoke at certain places where they can meet their friends before and after school. Most of them have been doing this for a long time. Why would they change now?

In this essay I have expressed my opinion on a smoking area on campus. As you can see, there are many different reasons why there shouldn't be a smoking spot. It's just a bad idea.

Essay 4
Smoking in the Schools

I think people have a right to smoke, as long as it doesn't bother others, and I would not mind if the schools set up a special place for smokers if the smoke did not effect the other people in the school. If a place for smokers was provided then smokers might stop smoking around people who don't smoke. This is important because many people are allergic to smoke and some of them could become sick.

The place set aside for smokers should in some way keep the smoke away from other areas so that it will not bother other people. We see this all the time in restaurants. In fact, it is now a law that restaurants must have a no-smoking area for people who don't smoke. If someone comes in with a cigarette, they have to sit in the smokers area. If the smoke still bothers someone in the restaurant, the smoker has to put out the cigarette or leave the restaurant. I work at Denny's on weekends and we have this happen all the time. Sometimes the smoker gets mad and refuses to put out the cigarette, but then the manager comes and forces him to either put it out or to leave.

This is a good idea because smoke causes so many diseases and it smells so bad. When I have to work the smoking section I come home with cigarette smoke on my clothes and in my hair. It doesn't do any good to wear a nice perfume because the smoke kills the fragrance so that all any-one can smell is cigarettes. Well the same thing happens at school in the restrooms because of all the girls in there sneaking a smoke. I come out stinking.

As I say, people have the right to smoke, but only if it doesn't bother anyone else. If the place on campus is set up for smokers and the smoke bothers the non-smokers, then the smoking area should be removed and smoking should be stopped in the school altogether.

Essay 5

Smokers seem to be everywhere on this campus. A person can't even go to the toilet without having to wade through clouds of smoke puffed into the air by all the guys hanging out in the restrooms sneaking a cigarette. A designated smoking area might put an end to this problem, but in my opinion it would create more trouble than it's worth.

Let's face it, smoking is a dirty habit that's not only bad for the person smoking but that's bad for the health of any innocent bystanders. In addition, it's illegal for minors to smoke. They aren't even supposed to *have* cigarettes. So what is the school going to do, help students break the law? That's stupid.

Also, think of what a mess a smoking area would be. In my experience, smokers are basically inconsiderate slobs. Rather than use an ashtray, most of them will just drop a butt on the floor. They also don't care where they put their ashes. They'll drop them anywhere. Concentrate a bunch of smokers in one small area, and you'll not only have ashes and butts to contend with, you'll have burned out matches and empty cartons everywhere. If you think covenient trash containers will help, you don't know many smokers. The result will be that our school will look trashy, which would bring the whole schools reputation down.

In all respects, of course, the area would be condouning the illegal possession and use of cigarettes by minors. Those who aren't of age are prohibited by law from buying cigarettes. So why should they be allowed to smoke them on campus? What would the parents of these children think if they didn't allow their son or daughter to smoke, only to find out later that the school districts not only allow them to smoke on campus, but even set up a reserved area for them? I don't think the parent would find this at all amusing.

And finally, there's the second hand smoke. Not only is smoke bad for the smoker but tests show that the second hand smoke is twice as bad for a person to breathe than what is going directly into the lungs of the smoker. If you concentrate all the smokers on this campus in one spot, you're going to generate a whole lot of smoke, and there's no way you're going to prevent it from affecting others. This means that the district would be endangering the lives and well being of innocent bystanders. Those who don't smoke would be getting a bad deal, and the school would be opening itself up to potential law suites.

Given all these reasons, I feel that to allow smoking on campus isn't right and shouldn't even be considered.

Essay 6
Smoking on Campus

The peer pressure applied on students in high school is very hard to cope with. Some people can ignore it, but most cannot. Those who are unfortunate get pulled into doing drugs, promiscuos sex, smoking, and other illegal acts. Probably the worst pressure would be to begin smoking, because unlike drugs it is more or less socially acceptable, and unlike promiscuos sex it is harmful. Cigarette smoking is proven to cause cancer and heart disease. The problem is that teens either don't know this or they don't believe it, so they experiment. This is where the problem starts, because once they try it they get addicted. I therefore feel that giving students a place to smoke is wrong because it will only encourage more students to smoke because of the peer pressure. It may also encourage teens to loiter, and it may turn into a "hang out" where kids can sell and take drugs.

Teens are already under a lot of peer pressure and giving them a place to smoke is almost like saying, "smoking is what everybody does." Everytime they get bored they'll go out to smoke a cigarette. This will probably be thier biggest reason for being tardy to class and for ditching or cutting class. It already is, of course, with teens hanging out in the restrooms and behind the gym. But it could be worse. Also, there is no guarante that this will stop students form smoking where they're not allowed.

Instead of adding to the problem, the school should be trying to do something about it. It should be trying to get teens off cigarettes. It should work on a way of controlling students urge to smoke, ending the addiction.

Maybe then some of these students would concentrate more on learning rather than on sneeking another smoke.

Essay 7
Essay

I think it would be all right if we had a smoking area on campus. I think then the kids wouldn't go the the liquor store and smoke there. It would be a good idea to get the smokers out in the open so the teachers could talk to them about quiting the habbit. This idea is to the bennafit of the people that smok, so they would support this idea.

On the other hand, I think that the smokers only smok to get atention. And having a smok area at school will only make it almost right for the High school kids to smoke. Also they would incorage the people that don't smok to smok too. Then you would just have more of a problum with smoking at Westminster High school. I also think it's a fier hazzard and we shouldnt have that at our school. We have enof to worrie about without this idea.

It is my opinion that there should be a smoking area on campus. If they want to muss up their lives by smoking it all right with me. I think it would be graet to teach the smokers the hard way just because they want to fit in. That way I think people suold be alowed to smok wereever they want or they suold stop selling cijrettes all together and take care of this problum once and for all!!

Essay 8

Upon entering high school students are faced with several important decisions. Among these decisions is whether or not to smoke. There is much pressure put upon the adolescences by their peers to "light up" with most parents having the oppisite veiws. Caught in the middle of this heated battle are the schools. A recent proposition made by the schools is to set aside an area for smoking on the schoolgrounds. Does this mean the school is condoning smoking? Yes, to a very large degree it does. If the students are given this area to use for smoking more students will begin "lighting up." There is no useful reason for such an area, and much to the dismay of may parents this proposition may someday come into affect.

With the awareness of the cancer-causing affects of the cigarettes the schools should be condemning their use. On each package reads a warning label to warn off that person from using the harmful product, yet millions of teenagers, and adults alike, are still smoking. Doctors warn of serious results from smoking, such as lung cancer, deadening of the cilia that lin the throat, and several others as well. Yet still we keep smoking. If areas are set aside in our schools we are leading our children into an addiction from which some may never return. The cons far outweight the pros in this situation, especially those from a medical stand point.

The future of these smoking teenagers is a factor as well. Studies have shown that smoking takes as much as five years off the life of a smoker, and that of those who begun smoking in their teens fewer were able to quit. Some of these students may die of concer before attaining their goals, and take away the contributions they might have put forth.

Essay 9
Smoking Area

I think setting aside an area on campus for students who smoke on their break is the most absurd idea I have ever heard. Smoking is bad enough already as it is and to even encourage it is something school administrators shouldn't be involved in. Most of the teenagers who smoke are too young. A person cannot purchase cigarettes legally until they are eighteen years of age, even though most liquor stores sell them to children well under the legal age.

By establishing this area on campus, smoking would be encouraged more among teenagers because it would be accepted. In no way would this eliminate smoke; high schoolers have thirty-five minutes of lunch to go off campus and smoke to their heart's content. Being an occasional smoker myself, I know that is plenty of time to have a few cigarettes. When there is an urge, even though seldom, I get tempted to spend class in a bathroom stall puffing on a cigarette, so somethimes I do. I never get caught, and if I did it wouldn't be a big deal like possession of drugs such as marijuana, alcohol, cocain, etc.

Smoking is a major cause of many diseases, we all know. So why should teachers, administrators, and the campus police augment the growth and popularity of smoking by providing a "special" place for teens to paractice their habit? Many people die each year of cigarette-related deaths. Smoking causes cancer, emphysema, high blood pressure and underweight babies at birth. These deadly diseases wouldn't show up in teenagers immdiately, but in ten or twnety years from now, many more people would be dying because smoking was accepted so much in the one place where drugs and alcohol weren't. And that's saying to students that smoking is okay.

References

Abbott, V., Black, J., & Smith, E. (1985). The representation of scripts in memory. *Journal of Memory and Language, 24*, 179–199.

Addison, R., & Homme, L. (1965). The reinforcenment of event (RE) menu. *National Society for Programmed Instruction Journal, 5*, 8–9.

Alloway, A., Carroll, J., Emig, J., King, B., Marcotrigiano, I., Smith, J., & Spicer, W. (1979). *The New Jersey writing project.* New Brunswick, NJ: Rutgers University Press.

Amastae, J. (1981). The writing needs of Hispanic students. In B. Cronnell (Ed.), *The writing needs of linguistically different students.* Washington, DC: SWRL Educational Research and Development.

Amastae, J. (1984). The Pan-American Project. In J. Ornstein-Galicia (Ed.), *Form and function in Chicano English.* Rowley, MA: Newbury House.

Anastasi, A. (1980). Culture-free testing. In G. Lindzey (Ed.), *A history of psychology in autobiography* (Vol. 7). San Francisco: W.H. Freeman.

Anastasi, A., & F. Cordova. (1953). Some effects of bilingualism upon the intelligence test performance of Puerto Rican children in New York City. *Journal of Educational Psychology, 44*, 1–19.

Aristotle. (1975). *The "art" of rhetoric* (J. Freese, Trans.). Cambridge, MA: Harvard University Press.

Bailey, R., & Fosheim, R. (Eds.). (1983). *Literacy for life: The demand for reading and writing.* New York: Modern Language Association.

Bain, A. (1866). *English composition and rhetoric.* New York: D. Appleton.

Bamberg, B. (1983). What makes a text coherent? *College Composition and Communication, 34,* 417–429.

Bateman, D., & Zidonis, F. (1966). *The effect of a study of transformational grammar on the writing of ninth and tenth graders.* Champaign, IL: National Council of Teachers of English.

Bates, E. (1976). *Language and context.* New York: Academic Press.

Bates, E. (1979). *The emergence of symbols: Cognition and communication in infancy.* New York: Academic Press.

Bates, E., Camaioni, C., & Volterra, V. (1975). *Communicazione nel primo anno di vita [Communication in the first year of life].* Rome: Mulino.

Baugh, J. (1983). *Black street speech: Its history, structure, and survival.* Austin: University of Texas Press.

Baugh, J. (1984). *Language in use: Readings in sociolinguistics.* Englewood Cliffs, NJ: Prentice-Hall.

Beach, R., & Liebman-Kleine, J. (1986). The writing/reading relationship: Becoming one's own best reader. In B. Petersen (Ed.), *Convergences: Transactions in reading and writing.* Urbana, IL: National Council of Teachers of English.

Beesley, M. (1986). The effects of word processing on elementary students' written compositions: Processes, products, and attitudes. *Dissertation Abstracts International, 47,* 11A.

Berthoff, A. (1981). *The making of meaning: Metaphors, models, and maxims for writing teachers.* Montclair, NJ: Boynton/Cook.

Berthoff, A. (1983). A comment on inquiry and composing. *College English, 45,* 605–606.

Bilingual Education Act. (1968). *United States Statutes at Large, 81,* 817.

Bissex, B. (1980). Patterns of development in writing: A case study. *Theory into Practice, 19,* 197–201.

Bizzell, P. (1984). William Perry and liberal education. *College English, 46,* 447–454.

Bizzell, P. (1987). What can we know, what must we do, what may we hope: Writing assessment. *College English, 49,* 575–584.

Bloom, B. (1956). *Taxonomy of educational objectives: The classification of educational goals.* New York: David McKay.

Bloom, L. (1970). *Language development: Form and function in emerging grammars.* Cambridge, MA: MIT Press.

Bloom, L. (1971). *The social psychology of race relations.* London: Allen & Unwin.

Bloom, L. (1973). *One word at a time: The use of single-word utterances before syntax.* The Hague: Mouton.

Bloomfield, L. (1933). *Language.* New York: Holt, Rinehart and Winston.

Boas, F. (1911). *Handbook of American Indian languages.* Washington, DC: Smithsonian Institution.

Bonner, S. (1977). *Education in ancient Rome: From the elder Cato to the younger Pliny.* Berkeley: University of California Press.

Braddock, R., Lloyd-Jones, R., & Schoer, L. (1963). *Research in written composition.* Champaign, IL: National Council of Teachers of English.

Britton, J., Burgess, T., Martin, N., McLeod, A., & Rosen, H. (1975). *The development of writing abilities (11–18).* London: Macmillan Education Ltd.

Brossell, G. (1983). Rhetorical specification in essay examination topics. *College English, 45,* 165–173.

Brown, G., & Yule, G. (1983). *Discourse analysis.* Cambridge: Cambridge University Press.

Bruck, M., Lambert, W., & Tucker, G. (1974). Bilingual schooling through the elementary grades: The St. Lambert project at grade seven. *Language Learning, 24,* 183–204.

Bruner, J., & Olson, D. (1979). Symbols and texts as the tools of intellect. In *The Psychology of the 20th Century, Vol. VII: Piaget's developmental and cognitive psychology within an extended context.* Zurich: Kindler.

Buffon, G. (1769). *Histoire naturelle générale et particulière [General and particular natural history].* Paris: L'Imprimerie Royale.

Buriel, R. (1975). Cognitive styles among three generations of Mexican American children. *Journal of Cross-Cultural Psychology, 7,* 417–429.

Burke, K. (1931). *Counter-statement.* Berkeley: University of California Press.

Burke, K. (1950). *A rhetoric of motives.* Berkeley: University of California Press.

Calkins, L. (1983). *Lessons from a child.* Exeter, NH: Heinemann.

Callaghan, T. (1978). The effects of sentence-combining exercises on the syntactic maturity, quality of writing, reading ability, and attitudes of ninth grade students. *Dissertation Abstracts International, 39,* 637-A.

Campbell, J. (1959). *The masks of God: Primitive mythology.* New York: Viking.

Caplan, D. (1987). *Neurolinguistics and linguistic aphasiology.* Cambridge: Cambridge University Press.

Caplan, R., & Keech, C. (1980). *Showing-writing: A training program to help students be specific.* Berkeley: University of California Press.

Cattel, R. (1971). The structure of intelligence in relation to the nature–nurture controversy. In R. Cancro (Ed.), *Intelligence.* New York: Grune & Stratton.

Chomsky, C. (1972). Write first, read later. *Childhood Education, 47,* 296–299.

Chomsky, N. (1957). *Syntactic structures.* The Hague: Mouton.

Chomsky, N. (1965). *Aspects of the theory of syntax.* Cambridge, MA: MIT Press.

Chomsky, N. (1968). *Language and mind.* New York: Harcourt Brace Jovanovich.

Chomsky, N. (1975). *Reflections on language.* New York: Pantheon.

Christensen, F. (1967). *Notes toward a new rhetoric: Six essays for teachers.* New York: Harper & Row.

Christiansen, T., & Livermore, G. (1970). A comparison of Anglo-American and Spanish-American children on the WISC. *Journal of Social Psychology, 81,* 9–14.

Cirello, V. (1986). The effect of word processing on the writing abilities of tenth grade remedial writing students. *Dissertation Abstracts International, 47,* 07A.

Clark, E. (1980). Here's the top: Nonlinguistic strategies in the acquisition of orientational terms. *Child Development, 51,* 329–338.

Clark, H., & Clark, E. (1977). *Psychology and language.* New York: Harcourt Brace Jovanovich.

Clark, I. (1986). *Perceived literacy in the home and its impact on the writing of college freshmen.* Unpublished manuscript, University of Southern California.

Clark, W. (1968). An evaluation of two techniques of teaching freshmen composition. *Final Report.* Colorado Springs: Air Force Academy.

Colby, B., & Cole, M. (1976). Culture, memory and narrative. In R. Horton & R. Finnigan (Eds.), *Modes of thought.* New York: Academic Press.

Combs, W. (1977). Sentence-combining practice: Do gains in judgments of writing "quality" persist? *Journal of Educational Research, 70,* 318–321.

Comrie, B. (1978). Ergativity. In W. Lehmann (Ed.), *Syntactic typology: Studies in the phenomenology of language.* Austin: University of Texas Press.

Comrie, B. (1981). *Language universals and linguistic typology.* Chicago: University of Chicago Press.

Conrad, R. (1972). Speech and reading. In J. Ravanaugh & I. Mattingly (Eds.), *Language by ear and eye.* Cambridge, MA: MIT Press.

Cooper, M. (1986). The ecology of writing. *College English, 48,* 364–375.

Corrigan, R. (1978). Language development as related to stage 6 object permanence development. *Journal of Child Language, 5,* 173–189.

Crane, L. (1970). The physiological response to the communication modes: Reading, listening, writing, speaking, and evaluating. *Journal of Communication, 20,* 231–240.

Crawford, J., & Haaland, G. (1972). Predecisional information seeking and subsequent conformity in the social influence process. *Journal of Personality and Social Psychology, 23,* 112–119.

Crowhurst, M., & Piche, G. (1979). Audience and mode of discourse effects on syntactic complexity in writing at two grade levels. *Research in the Teaching of English, 13,* 101–109.

Cummins, J. (1976). The influence of bilingualism on cognitive growth: A synthesis of research findings and explanatory hypothesis. *Working Papers on Bilingualism, 9*, 1–43.

Daiker, D., Kerek, A., & Morenberg, M. (1978). Sentence-combining and syntactic maturity in freshman English. *College Composition and Communication, 29*, 36–41.

Dance, F., & Larson, C. (1972). *Speech communication: Concepts and behavior.* New York: Holt, Rinehart and Winston.

Day, P., & Ulatowska, H. (1979). Perceptual, cognitive, and linguistic development after early hemispherectomy: Two case studies. *Brain and Language, 7*, 17–33.

Dennis, M., & Kohn, B. (1975). Comprehension of syntax in infantile hemiplegics after cerebral hemidecortication: Left hemisphere superiority. *Brain and Language, 2*, 475–486.

Dennis, M., & Whitaker, H. (1976). Language acquisition following hemidecortication: Linguistic superiority of the left over the right hemisphere of right-handed people. *Brain and Language, 3*, 404–433.

Diaz, D. (1986). The writing process and the ESL writer: Reinforcement from second language research. *Writing Instructor, 5*, 167–175.

Dillard, J. L. (1973). *Black English: Its history and usage in the United States.* New York: Vintage Books.

Dillon, G. (1981). *Constructing texts: Elements of a theory of composition and style.* Bloomington: Indiana University Press.

Dixon, E. (1970). Syntactic indexes and student writing performance. Unpublished doctoral dissertation, University of Chicago.

Donaldson, M. (1978). *Children's minds.* London: Fontana.

Donelson, K. (1967). Variables distinguishing between effective and ineffective writers in the tenth grade. *Journal of Experimental Education, 35*, 37–41.

Duin, A., & Graves, M. (1987). Intensive vocabulary instruction as a prewriting technique. *Reading Research Quarterly, 22*, 311–330.

Dulay, H., Burt, M., & Krashen, S. (1982). *Language two.* New York: Oxford University Press.

Duncan, S., & De Avila, E. (1979). Bilingualism and cognition: Some recent findings. *NABE Journal, 4*, 15–50.

Dyson, A. (1982). The emergence of visible language: The interrelationship between drawing and early writing. *Visible Language, 16*, 360–381.

Dyson, A. (1983). The role of oral language in early writing processes. *Research in the Teaching of English, 17*, 1–30.

Edelsky, C. (1986). *Writing in a bilingual program: Había una vez.* Norwood, NJ: Ablex.

Edfelt, A. (1960). *Silent speech and silent reading.* Chicago: University of Chicago Press.

Elbow, P. (1973). *Writing without teachers.* Oxford: Oxford University Press.

Elbow, P. (1983). Embracing contraries in the teaching process. *College English, 45,* 327–339.

Elley, W., Barham, I., Lamb, H., & Wyllie, M. (1976). The role of grammar in a secondary school English curriculum. *New Zealand Journal of Educational Studies, 10* (1), 26–42. Reprinted in *Research in the Teaching of English, 10,* 5–21.

Emig, J. (1971). *The composing process of twelfth graders.* Urbana, IL: National Council of Teachers of English.

Epstein, H. (1978). Growth spurts during brain development: Implications for educational policy and practice. In J. Chall & A. Mirsky (Eds.), *Education and the brain (Vol. 2).* Chicago: University of Chicago Press.

Erickson, F. (1984). Rhetoric, anecdote, and rhapsody: Coherence strategies in a conversation among black American adolescents. In D. Tannen (Ed.), *Coherence in spoken and written discourse.* Norwood, NJ: Ablex.

Faigley, L. (1979). Another look at sentences. *Freshman English News, 7* (3), 18–21.

Faigley, L. (1986). Competing theories of process: A critique and a proposal. *College English, 48,* 527–542.

Faigley, L., Cherry, R., Joliffe, D., & Skinner, A. (1985). *Assessing writers' knowledge and processes of composing.* Norwood, NJ: Ablex.

Farr, M., & Daniels, H. (1986). *Language diversity and writing instruction.* Urbana, IL: National Council of Teachers of English.

Farr, M., & Janda, M. (1985). Basic writing students: Investigating oral and written language. *Research in the Teaching of English, 19,* 62–83.

Farr Whitemann, M. (Ed.). (1981). *Variation in writing: Functional and linguistic–cultural differences.* Hillsdale, NJ: Lawrence Erlbaum.

Fasold, R. (1972). *Tense marking in Black English: A linguistic and social analysis.* Washington, DC: Center for Applied Linguistics.

Ferguson, C. (1977). Learning to pronounce: The earliest stages of phonological development in the child. In F. Minifie & L. Lloyd (Eds.), *Communication and cognitive abilities: Early behavioral assessment.* Baltimore: University Park Press.

Ferreiro, E., & Teberosky, A. (1982). *Literacy before schooling.* London: Heinemann.

Finegan, E. (1980). *Attitudes toward English usage: The history of a war of words.* New York: Teachers College Press, Columbia University.

Finnegan, R. (1970). *Oral literature in Africa.* London: Oxford University Press.

Finocchiaro, M. (1986). *English as a second language: From theory to practice.* New York: Regents.

Flavell, J. (1985). *Cognitive development.* Englewood Cliffs, NJ: Prentice-Hall.

Flavell, J., Botkin, P., Fry, C., Wright, J., & Jarvis, P. (1968). *The development of role-taking and communication skills in children.* New York: Wiley.

Flesch, R. (1955). *Why Johnny can't read—and what you can do about it.* New York: Harper.

Flinn, J. (1986). The role of instruction in revising with computers: Forming a construct for "good writing." (ERIC Document Reproduction Service No. ED 274 963.)

Flower, L., & Hayes, J. (1981). The pregnant pause: An inquiry into the nature of planning. *Research in the Teaching of English, 15,* 229–243.

Fodor, J. (1983). *The modularity of mind.* Cambridge, MA: MIT Press.

Fodor, J., Bever, T., & Garrett, M. (1974). *The psychology of language.* New York: McGraw-Hill.

Foster, S. (1985a). Linguistics and the writing instructor. *Writing Instructor, 4,* 108–112.

Foster, S. (1985b). The development of discourse topic skills by infants and young children. *Topics in Language Disorders,* March, 31–45.

Freire, P., & Macedo, D. (1987). *Literacy: Reading the word and the world.* South Hadley, MA: Bergin & Garvey.

Fries, C. (1962). *Linguistics and reading.* New York: Holt, Rinehart and Winston.

Furth, H. (1966). *Thinking without language: Psychological implications of deafness.* New York: Free Press.

Gale, I. F. (1968). An experimental study of two fifth-grade language-arts programs: An analysis of the writing of children taught linguistic grammar compared to those taught traditional grammar. *Dissertation Abstracts, 28,* 4156-A.

Garcia, E. (1983). *Early childhood bilingualism.* Albuquerque: University of New Mexico Press.

Gardner, R. C. (1980). On the validity of affective variables in second language acquisition: Conceptual, contextual, and statistical considerations. *Language Learning, 30,* 255–270.

Gardner, R. C. (1983). Learning another language: A true social psychological experiment. *Journal of Language and Social Psychology, 2,* 219–239.

Garibaldi, A. (1979). Teamwork and feedback: Broadening the base of collaborative writing. Paper presented at the annual meeting of the Conference on College Composition and Communication. (ERIC Document Reproduction Service No. ED 174 994.)

Gauntlett, J. (1978). Project WRITE and its effect on the writing of high school students. *Dissertation Abstracts International, 38,* 7189-A.

Gazdar, G., Klein, E., Pullum, G., & Sag, I. (1985). *Generalized phrase structure grammar.* Cambridge, MA: Harvard University Press.

Gee, T. (1972). Students' responses to teachers' comments. *Research in the Teaching of English, 6,* 212–221.

Genishi, C. (1981). Code switching in Chicano six-year-olds. In R. Duran (Ed.), *Latino language and communicative behavior.* Norwood, NJ: Ablex.

Gibson, E., & Levin, H. (1975). *The psychology of reading.* Cambridge, MA: MIT Press.

Giroux, H. (1983). *Theory and resistance in education: A pedagogy for the opposition.* South Hadley, MA: Bergin & Garvey.

Giroux, H. (1987). Literacy and the pedagogy of political empowerment. In P. Freire & D. Macedo, *Literacy: Reading the word and the world.* South Hadley, MA: Bergin & Garvey.

Glass, A., Holyoak, K., & Santa, J. (1979). *Cognition.* Reading, MA: Addison-Wesley.

Goodlad, J. (1984). *A place called school: Prospects for the future.* New York: McGraw-Hill.

Goodman, K. (1967). Reading: A psycholinguistic guessing game. *Journal of the Reading Specialist, 6,* 126–135.

Goodman, K. (1973). *Miscue analysis.* Urbana, IL: ERIC Clearinghouse on Reading and Communication Skills.

Goody, J. (Ed.). (1968). *Literacy in traditional societies.* Cambridge: Cambridge University Press.

Goody, J. (1972). Literacy and the non-literate. *Times Literary Supplement* (May 12). Reprinted in R. Disch (Ed.), *The future of literacy.* Englewood Cliffs, NJ: Prentice-Hall.

Goody, J. (1977). *The domestication of the savage mind.* Cambridge: Cambridge University Press.

Goody, J., & Watt, I. (1968). The consequences of literacy. In J. Goody (Ed.), *Literacy in traditional societies.* Cambridge: Cambridge University Press.

Graves, D. (1975). Examination of the writing processes of seven year old children. *Research in the Teaching of English, 9,* 227–241.

Graves, D. (1979). Let children show us how to help them write. *Visible Language, 13,* 16–28.

Graves, D. (1981). The growth and development of first grade writers. In D. Graves (Ed.), A case study observing the development of primary children's composing, spelling, and motor behaviors during the writing process. *Final Report.* Durham: University of New Hampshire Press.

Green, E. (1973). An experimental study of sentence-combining to improve written syntactic fluency in fifth-grade children. *Dissertation Abstracts International, 33,* 4057-A.

Greenberg, K., Wiener, H., & Donovan, T. (Eds.). (1986). *Writing assessment: Issues and strategies.* New York: Longman.

Greenfield, P. (1972). Oral or written language: The consequences for cognitive development in Africa, the United States and England. *Language and Speech, 15,* 169–177.

Greenfield, P., & Bruner, J. (1966). Culture and cognitive growth. *International Journal of Psychology, 1,* 23–59.

Grice, P. (1975). Logic and conversation. In P. Cole & J. Morgan (Eds.), *Syntax and semantics* (Vol. 3). Norwood, NJ: Ablex.

Griswold del Castillo, R. (1984). *La familia: Chicano families in the urban Southwest, 1848 to the present.* Notre Dame, IN: Notre Dame University Press.

Gumperz, J. J. (1976). The sociolinguistic significance of conversational code switching. *Working Paper No. 46.* Language Behavior Research Lab. Berkeley: University of California Press.

Gumperz, J. J. (1982). *Discourse strategies.* Cambridge: Cambridge University Press.

Gunderson, B., & Johnson, D. (1980). Promoting positive attitudes toward learning a foreign language by using cooperative learning groups. *Foreign Language Annuals, 13,* 39–46.

Gundlach, R. (1981). On the nature and development of children's writing. In C. Frederiksen, M. Whiteman, & J. Dominic (Eds.), *Writing: The nature, development, and teaching of written communication.* Hillsdale, NJ: Lawrence Erlbaum.

Gundlach, R. (1982). Children as writers: The beginnings of learning to write. In M. Nystrand (Ed.), *What writers know: The language, process, and structure of written discourse.* New York: Academic Press.

Gundlach, R. (1983). *How children learn to write: Perspectives on children's writing for educators and parents.* Washington, DC: National Institute of Education.

Guthrie, W. (1971). *The Sophists.* Cambridge: Cambridge University Press.

Hakuta, K. (1984). Bilingual education in the public eye: A case study of New Haven, Connecticut. *NABE Journal, 9,* 53–76.

Hakuta, K. (1986). *Mirror of language.* New York: Basic Books.

Hakuta, K., & Diaz, R. (1984). The relationship between bilingualism and cognitive ability: A critical discussion and some new longitudinal data. In K. Nelson (Ed.), *Children's language* (Vol. 5). Hillsdale, NJ: Lawrence Erlbaum.

Hall, M. (1972). *The language experience approach for the culturally disadvantaged.* Newark, DE: International Reading Association.

Halliday, M. (1973). *Explorations in the functions of language.* London: Edward Arnold.

Halliday, M. (1979). One child's protolanguage. In M. Bullowa (Ed.), *Before speech.* Cambridge: Cambridge University Press.

Hammer, D. (1986). The effectiveness of computer-assisted writing instruction for juniors who have failed the regents competency test in writing. *Dissertation Abstracts International, 47,* 11A.

Harder, B. (1984). Cultural attitudes and discourse analysis. *Canadian Journal of Linguistics, 29,* 115–130.

Hardyck, C., & Petrinovich, L. (1967). Subvocal speech and comprehension level as a function of the difficulty level of reading material. *Journal of Verbal Learning and Verbal Behavior, 9,* 647–652.

Harste, J., Burke, C., & Woodward, V. (1983). *Children's language and world: Initial encounters with print.* (Final Report NIE-G-79-0132.) Bloomington, IN: Language Education Departments.

Harter, M. T. (1978). A study of the effects of transformational grammar on the writing skills of seventh graders. *Dissertation Abstracts International, 39,* 2794-A.

Harter, S. (1981). A model of intrinsic mastery motivation in children: Individual differences and developmental change. In A. Collins (Ed.), *Minnesota Symposium on Child Psychology, 14.* Hillsdale, NJ: Lawrence Erlbaum.

Harter, S., & Connell, J. (1981). A model of the relationship among children's academic achievement and their self-perceptions of competence, control, and motivational orientation. In J. Nicholls (Ed.), *The development of achievement motivation.* Greenwich, CT: JAI Press.

Hatch, E. (1978). *Second language acquisition: A book of readings.* Rowley, MA: Newbury House.

Haugen, E. (1966). *Language conflict and language planning: The case of modern Norwegian.* Cambridge, MA: Harvard University Press.

Hausner, R. (1976). Interaction of selected student personality factors and teachers' comments in a sequentially-developed composition curriculum. *Dissertation Abstracts International, 36,* 5768-A.

Hawisher, G. (1987). The effects of word processing on the revision strategies of college freshmen. *Research in the Teaching of English, 21,* 145–159.

Hawkins, T. (1980). The relationship between revision and the social dimension of peer tutoring. *College English, 40,* 64-68.

Heath, S. (1981). *Language in the USA.* Cambridge: Cambridge University Press.

Heath, S. (1983). *Ways with words.* Cambridge: Cambridge University Press.

Hillocks, G. (1986). *Research on written composition: New directions for teaching.* Urbana, IL: National Conference on Research in English.

Hirsch, E. (1977). *The philosophy of composition.* Chicago: University of Chicago Press.

Hoffer, B. (1975). Spanish interference in the English written in South Texas high schools. In E. Dubois & B. Hoffer (Eds.), *Papers in Southwest English: Research techniques and prospects.* San Antonio, TX: Trinity University Press.

Holzman, M. (1986). The social context of literacy education. *College English, 48,* 27–33.

Howie, S. (1979). A study: The effects of sentence combining practice on the writing ability and reading level of ninth grade students. *Dissertation Abstracts International, 40,* 1980-A.

Hudson, R. (1980). *Sociolinguistics.* Cambridge: Cambridge University Press.

Huff, R., & Kline, C. (1987). *The contemporary writing curriculum: Rehearsing, composing, and valuing.* New York: Teachers College Press, Columbia University.

Hughes, M. (1975). Egocentrism in pre-school children. Unpublished doctoral dissertation, Edinburgh University.

Hunt, J. (1975). Reflections on a decade of early education. *Journal of Abnormal Child Psychology, 3,* 275–336.

Hunt, K. (1965). *Grammatical structures written at three grade levels.* NCTE Research Report Number 3. Champaign, IL: National Council of Teachers of English.

Hymes, D. (1971). Competence and performance in linguistic theory. In R. Huxley & E. Ingram (Eds.), *Language acquisition: Models and methods.* New York: Academic Press.

Jencks, C. (1972). *Inequality: A reassessment of the effect of family and schooling in America.* New York: Basic Books.

Jensen, A. (1969). How much can we boost IQ and scholastic achievement? *Harvard Educational Review, 39,* 1–123.

Johnson, B. (1980). *The critical difference: Essays in the contemporary rhetoric of reading.* Baltimore: Johns Hopkins.

Johnson, D. (1980). Group processes: Influences of student-vs-student interaction on school outcomes. In J. McMillan (Ed.), *The social psychology of school learning.* New York: Holt, Rinehart and Winston.

Johnson, D., & Ahlgren, A. (1976). Relationship between students' attitudes about cooperation and competition and attitudes toward schooling. *Journal of Educational Psychology, 68,* 92–102.

Johnson, D., Johnson, R., & Maruyama, G. (1983). Interdependence and interpersonal attraction among heterogeneous and homogeneous individuals: A theoretical formulation and a meta-analysis of the research. *Review of Educational Research, 53*(1), 5–54.

Johnson, D., Maruyama, G., Johnson, R., Nelson, D., & Skon, L. (1981). The effects of cooperative, competitive, and individualistic goal structures on achievement: A meta-analysis. *Psychology Bulletin, 89*(1), 47–62.

Johnson, T., & Louis, D. (1985). *Literacy through literature.* Melbourne: Methuen Australia.

Johnson-Laird, P. (1983). *Mental models.* Cambridge, MA: Harvard University Press.

Jones, S. (1982). Attention to rhetorical information while composing in a second language. Proceedings of the 4th Los Angeles Second Language Research Forum.

Jones, S., & Tetroe, J. (1983). Composing in a second language. In A. Matsuhashi (Ed.), *Writing in real time.* Norwood, NJ: Ablex.

Kagan, S., & Buriel, R. (1977). Field dependence-independence and Mexican-American culture and education. In J. Martinez (Ed.), *Chicano psychology.* New York: Academic Press.

Kagan, S., & Zahn, G. (1975). Field dependence and the school achievement gap between Anglo-American and Mexican-American children. *Journal of Educational Psychology, 67,* 643–650.

Kantor, K. (1985). Questions, explorations, and discoveries. *English Journal, 74,* 90–92.

Kaplan, R. (1972). *The anatomy of rhetoric: Prolegomena to a functional theory of rhetoric.* Philadelphia: Center for Curriculum Development.

Katstra, J., Tollefson, N., & Gilbert, E. (1987). The effects of peer evaluation, attitude toward writing, and writing fluency on ninth grade students. *Journal of Educational Research, 80,* 168–172.

Kay, P., & Sankoff, G. (1974). A language-universals approach to pidgins and creoles. In D. DeCamp & I. Hancock (Eds.), *Pidgins and creoles: Current trends and prospects.* Washington, DC: Georgetown University Press.

Kennedy, G. (1980). *Classical rhetoric and its Christian and secular tradition from ancient to modern times.* Chapel Hill: University of North Carolina Press.

Kerek, A., Daiker, D., & Morenberg, M. (1980). Sentence combining and college composition. *Perceptual and Motor Skills, 51,* 1059–1157.

Killian, L. (1971). WISC, Illinois test of psycholinguistic abilities and Bender Visual-Motor Gestalt test performance of Spanish-American kindergarten and first grade school children. *Journal of Consulting and Clinical Psychology, 37,* 38–43.

Kimberling, R., Wingate, L., Rosser, A., DiChiara, R., & Krashen, S. (1978). Cited in S. Krashen, On the acquisition of planned discourse: Written English as a second dialect. In M. Douglas (Ed.), *Claremont reading conference 42nd yearbook* (pp. 173–185). Claremont, CA: Claremont Graduate School.

Kinneavy, J. (1971). *A theory of discourse.* Englewood Cliffs, NJ: Prentice-Hall. Reprinted (1980), New York: Norton.

Kinneavy, J. (1979). Sentence combining in a comprehensive language framework. In D. Daiker, A. Kerek, & M. Morenberg (Eds.), *Sentence combining and the teaching of writing.* Conway, AR: University of Akron and University of Central Arkansas.

Kintsch, W., & van Dijk, T. (1978). Toward a model of text comprehension and production. *Psychological Review, 85,* 363–394.

Kohn, B. (1980). Right-hemisphere speech representation and comprehension of syntax after left cerebral injury. *Brain and Language, 9,* 350–361.

Kozol, J. (1985). *Illiterate America.* Garden City, NJ: Anchor.

Krashen, S. (1978). On the acquisition of planned discourse: Written English as a second dialect. In M. Douglas (Ed.), *Claremont reading conference 42nd yearbook* (pp. 173–185). Claremont, CA: Claremont Graduate School.

Krashen, S. (1980). The input hypothesis. In J. Alatis (Ed.), *Current issues in bilingual education.* Washington, DC: Georgetown University Press.

Krashen, S. (1981a). *Second language acquisition and second language learning.* Oxford: Pergamon.

Krashen, S. (1981b). The role of input (reading) and instruction in developing writing ability. Working paper, University of Southern California.

Krashen, S. (1982). *Principles and practice in second language acquisition.* Oxford: Pergamon.

Krashen, S. (1985). *Writing research, theory, and applications.* New York: Pergamon.

Kurth, R. (1986). Using word processing to enhance revision strategies during student composing. Paper presented at the annual meeting of the American Educational Research Association, San Francisco. (ERIC Document Reproduction Service No. ED 277 049.)

Labov, W. (1964). Phonological indices to social stratification. In J. Gumperz & D. Hymes (Eds.), *The ethnography of communication.*

Labov, W. (1966). *The social stratification of English in New York City.* Washington, DC: Georgetown University Press.

Labov, W. (1969). Contraction, deletion, and inherent variability of the English copula. *Language, 45,* 715–762.

Labov, W. (1970). *The study of nonstandard English*. Urbana, IL: National Council of Teachers of English.

Labov, W. (1971). The notion of system in creole studies. In D. Hymes (Ed.), *Pidginization and creolization of language*. Cambridge: Cambridge University Press.

Labov, W. (1972a). *Language in the inner city: Studies in the Black English vernacular*. Philadelphia: University of Pennsylvania Press.

Labov, W. (1972b). *Sociolinguistic patterns*. Philadelphia: University of Pennsylvania Press.

Labov, W., & Harris, W. (1983). De facto segregation of black and white vernaculars. Paper presented at the Annual Conference on New Ways of Analyzing Variation in English, Montreal.

Lakoff, G. (1987). *Women, fire, and dangerous things*. Chicago: University of Chicago Press.

Lakoff, R. (1973). Pronominalization and the chain command. In D. Reibel & S. Schane (Eds.), *Modern studies in English*. Englewood Cliffs, NJ: Prentice-Hall.

Lambert, W. (1977). The effects of bilingualism on the individual: Cognitive and socio-cultural consequences. In P. Hornby (Ed.), *Bilingualism: Psychological, social, and educational implications*. New York: Academic Press.

Lambert, W. (1978). Cognitive and socio-cultural consequences of bilingualism. *Canadian Modern Language Review, 34*, 537–547.

Lambert, W. E., & Tucker, G. R. (1972). *Bilingual education of children: The St. Lambert experiment*. Rowley, MA: Newbury House.

Lareau, E. (1971). Comparison of two methods of teaching expository composition and evaluation of a testing instrument. *Dissertation Abstracts International, 32*, 2437-A.

Laughlin, P., & McGlynn, R. (1967). Cooperative versus competitive concept attainment as a function of sex and stimulus display. *Journal of Personality and Social Psychology, 7*, 398–402.

Lee, J. (1987). Prewriting assignments across the curriculum. In C. Olson (Ed.), *Practical ideas for teaching writing as a process*. Sacramento, CA: State Department of Education.

Lehmann, W. (1983). *Language: An introduction*. New York: Random House.

Leiber, J. (1975). *Noam Chomsky: A philosophic overview*. New York: St. Martin's.

Lenneberg, E. (1967). *Biological foundations of language*. New York: Wiley.

Lévi-Strauss, C. (1966). *The savage mind*. Chicago: University of Chicago Press.

Levinson, S. (1983). *Pragmatics*. Cambridge: Cambridge University Press.

Levy-Bruhl, L. (1975). *The notebooks on primitive mentality* (P. Riviere, Trans.). New York: Harper & Row.

Lindemann, E. (1987). *A rhetoric for writing teachers.* New York: Oxford University Press.

LoCoco, V. (1975). An analysis of Spanish and German learners' errors. *Working Papers on Bilingualism, 7,* 96–124.

Love, G., & Payne, M. (Eds.). (1969). *Contemporary essays on style.* New York: Scott, Foresman.

Luria, A. (1973). *The working brain: An introduction to neuro-psychology* (B. Haigh, Trans.). New York: Basic Books.

Luria, A. (1976). *Cognitive development: Its cultural and social foundations* (M. Lopez-Morrillas & L. Solotaroff, Trans.). Cambridge, MA: Harvard University Press.

Lyons, J. (1970). *Noam Chomsky.* New York: Penguin.

Lyons, J. (1977). *Semantics* (Vol. 1 & 2). Cambridge: Cambridge University Press.

Macaulay, R. (1973). Double standards. *American Anthropologist, 75,* 1324–1337.

McClure, E. (1981). Formal and functional aspects of the code-switched discourse of bilingual children. In R. Duran (Ed.), *Latino language and communicative behavior: Advances in discourse processes* (Vol. 6). Norwood, NJ: Ablex.

McCrum, R., Cran, W., & MacNeil, R. (1986). *The story of English.* New York: Viking.

McGuigan, F. (1966). *Thinking: Studies of covert language processes.* New York: Appleton.

McGuigan, F. (1978). *Cognitive psychophysiology: Principles of covert behavior.* Englewood Cliffs, NJ: Prentice-Hall.

Macnamara, J. (1972). Cognitive basis of language learning in infants. *Psychological Review, 79,* 1–13.

Macrorie, K. (1970). *Uptaught.* Rochelle Park, NJ: Hayden.

Malt, B. (1985). The role of discourse structure in understanding anaphora. *Journal of Memory and Language, 24,* 271–289.

Mano, S. (1986). Television: A surprising acquisition source for literacy. *Writing Instructor, 5,* 104–111.

Martin, W. (1981). The effects of a program of models-imitation on the writing of seventh grade students. *Dissertation Abstracts International, 41,* 3067-A.

Mathews, M. (1966). *Teaching to read, historically considered.* Chicago: University of Chicago Press.

Matsuhashi, A. (1981). Pausing and planning: The tempo of written discourse production. *Research in the Teaching of English, 15,* 113–134.

Mellon, J. (1969). Transformational sentence-combining: A method for enhancing the development of syntactic fluency in English composition. *NCTE Research Report Number 10.* Champaign, IL: National Council of Teachers of English.

Mencken, H. L. (1936). *The American language: An inquiry into the development of English in the United States.* New York: Knopf.

Metviner, E. (1981). Rhetorically based and rhetorically deficient writing: The effects of purpose and audience on the quality of ninth grade students' compositions. *Dissertation Abstracts International, 41,* 3977-A.

Miller, G. A. (1962). Some psychological studies of grammar. *American Psychologist, 17,* 748–762.

Miller, G., & McKean, K. (1964). A chronometric study of some relations between sentences. *Quarterly Journal of Experimental Psychology, 16,* 297–308.

Miller, J., Chapman, R., Branston, M., & Reichle, J. (1980). Language comprehension in sensorimotor stages V and VI. *Journal of Speech and Hearing Research, 23,* 284–311.

Moffett, J. (1968). *Teaching the universe of discourse.* Boston: Houghton Mifflin.

Moffett, J. (1982). Writing, inner speech, and meditation. *College English, 44,* 231–244.

Moffett, J. (1985). Liberating inner speech. *College Composition and Communication, 36,* 304–308.

Murray, D. (1982). *Learning by teaching.* Montclair, NJ: Boynton/Cook.

Nelson, K. (1973). Structure and strategy in learning to talk. *Monographs of the Society for Research in Child Development, 38* (1–2, Serial No. 149).

Nold, E., & Freedman, S. (1977). An analysis of readers' responses to essays. *Research in the Teaching of English, 11,* 164–174.

O'Donnell, R., Griffin, W., & Norris, R. (1967). Syntax of kindergarten and elementary school children: A transformational analysis. *NCTE Research Report Number 8.* Champaign, IL: National Council of Teachers of English.

O'Hare, F. (1973). Sentence combining: Improving student writing without formal grammar instruction. *NCTE Committee on Research Report Series, Number 15.* Urbana, IL: National Council of Teachers of English.

Ohmann, R. (1969). Prolegomena to the analysis of prose style. In G. Love & M. Payne (Eds.), *Contemporary essays on style.* Glenview, IL: Scott, Foresman.

Olson, D. (1977). From utterance to text: The bias of language in speech and writing. *Harvard Educational Review, 47,* 257–281.

Olson, M., & DiStephano, P. (1980). Describing and testing the effectiveness of a contemporary model for in-service education in teaching composition. *English Education, 12,* 69–76.

Ong, W. (1978). Literacy and orality in our time. *ADE Bulletin, 58,* 1–7.

Ong, W. (1982). *Orality and literacy: The terminologizing of the word.* London: Methuen.

Parker, R. (1979). From Sputnik to Dartmouth: Trends in the teaching of composition. *English Journal, 68* (6), 32–37.

Peal, E., & Lambert, W.E. (1962). The relation of bilingualism to intelligence. *Psychological Monographs, 76* (27, Whole #546).

Peck, M. (1982). *An investigation of tenth-grade students' writing.* Washington, DC: United Press of America.

Pedersen, E. (1978). Improving syntactic and semantic fluency in writing of language arts students through extended practice in sentence-combining. *Dissertation Abstracts International, 38,* 5892-A.

Penalosa, F. (1980). *Chicano sociolinguistics: A brief introduction.* Rowley, MA: Newbury House.

Penfield, J., & Ornstein-Galicia, J. (1985). *Chicano English: An ethnic contact dialect.* Amsterdam: John Benjamins.

Perelman, C., & Olbrechts-Tyteca, L. (1969). *The new rhetoric: A treatise on argumentation.* Notre Dame, IN: University of Notre Dame Press.

Perl, S., & Wilson, N. (1986). Through teachers' eyes: Portraits of writing teachers at work. New York: Heinemann.

Perron, J. (1977). *The impact of mode on written syntactic complexity.* Athens: University of Georgia Studies in Language Education Series.

Perry, M. (1980). A study of the effects of a literary models approach to composition on writing and reading achievement. *Dissertation Abstracts International, 40,* 6137-A.

Piaget, J. (1953). *The origins of intelligence in the child.* London: Routledge & Kegan Paul.

Piaget, J. (1955). *The child's construction of reality.* London: Routledge & Kegan Paul.

Piaget, J. (1962). *Plays, dreams, and imitation in childhood.* New York: Norton.

Piaget, J. (1974). *The language and thought of the child.* New York: New American Library.

Piaget, J., & Inhelder, B. (1969). *The psychology of the child.* New York: Basic Books.

Pinkham, R. (1969). The effect on the written expression of fifth grade pupils of a series of lessons emphasizing the characteristics of good writing as exemplified in selected works from the area of children's literature. *Dissertation Abstracts, 29,* 2613-A.

Puttenham, G. (1589). *The arte of English poesie.* Facsimile reproduction (1970). Kent, OH: Kent State University Press.

Raimes, A. (1985). What unskilled ESL students do as they write: A classroom study of composing. *TESOL Quarterly, 19,* 229–258.

Raimes, A. (1986). Teaching ESL writing: Fitting what we do to what we know. *Writing Instructor, 5,* 153–166.

Ramirez, M., & Casteneda, A. (1974). *Cultural democracy, bicognitive development and education.* New York: Academic Press.

Ramirez, M., & Price-Williams, D. (1974). Cognitive styles in children: Two Mexican communities. *Interamerican Journal of Psychology, 8,* 93–100.

Reedy, J. (1966). A comparative study of two methods of teaching the organization of expository writing to ninth grade pupils. *Dissertation Abstracts, 26,* 5923-A.

Reither, J. (1985). Writing and knowing: Toward redefining the writing process. *College English, 47,* 620–628.

Restak, R. (1979). *The brain: The last frontier.* New York: Warner.

Rice, M., & Kemper, S. (1984). *Child language and cognition.* Baltimore: University Park Press.

Richards, J. (1985). *The context of language teaching.* Cambridge: Cambridge University Press.

Rickford, J. (1975). Carrying the new wave into syntax: The case of Black English *been.* In R. Fasold & R. Shuy (Eds.), *Analyzing variation in language.* Washington, DC: Georgetown University Press.

Rohman, D., & Wlecke, A. (1964). *Prewriting: The construction and application of models to concept formation in writing.* East Lansing: Michigan State University Press.

Ronald, K. (1986). The self and the other in the process of composing: Implications for integrating the acts of reading and writing. In B. Petersen (Ed.), *Convergences: Transactions in reading and writing.* Urbana, IL: National Council of Teachers of English.

Rosch, E. (1978). *Principles of categorization.* Hillsdale, NJ: Wiley.

Rose, M. (1984). *Writer's block: The cognitive dimension.* Carbondale: Southern Illinois University Press.

Russell, D. (1987). Writing across the curriculum and the communications movement: Some lessons from the past. *College Composition and Communication, 38,* 184–194.

Sanchez, N. (1987). Bilingual training can be a barrier to academic achievement for students. *Chronicle of Higher Education,* June 10.

Sanchez, R. (1983). *Chicano discourse: Socio-historic perspectives.* Rowley, MA: Newbury House.

Sanford, A., & Garrod, S. (1981). Understanding written language. New York: Wiley.

Scardamalia, M., & Bereiter, C. (1983). The development of evaluative, diagnostic, and remedial capabilities in children's composing. In M. Martlew (Ed.), *The psychology of written language: A developmental approach.* London: Wiley.

Scargill, M., & Penner, P. (Eds.). (1966). *Looking at language: Essays in introductory linguistics.* Glenview, IL: Scott, Foresman.

Schank, R., & Abelson, R. (1977). *Scripts, plans, goals and understanding.* Hillsdale, NJ: Lawrence Erlbaum.

Schecter, B. (1987). How to make your own superconductors. *Omni, 10*(2), 72–76.

Schlesinger, I. (1971). The production of utterances and language acquisition. In D. Slobin (Ed.), *The ontogenesis of grammar.* New York: Academic Press.

Schroeder, T. (1973). The effects of positive and corrective written teacher feedback on selected writing behaviors of fourth-grade children. *Dissertation Abstracts International, 34,* 2935-A.

Scinto, L. (1986). *Written language and psychological development.* San Diego: Harcourt Brace Jovanovich.

Scollon, R., & Scollon, S. (1979). *The literate two-year-old: The fictionalization of self.* Austin, TX: Southeast Regional Laboratory.

Scribner, S., & Cole, M. (1981). *The psychology of literacy.* Cambridge, MA: Harvard University Press.

Sealey, R. (1976). *A history of the Greek city states, 700–338 b.c.* Berkeley: University of California Press.

Searle, J. (1983). *Intentionality: An essay in the philosophy of mind.* Cambridge: Cambridge University Press.

Self, C. (1986). Reading as a writing strategy: Two case studies. In B. Petersen (Ed.), *Convergences: Transactions in reading and writing.* Urbana, IL: National Council of Teachers of English.

Shankweiler, D., & Crain, S. (1986). Language mechanisms and reading disorder: A modular approach. *Cognition, 10,* 139–168.

Shaughnessy, M. (1977). *Errors and expectations: A guide for the teacher of basic writing.* New York: Oxford University Press.

Shayer, D. (1972). *The teaching of English in schools, 1900–1970.* London: Routledge and Kegan Paul.

Slobin, D. (1973). Cognitive prerequisites for the development of grammar. In C. Ferguson & D. Slobin (Eds.), *Studies of child language development.* New York: Holt, Rinehart and Winston.

Slobin, D. (1977). Language change in childhood and history. In J. Macnamara (Ed.), *Language, learning and thought.* New York: Academic Press.

Slobin, D. (1982). Universal and particular in the acquisition of language. In L. Gleitman & E. Wanner (Eds.), *Language acquisition: State of the art.* New York: Cambridge University Press.

Slobin, D., & Welsh, C. (1973). Elicited imitation as a research tool in developmental psycholinguistics. In C. Ferguson & D. Slobin (Eds.), *Studies of child language development.* New York: Holt, Rinehart and Winston.

Smith, F. (1972). *Understanding reading*. New York: Holt, Rinehart and Winston.

Smith, F. (1983). *Essays into literacy*. London: Heinemann.

Smith, M. (1939). Some light on the problem of bilingualism as found from a study of the progress in mastery of English among pre-school children of non-American ancestry in Hawaii. *Genetic Psychology Monographs, 21,* 119–284.

Snipper, G. (1985). The implementation and effects of the reclassification criteria in transitional bilingual education programs. Paper presented at the 29th Comparative and International Education Annual Conference, Stanford University.

Sokolov, A. (1972). *Inner speech and thought* (G. Onischenko, Trans.). New York: Plenum.

Sommers, N. (1982). Responding to student writing. *College Composition and Communication, 33,* 148–156.

Sponsler, M. (1971). The effectiveness of literary models in the teaching of written composition. *Dissertation Abstracts International, 32,* 2322-A.

Staats, A., & Butterfield, W. (1965). Treatment of nonreading in a culturally deprived juvenile delinquent: An application of reinforcement principles. *Child Development, 4,* 925–942.

Stefl, L. (1981). The effect of a guided discovery approach on the descriptive paragraph writing skills of third grade pupils. *Dissertation Abstracts International, 42,* 2493-A.

Sullivan, M. (1978). The effects of sentence-combining exercises on syntactic maturity, quality of writing, reading ability, and attitudes of students in grade eleven. *Dissertation Abstracts International, 39,* 1197-A.

Sullivan, M. (1979). Parallel sentence-combining studies in grades nine and eleven. In D. Daiker, A. Kerek, & M. Morenberg (Eds.), *Sentence combining and the teaching of writing*. Conway, AR: University of Akron and University of Central Arkansas.

Swain, M., & Cummins, J. (1979). Bilingualism, cognitive functioning and education. *Language Teaching and Linguistics: Abstracts, 4–18.*

Swain, M., & Lapkin, S. (1982). *Evaluating bilingual education: A Canadian case study*. Avon, England: Multilingual Matters.

Swift, J. (1712). A letter to a young gentleman lately entered into holy orders. In R. Greenberg & W. Piper (Eds.), *The writings of Jonathan Swift* (1973). New York: Norton.

Tannen, D. (1982). Oral and literate strategies in spoken and written narratives. *Language, 58,* 1–21.

Tarvers, J. (1988). *Teaching writing: Theories and practices*. Glenview, IL: Scott, Foresman.

Teichman, M., & Poris, M. (1985). Word processing in the classroom: Its effects on freshman writers. (ERIC Document Reproduction Service No. ED 276 062.)

Thaiss, C., & Suhor, C. (Eds.). (1984). *Speaking and writing, K–12*. Urbana, IL: National Council of Teachers of English.

Thibodeau, A. (1964). Improving composition writing with grammar and organization exercises utilizing differentiated group patterns. *Dissertation Abstracts, 25*, 2388.

Thonis, E. (1983). *The English–Spanish connection*. Northvale, NJ: Santillana.

Trevarthen, C. (1974). Communication and cooperation in early infancy: A description of primary intersubjectivity. In M. Bullowa (Ed.) *Before speech: The beginnings of human communication*. Cambridge: Cambridge University Press, 1979.

Trimbur, J. (1987). Beyond cognition: The voices of inner speech. *Rhetoric Review, 5*, 211–221.

Trudgill, P. (1974). *Sociolinguistics: An introduction*. New York: Penguin.

Tufte, V. (1971). *Grammar as style*. New York: Holt, Rinehart and Winston.

Turner, G. (1973). *Stylistics*. London: Penguin.

Ullmann, J. (1963). *Semantics: An introduction to the study of meaning*. Oxford: Basil Blackwell & Mott.

van Dijk, T. (1980). *Macrostructures*. Hillsdale, NJ: Lawrence Erlbaum.

Vinson, L. (1980). The effects of two prewriting activities upon the overall quality of ninth graders' descriptive paragraphs. *Dissertation Abstracts International, 41*, 927-A.

Vygotsky, L. S. (1962). *Thought and language*. Cambridge, MA: MIT Press.

Vygotsky, L. S. (1978). *Mind in society*. M. Cole, V. John-Steiner, S. Scribner, & E. Souberman (Eds.). Cambridge, MA: Harvard University Press.

Wadsworth, O. (1971). *Over in the meadow*. New York: Scholastic.

Wald, B. (1985). Motivation for language choice behavior of elementary Mexican American children. In E. Garcia & R. Padilla (Eds.), *Advances in bilingual education research*. Tucson: University of Arizona Press.

Warren, R., & Warren, R. (1970). Auditory illusions and confusions. *Scientific American, 223*, 30–36.

Warriner, J. (1986). *English grammar and composition*. Orlando, FL: Harcourt Brace Jovanovich.

Waterfall, C. (1978). An experimental study of sentence-combining as a means of increasing syntactic maturity and writing quality in the compositions of college-age students enrolled in remedial English classes. *Dissertation Abstracts International, 38*, 7131-A.

Watson, R. (1985). Toward a theory of definition. *Journal of Child Language, 12,* 181–197.

Weber, H. (1968). The study of oral reading errors: A survey of the literature. *Reading Research Quarterly, 4,* 96–119.

West, W. (1967). A comparison of a "composition equivalencies" approach and a traditional approach to teaching writing. *Dissertation Abstracts, 27,* 4178-A.

White, E. (1986). *Teaching and assessing writing.* San Francisco: Jossey-Bass.

White, L. (1977). Error analysis and error correction in adult learners of English as a second language. *Working Papers in Bilingualism, 13,* 42–58.

White, R. (1965). The effect of structural linguistics on improving English composition compared to that of prescriptive grammar or the absence of grammar instruction. *Dissertation Abstracts, 25,* 5032.

Whitehead, C. (1966). The effect of grammar-diagramming on student writing skills. *Dissertation Abstracts, 26,* 3710.

Whorf, B. L. (1956). *Language, thought and reality: Selected writings of Benjamin Lee Whorf.* J. B. Carroll (Ed.). Cambridge, MA: MIT Press.

Williams, J. D. (1983). Covert language behavior during writing. *Research in the Teaching of English, 17,* 301–312.

Williams, J. D. (1985). Coherence and cognitive style. *Written Communication, 2,* 473–491.

Williams, J. D. (1987). Covert linguistic behavior during writing tasks: Psychophysiological differences between above-average and below-average writers. *Written Communication, 4,* 310–328.

Winterowd, W. R. (Ed.). (1975). *Contemporary rhetoric: A conceptual background with readings.* New York: Harcourt Brace Jovanovich.

Witte, S. (1980). Toward a model for research in written composition. *Research in the Teaching of English, 14,* 73–81.

Witte, S. (1985). Revising, composing theory, and research design. In S. Freedman (Ed.), *The acquisition of written language: Response and revision.* Norwood, NJ: Ablex.

Witte, S. (1987). Pre-text and composing. *College Composition and Communication, 38,* 397–425.

Witte, S., & Cherry, R. (1986). Writing processes and written products in composition research. In C. Cooper & S. Greenbaum (Eds.), *Studying writing: Linguistic approaches.* Beverly Hills: Sage.

Witte, S., & Faigley, L. (1981). Coherence, cohesion, and writing quality. *College Composition and Communication, 32,* 189–204.

Wittrock, M. (1977). The generative processes of memory. In M. Wittrock (Ed.), *The human brain.* Englewood Cliffs, NJ: Prentice-Hall.

Wolfram, W. (1969). *A sociolinguistic description of Detroit Negro speech*. Washington, DC: Center for Applied Linguistics.

Woodward, J., & Phillips, A. (1967). Profile of the poor writer. *Research in the Teaching of English, 1*, 41–53.

Woodworth, P., & Keech, C. (1980). The write occasion. *Collaborative Research Study Number 1*. Berkeley: University of California School of Education.

Yoshioka, J. G. (1929). A study of bilingualism. *Journal of Genetic Psychology, 36*, 473–479.

Zamel, V. (1983). The composing processes of advanced ESL students: Six case studies. *TESOL Quarterly, 17*, 165–187.

Ziv, N. (1980). The effect of teacher comments on the writing of four college freshmen. (ERIC Document Reproduction Service No. ED 203 317.)

Zoellner, R. (1969). Talk-write: A behavioral pedagogy for composition. *College English, 30*, 267–320.

Index

Action, language as, 17, 27–37. *See
also* Writing as a psychosocial
action
Active modeling, 66
Addison, R., 209
Amastae, Jon, 174
American Indian tribal languages,
grammar, 78, 88–89
Anastasi, A., 140
Argumentation
in ancient Greek rhetoric, 19–22
purpose, intention and, 33–35
use in sequenced writing as-
signments, 236, 245, 246–48
Argumentative essay, 22, 34
rubrics for, 270–72
Aristotle, 17
on rhetoric, 20
'Art' of Rhetoric, The (Aristotle), 20
Asian English, 158–59, 164
Aspect, 168
Assertions, 28–29
Assessment of writing, 255–99
conclusions on, 298–99

under curriculum constraints,
261–62
holistic scoring, 256, 266–73
overview, 255–56
portfolio grading, 256, 277–98
reducing paper load in, 262–66,
278
reliability of, 255–56, 260–61
rubrics (*see* Rubric[s])
scoring student papers, 274–77
validity and, 243, 255, 256–60
Assignments. *See* Writing
assignment(s)
Athens, rhetoric in ancient, 19–24
Audience, composition for a specific, 32

Bailey, R., 11
Barham, H., 111
Basque language, 87
Bateman, D., 111
Bates, E., 181
Berthoff, Ann, 38
Bible, rhetoric and, 16, 24–25

340